What
Would
MADISON
Do?

The
FATHER OF THE CONSTITUTION
Meets
MODERN AMERICAN POLITICS

What
Would
MADISON
Do?

BENJAMIN WITTES *and* PIETRO S. NIVOLA
EDITORS

Brookings Institution Press
WASHINGTON, D.C.

The Brookings Institution is a private nonprofit organization devoted to research,
education, and publication on important issues of domestic and foreign policy. Its
principal purpose is to bring the highest quality independent research and analysis
to bear on current and emerging policy problems. Interpretations or conclusions in
Brookings publications should be understood to be solely those of the authors.

Library of Congress Cataloging-in-Publication data
What would Madison do? : the Constitution's architect meets modern American
government / Benjamin Wittes and Pietro Nivola, editors.
pages   cm
Includes bibliographical references and index.
ISBN 978-0-8157-2657-9 (hardcover : alk. paper)
ISBN 978-0-8157-2674-6 (pbk. : alk. paper)
ISBN 978-0-8157-2658-6 (epub)
ISBN 978-0-8157-2743-9 (pdf)
1. Madison, James 1751–1836—Political and social views. 2. United States—
Politics and government—Philosophy. I. Wittes, Benjamin, editor.
II. Nivola, Pietro S., editor.
E342.W48   2015
973.5'1092—dc23   2015019158

9 8 7 6 5 4 3 2 1

Typeset in Adobe Caslon
Composition by Elliott Beard

In memory of Martha A. Derthick (1933–2015)
teacher, colleague, friend

Contents

Acknowledgments

A number of people whose names do not appear as authors or editors in this volume played essential roles in making it happen. Thanks, first off, to the employees and staff of James Madison's Montpelier and its Robert H. Smith Center for the Constitution, with whom Brookings partnered for a multi-year collaboration that ultimately resulted in this book. Kat Imhoff, Montpelier's president, and C. Douglas Smith were unstinting in their support of the project. Two other people at Montpelier deserve special mention: Sean O'Brien and Jennifer Patja Howell, who have shepherded the relationship with Brookings for the entirety of its history. They have been great partners, essential collaborators, and good friends. We are especially indebted to Eileen Hughes, our skilled editor at the Brookings Press, who worked patiently over several months on the papers contributed by the book's multiple authors. We also are grateful to Janet Walker, the managing editor at the press, for her assistance in overseeing the editing and publication process and to Cody Poplin, who helped edit early drafts of the volume's contents.

What
Would

MADISON

Do?

One

INTRODUCTION

*Perspectives on Madison's Legacy for
Contemporary American Politics*

BENJAMIN WITTES AND PIETRO S. NIVOLA

*I*n 1785, while serving as a member of the Virginia legislature, James Madison wrote a letter to a friend who was contemplating the possible parameters of a constitution for Kentucky, which was soon to become independent of Virginia. His friend, Caleb Wallace, had asked him a number of questions, including one on a lot of people's minds today: "Should there be a periodical review of the Constitution?"

Madison responded noncommittally. He noted that the idea was good in theory but had not been tried much, and he mentioned a couple of schemes by which review of a constitution could be built into its fabric. He concluded that perhaps a temporary constitution made sense for Kentucky. "In your situation," he wrote, "I should think it both imprudent & indecent not to leave a door open for at least one revision of your first Establishment, imprudent because you have neither the same resources for supporting nor the same lights for framing a good establishment now as you will have 15 or 20 Years hence, indecent because a handful of early settlers ought not to preclude a populous Country from a choice of the Government under which they & their posterity are to live."[1]

By the end of his long life, Madison was firmly committed to the young nation's constitutional arrangement, especially its stronger union, which he had done more than anyone else to design. His 1834 "Advice to My Country," one of the last things he ever wrote, is brief: "The advice nearest to my heart and deepest in my convictions is that the Union of the States be cherished and perpetuated. Let the open enemy to it be regarded as a Pandora with her box opened; and the disguised one, as the Serpent creeping with his deadly wiles into Paradise."[2]

There is no shortage of academic tracts pondering whether the American constitutional order, so influenced by Madison's thinking, has grown outmoded in important respects. Periodically, the discontents express concern that the old Madisonian framework may not be up to the challenge of addressing modern society's most pressing problems. Isn't the framework, at least in part, an anachronism that perpetuates governmental inefficiencies and inequities, the critics ask? Their qualms are somewhat reminiscent of Madison's own in 1785. What right, they ask, does the "handful of early settlers" who established the U.S. Constitution now have to "preclude a populous Country" of 300 million people from modernizing it?

Defenders of the American political system today rejoin that while much of it continues to reflect the exigencies of its original framers, the Constitution also has proven resilient and innovative, and they warn that those who call for fundamental reform should be careful what they wish for. This view is closer to Madison's advice to his country in 1834—to his insistence that the Constitution was not to be trifled with and to his warnings about renegotiating a hard-won compact.

This book joins the debate: How well—or at least how consequentially—*does* the Madisonian system perform? But the book also asks an additional question: If Madison could peer at the present, how would he regard the current condition of the key political institutions that he helped originate and the government policies that they make? The book, in short, explores what Madison might think of contemporary U.S. politics and how reverential we should remain toward the system that he bequeathed to the nation.

To contemplate these matters, a group of scholars convened at Montpelier, James Madison's home, in Orange, Virginia, during the fall of 2013, under the joint auspices of Montpelier's Robert H. Smith Center for the Constitution and the Brookings Institution. This volume contains the papers presented at that conclave. The book, in accordance with the questions posed, has two parts. The first comprises five chapters concerned primarily with systemic performance: Does the intricate edifice that Madison and his colleagues engineered still measure up? The second comprises five chapters that illustrate the extent to which the Father of the Constitution, were he with us today, might be discomfited by contemporary developments in American politics and public policy.

In chapter 2, John DiIulio Jr., of the University of Pennsylvania, examines a contemporary political shortcoming that Madison and the Founders arguably had a hand in bequeathing: the failure of policymakers these days to address fully the nation's long-range financial liabilities. "American citizens yet to be born," DiIulio writes, "are being stuck with an entitlement benefits bill that is about five times the country's current annual GDP." He suggests more than one reason that America has not broken the habit of "legally robbing future citizens in order to enjoy present benefits without having to pay for them itself." Not least among his explanations is the power of organized groups with a vested interest in feeding and fattening the public sector. Another, however, is simply public opinion: substantial majorities oppose genuine retrenchment of the welfare state and will not hesitate to punish elected officials who attempt more than token tweaks to either entitlements or the tax revenues necessary to support them.

DiIulio's diagnosis of what ails the U.S. polity is important because, at the end of his chapter, he countenances potentially far-reaching constitutional reforms. He boldly stipulates that the Constitution is now an ill-fitting suit for a government that has outgrown it. Yet, if, as DiIulio's analysis implies, the weight of the people's preferences is a big part of the underlying problem, the reform agenda would have to include not only greater restraints on the excesses of participatory democracy (a challenge discussed in the subsequent chapter) but also, let's face it, on the norm of majoritarian rule, which Madison basically favored and which lies at the core of any democratic regime. That is a very tall order.

In chapter 3, Brookings Institution senior fellow William Galston reviews a number of respects in which the country's politics have deviated from the Framers' intentions. His observations, at least implicitly, have a bearing on whether certain constitutional corrections might be in order. Some of what Galston cites—the expansion of executive power, federal authority poaching on the traditional purview of the states—also comes up elsewhere in the volume. But two other big changes do not: the rise of political parties (forces that, for better or worse, the Founders sought to discourage), and, related to it, what Galston terms the ascent of "direct versus representative democracy."

This latter populist element may be, as Galston suggests, the single most nettlesome deviation to have occurred in the American political arena. A committed republican, Madison decidedly championed governance with the consent of the people, perhaps even to the point of permitting "them" the final say in determining the constitutionality of statutes. But—and this is a crucial distinction—he eschewed any form of direct rule by the populace. Rather, he envisioned, as Galston describes, a modified democracy, one in which popular participation is suitably subject to "filtration through representation."

No major democracy is more sensitive to popular moods and grassroots pressures than the United States. Some of that sensitivity is baked into the constitutional design: consider the implications of the system's unique biennial elections for the House of Representatives—an instrument of democratic expression that Madison himself considered excessive. (He had preferred at least a three-year term for House members.) Much of it, however, is of more recent vintage: the dominance of party primaries and caucuses, which has challenged, as Galston calls it, "the culture of deference" to seasoned political leaders—that is, the "filter" that Madison deemed so necessary to represent the people responsibly and attain for them what he called the "real" public good.

In chapter 4, Pietro Nivola, a senior fellow emeritus at Brookings, takes another tack. Although he, like DiIulio, recognizes the democratic predicament presented by the need to face up to long-term fiscal challenges, his first concern is how American democracy performed in an immediate crisis of epic proportions: the global economic collapse that began in 2008. Commentators who ritually chastise "Washington" for its deficient policies ought to ask themselves: Deficient compared with what? The Great Recession was a very big test—and, as a matter of fact, the U.S. government arguably handled it better than governments in many other advanced economies did, most notably several in Europe. The comparative U.S. success has been evident: U.S. GDP has grown, mostly at a respectable pace, and unemployment has dropped below the pre-recession level. The recovery in much of Europe was slower. Although growth there has finally regained momentum recently, unemployment in the Eurozone has remained disturbingly high.

How did America's supposedly "gridlocked" political system manage this feat, in contrast to regimes overseas? The answer, Nivola posits, is that first of all, the gridlock itself was actually helpful. The political parties were at odds. There was reluctance to cut public spending (chiefly on the part of Democrats) and to raise taxes (most intensely on the part of Republicans). Felicitously, the combination of those positions prevented premature adoption of austerity measures. Second, where activism was imperative—to secure various countercyclical initiatives—the government was anything but gridlocked; in large part, it responded promptly, creatively, and energetically. What does this story imply about America's Madisonian mix of institutional constraints and capabilities? It still works, Nivola argues—indeed, at times impressively—at least if the comparison is with other societies in the real world, not with some utopia.

Granted, the remarkable response to a near-term crisis may say little about the prospects for prudent policies that anticipate dangers in the more distant future. DiIulio harbors that reservation about fiscal policymaking in this country—and Nivola shares some of his unease. Where these two old friends might part company, however, is on the question of how many examples there are of other democracies that unquestionably excel at taking the long view. Glancing abroad, Nivola suspects that distinctive profiles in courage are scarce.

A healthy debate has been joined. DiIulio's case for considering some judicious constitutional adjustments in the United States cannot be dismissed out of hand. In a famous letter to Madison in 1789, Thomas Jefferson had insisted that no constitution should be immutable—indeed, that all should have an expiration date.[3] And Madison did not wholly disagree. Replying the following year, he concurred that from time to time improvements might well be called for, especially to provide "a salutary curb on the living generation from imposing unjust or unnecessary burdens on their successors."[4] That is precisely the broad rationale that DiIulio advances.

In chapter 5, R. Shep Melnick of Boston College contributes his keen insights on whether the nation's Madisonian regime now is plainly malfunctioning. Melnick's essay is a wide-ranging *tour d'horizon*, probing most comprehensively the *real*, not merely the rhetorical, record of policy outcomes in the past couple of decades. He begins by observing that critics of the nation's Madisonian order have long bemoaned its biases. The main flaw, the dissenters allege, is a systemic propensity for evasion and inaction. In the 1950s, they complained of "stalemate." In more current parlance, the label is "gridlock." But are such characterizations warranted? Whatever the catchphrase of the day, Melnick shows that no serious analysis of what has actually transpired in the United States during this century and much of the last can conclude that U.S. politics has been paralytic. His list of major new policies is robust and extensive. While the political process can erect roadblocks, it also can (and does) clear new paths to get around them.

Furthermore, Melnick's chronicle does a special service: he notices how a great deal of innovation emanates from venues that too often remain under-recognized. While the media may fixate on this or that "do nothing" Congress, elsewhere—in the courts, the regulatory bureaucracy, the Federal Reserve, the states—a lot of significant undertakings fill the space. Suffice it to look at this astonishing train of events, for example: the revolutionary change that has occurred in marital law. Almost overnight, the legalization of same-sex marriage has hopscotched from state to state, and in June 2015, the Supreme Court itself ruled on the question.

In chapter 6, the last in this half of the book, Jonathan Rauch, another senior fellow at Brookings, also runs against the grain of prevailing commentary, which tends to depict the U.S. political scene as a sorry spectacle, hopelessly deadlocked and "dysfunctional." To the contrary, writes Rauch, the system continues to do what the Framers, particularly Madison, intended: It duly applies a "brake" on precipitous change, but it also has a vigorous capacity for "adaptation." Why is that possible? Because, even amid today's partisan polarization and obstructionism, the Madisonian design still encourages pragmatism: "It forces politicians to compromise, by creating competing power centers and depriving any of them of the power to impose its will on the others." The arrangement can be "an engine of innovation"—albeit one that typically innovates in measured, incremental ways. Rauch presents a compelling example. Not long ago, the divided government accomplished the seemingly impossible: it initiated (albeit on the margins) the painful process of cutting federal spending and hiking taxes. However tentatively, in other words, it took steps to begin putting the nation's fiscal house in order.

In the second half of his essay, Rauch takes aim at the "anti-compromise movement" in recent party politics, arguing respectfully that it is not in keeping with the political tradition credited to Madison. For now we live in an era when bands of uncompromising partisans, empowered directly by impassioned voters, sometimes appear to exert outsized influence on the national agenda—and have kicked aside some overdue business that parties controlled by practical politicians probably would have resolved by now.

Part 2 of the book turns from what we should think of Madison's legacy to what Madison might think of the United States today. It begins with chapter 7, by Jack Rakove, a historian at Stanford University. Rakove focuses on the contemporary conduct of the U.S. Senate. Nowadays, far from being a consistent source of "wisdom and stability" in legislative deliberations, as Madison had hoped, Congress's upper body has inordinately expanded its methods of obstruction. Its bag of tricks includes the secret holds that individual senators frequently slap on confirmation proceedings for prospective executive or judicial appointments, leaving the courts and essential administrative agencies with critical vacancies. Perhaps worse, by regularly threatening to resort to filibusters, the modern Senate has all but imposed a new procedural norm for lawmaking: the requirement for a supermajority to pass even ordinary legislation. Rakove makes a case that Madison, a firm believer in the "republican principle" of majority rule, would have disapproved of such parliamentary practices.

In chapter 8, the late Martha Derthick of the University of Virginia traces the profound transformation that has taken place in another cornerstone of the Constitution: federalism. In *Federalist* No. 45, Madison had expected the state governments, to which the people would be closely attached, to form a firm bulwark against overweening encroachments by the central government. That expectation proved wrong. In sphere after sphere, the balance of power has shifted to the central authorities in the course of the country's history. Derthick delves into the trends in certain health care programs (notably the steady expansion of Medicaid) and in education policy, describing in granular detail the stealthy policy entrepreneurship of administrators as well as legislators. Her larger point is that Madison might be startled by how extensively the government in Washington has come to micromanage the strictly "local and particular" concerns that used to be the province of the states and municipalities (*Federalist* No. 10). And, Derthick infers, Madison would be no less disturbed by how much of this vast body of national law "is being made outside of legislatures."

Had Martha Derthick lived to revisit her essay, she almost certainly would have enhanced it by further stressing yet another characteristic of the euphemistically termed "cooperative federalism" of modern times: its stupefying legal complexity. Observers since de Tocqueville have recognized that, as he noted, "complication" is one of the "vices in every federal system." But the sheer amount of complication associated with American state-*cum*-federal law today would surely dismay Madison, much as it does many ordinary citizens. Too much law is "a nuisance of the most pestilent kind," wrote Madison in 1787.[5]

In chapter 9, Eugene Hickok, a former deputy secretary of education and fellow at the Heritage Foundation, also examines what has happened in the field of education. He discusses in depth Madison's grasp of the essential role of educational institutions in society. Like Jefferson, Madison viewed an educated citizenry as vital to a vibrant republic. In some ways, the United States has duly heeded his aspiration. This country spends more per pupil than any other advanced democracy. Like Derthick, Hickok shows that investment in education is no longer just a state and local priority; it has become a national one, with the federal government increasingly engaged at all levels.

But it must also be said that Madison would likely be troubled by the often mediocre return on this expensive investment. Despite the massive spending, Hickok observes, the upshot according to most indicators has been that "student achievement in reading, math, and science has been flat for more than twenty years. Moreover, the performance of U.S. students is lower than that of students in many other countries." Not only that, but assessments of civic literacy—even among graduates of the nation's vaunted system of higher education—can look decidedly discouraging. The finding of one multiyear study cited by Hickok was that "a college education had almost no influence on students' understanding and awareness of civics and government." Madison would be troubled by that outcome. As Hickok emphasizes, no founder was more mindful than Madison of the importance to Americans of obtaining "a good education in order to fulfill the responsibilities of self-government."

Chapter 10 opens with the Affordable Care Act (ACA), which is in some ways a poster child for the reach—and, more important, the extraordinarily complex form—of federal domestic policy in the twenty-first century. A law of this sort would have been so unimaginable in Madison's day that it seems strained to wonder what Madison would think of it. An indisputably relevant query, however, is whether he would have been comfortable with how the law's constitutional legitimacy was ultimately decided: through the judiciary. Lynn Uzzell, a scholar in residence at Montpelier, directs her attention to this inquiry. She concludes that, at bottom, Madison would have preferred the court of public opinion—not the litigants and judges at federal tribunals—to have the last word on so ambitious and controversial a national policy initiative and one so hobbled by lukewarm popular support. Madison had indeed asserted at times that the people should be the final arbiters of laws that arguably strain, or "usurp," constitutional boundaries: "in the last resort a remedy must be obtained from the people who can, by the election of more faithful representatives, annul the acts of the usurpers."[6] As author of the Virginia Resolution in 1798, he more or less practiced what he preached.

That said, some of Madison's other reflections might seem at odds with Uzzell's take. In *Federalist* No. 37, for example, he ruminated on the inevitable need for interpretive jurisprudence: "All new laws," he argues, "are considered as more or less obscure and equivocal until their meaning be liquidated and ascertained by a series of particular discussions *and adjudications*" (italics added). For, he implied, in legislation as in the human expression of practically any sophisticated idea, there tends to be "unavoidable inaccuracy," all the more so when the "objects" in question inherently involve "complexity and novelty."[7] The ACA could certainly be considered a case in point.

In the book's final chapter, Benjamin Wittes and Ritika Singh tackle the momentous issue of how, if at all, James Madison's inclinations might be said to square with America's modern national security regime. For politicians, then as now, where one stands frequently depends on where one sits. Wittes and Singh remind us, in essence, that the old adage also applies to

Madison, who was a pragmatic practitioner of politics, not merely a theorist. As a coauthor of the *Federalist Papers*, he had joined Hamilton in calling for a stronger national government. Afterward, as a member of the Anti-Federalist opposition, he was less inclined to do so (note the Virginia Resolution). Later, as secretary of state and then president, he tilted again toward various nationalist stances—sanctioning expansion into the territories of the Louisiana Purchase and part of Florida, appealing to Congress for resources to prosecute the War of 1812 ("Mr. Madison's War"), and, in his final message to Congress in December of 1815, at last largely embracing a Hamiltonian case for maintaining adequate military strength in peacetime.

The nub of the thesis that Wittes and Singh exposit is this: If Madison appeared to fluctuate between assertions of national power on one hand and grave misgivings on the other, a similar pattern persists to this day in the pursuit of the nation's security. At times, the government asserts the national security interest aggressively; at other times, amid mounting public skepticism, it retreats. In the age-old contest between the competing values of security and civil liberties, in some ways America still wrestles with its constitutional scruples, as did Madison. And in no small part, we have him to thank for that.

Fair enough. One has to be careful not to overstate the parallels, however—and sensibly, Wittes and Singh don't. Madison's moves in the name of national security pale in comparison with those of subsequent presidents. His wartime measures were small-bore, almost quaint, even by the standards of his time. As Martha Derthick notes, whereas Madison had believed that wars would be rare, now they seem perpetual, summoning up a military establishment and security apparatus so formidable that nothing like it exists anywhere else. What would a president who declined to prosecute even flagrant traitors during the War of 1812 say about the likes of the USA Patriot Act or the scope of NSA surveillance? How would he react to modern America's permanent state of being under threat and on a war footing?

This much is clear: the foundation that Madison helped lay has proven neither static nor unproductive in the modern age. How radically the modern American state has stretched the original constitutional limits that he held dear remains a contested question.

Notes

1. James Madison, "Letter to Caleb Wallace, August 23, 1785," in *Selected Writings of James Madison*, edited by James Ketcham (Indianapolis/Cambridge: Hackett Publishing Company, 2006), pp. 29–34.

2. James Madison, "Advice to My Country," in *Selected Writings of James Madison*, edited by Ketcham, pp. 362–63.

3. Letter from Thomas Jefferson to James Madison, September 6, 1789, in *The Republic of Letters: The Correspondence between Thomas Jefferson and James Madison, 1776–1826*, edited by James Morton Smith (New York: Norton, 1995), pp. 631–36.

4. Letter from James Madison to Thomas Jefferson, February 4, 1790, in *Life of Thomas Jefferson, Third President of the United States*, vol. 1, edited by James Parton (Boston: J.R. Osgood, 1874), pp. 326–30.

5. James Madison, *Vices of the Political System of the U. States*, vol. 2, in *The Writings of James Madison: 1783–1787*, edited by Gaillard Hunt (New York: G.P. Putnam's Sons, 1901), pp. 361–69.

6. James Madison, *"Federalist* No. 44," in *The Federalist*, edited by Robert A. Ferguson (New York: Barnes and Noble, 2006), pp. 248–55.

7. James Madison, *"Federalist* No. 37," in *The Federalist*, edited by Ferguson, pp. 194–201.

Part I

AN OUTMODED MODEL?

Two

Mr. Madison's Communion Suit

*Implementation-Group Liberalism and
the Case for Constitutional Reform*

John J. DiIulio Jr.

Until the day that she died in 2010, my mother loved showing anybody who would look—doctors, nurses, even, on one occasion, an ambulance driver who later confided that he thought she was reaching for pills or a ventilator—her favorite photograph: me in 1965, wearing my First Holy Communion suit.

I can't say that I blamed her; I did look awfully angelic. Then as now, I was what my mother insisted on calling "husky" (a.k.a. having sky-high BMI). The jacket strained at the waist. The shirt collar and knot of the blue tie folded into a chubby (sorry, Mama, "husky") double chin. The pants rode up high above my ankles (as in "Why don't you have a party and invite your pants down?") Still, it was '60s urban Catholic school cool.

But not even Mama wanted me to keep wearing my communion suit as I got older. Not even she lamented that I stopped wearing it well before middle school and could not possibly wear it when I reached middle age. The Incredible Hulk's pants get frayed but somehow still fit after he morphs from normal-sized man to outsized monster. Me? As an adult, I might have been able to get one "husky" arm into the suit's pant leg, but that would be about it. In fact, in 2002, when Mama moved in with me and my wife and children after my father died, she finally threw out my communion suit (along with other clothes dating back to God knows when). It was tearfully but totally gone.

Metaphorically speaking, is the Constitution America's communion suit? It was tailored for a slave-holding, Anglo-Protestant–dominated, horse-and-carriage, eighteenth-century nation peopled by roughly 4 million mostly Eastern Seaboard–hugging souls. It underwent twenty-seven post-ratification alterations (or sixteen if you count the first ten plus the twenty-seventh, which was originally proposed along with the first ten, as just one). Albeit not without busted seams and threadbare patches, the Constitution proved elastic enough for the democracy to keep wearing through territorial expansions, waves of immigration, technological leaps, a civil war, economic crises, two world wars, a global cold war, and a domestic civil rights revolution. In 1965, when my communion suit fit me the best, the Constitution still fit the country.

Over the last half-century, however, America has become a demographically diverse country that more than 300 million citizens call home. Since 1965, the American people's duly elected national leaders at both ends of Pennsylvania Avenue have birthed six new federal cabinet departments: Housing and Urban Development (1965); Transportation (1966); Energy (1977); Education (1979); Veterans Affairs (1989); and Homeland Security (2002). Enacted in 1965, Medicare and Medicaid, the two major federal health care programs, together account for about one-fifth of annual federal spending. Environmental protection, education, crime, and other issues that were barely on the federal agenda in 1965 are major agenda items today.

Adjusted for inflation, the size of the federal budget today is more than five times as large as it was in 1960. In 2011 dollars, the federal government spent roughly $712 billion in 1960. In 1970, it spent about $1.2 trillion; in 1980, $1.7 trillion; in 1990, $2.3 trillion; in 2000, $2.5 trillion; and in 2010, $4 trillion. State and local governments combined spend about $3 trillion each year. Total government spending (federal, state, and local) per capita is now about $20,000, and the annual debt per capita is about $50,000.

The Constitution's founding tailors, led by James Madison, were by no means allergic to a strong national government (see the Virginia Plan; see

Alexander Hamilton). They favored structures that could be changed and powers that could be expanded over time (see Article V). Compared with that of their antifederalist adversaries (see Patrick Henry), their vision for America was remarkably cosmopolitan (Exhibit A: no religious test required to hold federal office). Still, Madison's Constitution was not designed to fit a big or ever-growing government. It was more nearly designed to prevent one, and it most surely comprehended nothing like today's "husky" federal bureaucracy. Over the last half-century, formal, legal, and customary constitutional restraints on government growth were progressively relaxed, reduced, or removed. For example:

—The great majority of members of the House of Representatives have come to be incumbents holding fairly safe seats; primary elections and activists have supplanted party conventions and party bosses as the decisive means of selecting presidential candidates; and the number and variety of interest groups have increased enormously, as has the amount of money flowing into campaigns.

—The federal courts have altered their interpretation of the Constitution in ways that have not only permitted but required government action.

—Public opinion and the voting public have changed in ways that have legitimated and supported an expanded role for the federal government.

—Checks and balances have persisted, but whereas they once made it hard for the federal government to start a new program, they later made it hard, if not impossible, to cut or kill a program or to change how Washington directly administers or, more commonly, leverages what it funds.

Over the last thirty years, I have taught introductory American politics and government courses to undergraduates at Harvard University (in the 1980s), Princeton University (in the 1980s and 1990s), and the University of Pennsylvania (from 1999 to the present). Among the students in my courses, I am famous (or infamous) for assigning *The Federalist Papers* and requiring students to read Madison's No. 10 over and over again (seven times on my spring semester 2014 syllabus). No. 10 is the essay in which Madison explicates his hope that America's representative democracy—if structured as proposed in the yet-to-be-ratified Constitution and without depending on "enlightened statesmen" to "always be at the helm"—will generally succeed in taming "the mischiefs of faction." Most important, he hoped that it would tame the potentially fatal-to-democracy mischiefs of majority factions. Madison reasoned that through the constitutional contrivances to be described and defended in later numbers of the papers (separation of powers, checks and balances, federalism, the bicameral legislature, staggered elections, and others)—and given a bit of *buona fortuna*—the republic's "various and interfering interests" would likely be subjected regularly to public-spirited "regulation" by duly elected legislators (whether average leaders, self-loving louts, or the occasional Solon) functioning in the main as "proper guardians of the public weal."

The Madison who wrote No. 10 reckoned that the national government of "We the People," in its "necessary and ordinary operations," would cope successfully with the ever-present "spirit of party and faction," respect citizens' liberties, protect citizens' rights, and serve "the permanent and aggregate interests of the community" (what elsewhere in No. 10 and throughout *The Federalist Papers* is rendered in shorthand as the "public good"). As is plain from the Preamble of the Constitution as well as from so much else that Madison and the other Framers did and wrote, the "people," the "public," the "community" whose "permanent and aggregate interests" the "more perfect Union" was to serve" encompassed both "ourselves and our Posterity."

WE THE DEBT-FINANCED FACTION

Despite the Framers' reference to "ourselves and our Posterity," for a half-century or so, a persistent majority faction, consisting of Americans of every demographic description and socioeconomic status, supported by elected leaders in both parties and unbridled by the federal judiciary, has broken through virtually every constitutional barrier in order to benefit "ourselves" at the expense of "our Posterity," saddling the republic's future generations with tens of trillions of dollars in public debt.[1]

Lest my reader begin to get the wrong impression and smell a tea party brewing here, I am a lifelong Democrat who carries a torch for the New Deal.[2] I am highly sympathetic to the FDR-initiated, Eisenhower-consolidated, LBJ-expanded, and Reagan-survived entitlement state. I have never been philosophically allergic to "big government."[3] Rather, I contend that having mega-programs like Medicare, Medicaid, and "Obamacare" (a.k.a. the Patient Protection and Affordable Care Act of 2010) is a civic blessing. In fact, I favor a single-payer universal health system.[4] In short, I have faith that the federal government, together with state and local governments, can yet be made to work better and cost less, including through surgical—not sweeping—administrative reforms and through public-private partnerships involving for-profit businesses, secular nonprofits, and (my personal favorite) faith-based organizations.[5]

What I do oppose strongly enough to now contemplate a possible cure that I have hitherto thought worse than the disease—far-reaching constitutional reforms—is big government by a tax less, spend more, fifty-plus-year-old majority faction that has gorged itself on entitlements and other government-supplied goodies for which future generations must foot the bill. To be clear, I am defining entitlements as benefits that every eligible person has a legal right to claim and that the government may not legally deny. Social Security benefits and Medicare benefits are entitlements—big ones. Entitlements also include all the government benefits legally due to an individual who can demonstrate a need for those benefits—like nursing home payments for old folks who qualify for Medicaid or meals and snacks in the summer months for children who are eligible for the U.S. Department of Agriculture's summer food service programs.

The entitlement state that began during the New Deal was born from the noble conviction that to serve the common good, the federal government could and should work to create conditions under which average men, women, and children could lead peaceful and productive, if not uniformly prosperous, lives. The entitlement state today is far more extensive than anyone dreamed it would be in 1935 or, for that matter, in 1965. For instance, Medicare, the program serving mainly people age sixty-five and older, now has about 50 million beneficiaries and costs more than $550 billion a year. Medicaid, the federal-state program that mainly covers low-income children and adults plus people with certain disabilities, now has about 60 million beneficiaries and costs roughly $350 billion a year. Together, Medicare, Medicaid, and Social Security account for about 40 percent of the federal budget.[6]

Still, so far, so good, at least as far as I am concerned. As I see it, the problem is *not* the entitlement state per se. Nor, I would argue, is the problem that the entitlement state's expansion has propelled the aforementioned increase in total government (federal, state, and local) spending, which was equal to about 42 percent of GDP in 2010, up from about 27 percent of GDP in 1960. Rather, the problem is that the entitlement state has expanded mainly through fake political compromises, ever-goofier budgetary gimmicks, and long-term debt financing. For instance, according to a 2012 report by the Medicare Board of Trustees, the Medicare Trust Fund could be exhausted in 2024. Add the unfunded liabilities of Medicare, Social Security, and federal employees' future retirement benefits and the bill being foisted on future generations of Americans is more than $80 trillion (about $40 trillion for Medicare alone).[7]

In other words, American citizens yet to be born are being stuck with an entitlement benefits bill that is about five times the country's current annual GDP. And why is that? A persistent public majority says that it dislikes Congress and has big qualms about "big government." Yet in twenty-five national plebiscites between 1960 and 2014, voters reelected House incumbents at a rate north of 90 percent and Senate incumbents at a rate of about 80 percent.[8]

The 1980s brought both Ronald Reagan to the White House and the first waves of incontrovertible evidence that the entitlement state was becoming ever more financially wobbly. In 1986, Washington overhauled the federal tax system. The leading journalistic account of the law characterized it as reflecting an unlikely triumph of bipartisan legislators over Beltway bandits, lawyers, and lobbyists,[9] and a leading academic account of the law described it as a prime example of how Congress, warts and all, sometimes manages to produce "general interest" legislation.[10] But what actually followed was not a slow but steady return to fiscal discipline or tax-as-you-entitle politics. Instead, what followed were more federal programs; more federal program benefits; more federal spending; lower federal taxes; reborn federal tax breaks, deductions, and credits; even more reaching recklessly and unfairly into "our Posterity's" pockets; and ever fewer degrees of financial freedom for future democratic generations to set their own public priorities.

The "Reagan revolution" involved a conservative president that wanted three things: lower taxes, increased defense spending, and sizable long-term cuts in entitlement spending. To get the first two, he traded off the third.

But his 1986 deal with House Democratic leader Thomas P. "Tip" O'Neill was not a classic, bipartisan political compromise. It was the first of the "you tax less, we spend more" corrupt bargains that have defined federal "fiscal policy" for the last quarter-century and persist down to the present day.

Partisan and ideological fights like the post-2009 clashes over budgets and the debt ceiling fog the fact that nobody in official Washington at either end of Pennsylvania Avenue—*nobody*—is both willing and able to do anything that would *either* actually cut big-budget programs *or* raise more revenues from today's taxpayers to pay for them anytime soon. For instance, in 2011, Senator Ron Wyden (D-Ore.) and Representative Paul Ryan (R-Wis.) introduced a Medicare reform plan. Among other provisions, the plan reduced certain benefits for the wealthiest senior citizens. It featured a "premium support" voucher-type option under which beneficiaries could choose either a traditional Medicare plan or a Medicare-approved private plan. Total annual out-of-pocket Medicare costs were to be capped at $6,000 per person, and low-income citizens who could not pay the cap would receive a subsidy from the government.[11]

But for all the controversies that swirled around it, the Wyden-Ryan proposal contemplated neither deep cuts in benefits nor steep tax increases. Instead, its first lines were a rhapsody regarding the need to "strengthen Medicare and health security for all," with "no changes for those in or near retirement," and guaranteeing that Americans age fifty-six and older "would see no changes to the structure of their benefits." The proposal reflected the "We, the Majority" faction's desire to continue to get benefits without increasing taxes except, perhaps, on the richest citizens: 92 percent of respondents opposed "major cuts"; 65 percent opposed "minor cuts"; 51 percent opposed increasing program tax rates.[12]

"Errors and Delusions" Are Us

In December 2010, Erskine Bowles, the co-chair of the National Commission on Fiscal Responsibility and Reform, suggested that federal spending and revenues be balanced at no more than 21 percent of GDP.[13] He did not pick 21 percent out of a hat: that was roughly the average level of federal spending from 1970 to 2010.[14] The conservative Heritage Foundation was all for it.[15] The left-leaning Center on Budget and Policy Priorities was not: 21 percent of GDP would prove too little given "the aging of the population, substantial increases in health care costs, and new federal responsibilities in areas such as homeland security, education, and prescription drug coverage for seniors."[16] At 21 percent of GDP, it would not "be possible to maintain federal expenditures at their average level for decades back to 1970 without making draconian cuts in Social Security, Medicare, and an array of other vital federal activities."[17]

The Center on Budget and Policy Priorities was right. And since I share the progressive values that informed its factual analysis, I also share its conclusion that "higher levels of federal spending and revenues over the next 40 years" might prove both necessary and desirable.[18] But is an ever bigger debt-financed big government—a big government that increases spending to pay for increased benefits without commensurately increasing taxes enough to cover the next entitlement explosions—just fine so long as it does not involve any entitlement program cuts or result in immediate economic calamities? Self-styled centrists like Mr. Bowles and his bipartisan commission colleagues think not, and I agree. Their December 2010 report was entitled *The Moment of Truth*. It called for $4 trillion in deficit reduction through 2020, "more than any effort in the nation's history."[19] In public speeches and myriad other public communications, Bowles and his commission colleagues repeatedly called $4 trillion in deficit reduction over ten years a "go big" plan.

Bravo, but this "go big" plan symbolized just how far from anything like real "fiscal responsibility and reform" the country has drifted. For one thing, the "go big" plan did not deal at all adequately with the state and local government fiscal crises that are inextricably linked to Washington's financial mess. Subnational governments will spend about $3 trillion a year or so for decades to come. Their public employee pensions are somewhere between $1 trillion and $3 trillion in the hole (depending on which investment assumptions you buy), and their unfunded liabilities for their retirees' health care benefits are more than $1 trillion.[20]

America taxes and borrows its way to about $7 trillion a year in total (federal, state, and local) government spending (including more than $600 billion a year that the feds alone spend on more than 200 intergovernmental programs)—$70 trillion or so in the decade ahead. If aiming to cut $4 trillion out of $70 trillion over ten years is a "go big" deficit reduction plan, then a 700-pound, 40-year-old man hoping to lose 35 pounds by his 50th birthday is on a "moment-of-truth diet."

In late 2011, the so-called congressional supercommittee failed to find and agree on as much as $1.5 trillion (never mind $4 trillion or more) in deficit reduction over ten years. The country is approaching $20 trillion in national debt and witnessing big and mid-sized American cities go bankrupt and into receivership. Still, I am not an economist, though I majored in economics when gas cost less than a dollar a gallon. Today, many top economists are unsure about how much we should worry about any level of government debt (starting with how, exactly, we should measure it). With Harry Truman, I long for a one-handed economist. In the meantime, I am heeding what Paul A. Volcker, Richard Ravitch, and the State Budget Crisis Task Force had to say in January 2014 about the collective responsibility of the federal and state governments: _"It is, after all, our children and grandchildren who will pay the price of failure, and will have to cope with the diminished strength and competitiveness of the American republic."_[21]

I do not share the fawning assessments that Henry A. Kissinger and a Who's Who of government, business, academic, and other VIPs offered in their respective endorsements of a 2012 book showcasing "insights on China, America, and the world" by Lee Kuan Yew, a former prime minister of Singapore. In the book, his "insights" include the claim that "multiculturalism will destroy America" and the view that Deng Xiaoping was right "when he said: if 200,000 students have to be shot, shoot them."[22] Still, I am with Kissinger and company when it comes to Mr. Lee's take on the leadership failures behind America's mega-debt government:

> Presidents do not get reelected if they give a hard dose of medicine to their people. So, there is a tendency to procrastinate, to postpone unpopular policies in order to win election. . . . Governments took the easy way out by borrowing to give higher benefits to the current generation of voters and passing the costs on to the future generation who are not yet voters. This resulted in persistent government deficits and high public debt. . . . Medicare is going to cost them an extra $1.2 trillion in ten years—I do not know where the money is going to come from. . . . America's debt is what worries me most.[23]

In *Federalist* No. 10, Madison cautioned, "Enlightened statesmen will not always be at the helm."[24] (The "always" was his subtle way of saying "But they are now.") While confident in the constitutional arrangement that he and the other Founders had designed, he did not doubt for a moment that the republic's future would depend in part on enlightened leadership. For example, in *Federalist* No. 63, he pointed to "a well-constructed Senate" as "a defense to the people against their own temporary errors and delusions."[25] There are "particular moments in public affairs," he reasoned, when "the people . . . may call for measures which they themselves will afterwards be the most ready to lament and condemn." He banked on a "temperate and re-spectable body of citizens" to counter the public's misguided adventures and block "the blow mediated by the people against themselves, until reason, justice, and truth can regain their authority over the public mind."

For a half-century and counting, Americans have demanded and, in effect, voted for what it is impossible for their government to deliver all at once—ever more benefits, ever lower taxes, and no big budget deficits. There is nothing "temporary" about these public "errors and delusions." Reasonable scholars disagree about whether the Senate has ever played a robust role in restraining misguided but popular "measures." (I think it often has.) But, or so I would argue, senators who are "temperate and respectable" enough to lead and leaven public debates focused on fiscal responsibility and reform are many fewer and far less influential today than they were in 1965. (Name ten; I cannot.)

As Thomas E. Mann and Norman J. Ornstein have argued, in Congress as a whole, most particularly in the House and most emphatically among the GOP leaders, "It's even worse than it looks."[26] And, from Reagan right through Obama, the White House has fiddled right, fiddled left, and served mainly to reinforce and legitimate the public's false notions and unrealistic expectations about big government and its finances. The epitomizing presidential "moment of truth" here came in President Clinton's January 1996 State of the Union Ad-dress, when he proclaimed that the "era of big government is over."

Of course, the truth was and remains that post-1965 America has a big government that by popular demand (all reported mass discontent and muddled thinking about it aside) has added ever more federal policies, pro-grams, and regulations and become ever more debt-financed. And, as we now turn to discuss, rather than being "reinvented" in the last half-century,

America's Washington-leveraged big government has become ever more poorly administered by federal proxies that include state and local government supplicants and self-dealing for-profit and nonprofit groups.

IMPLEMENTATION-GROUP LIBERALISM

In 1969, in his classic work, *The End of Liberalism*, Theodore J. Lowi discerned how "interest-group liberalism" had arisen and remade the nation's constitutional republic—mostly for the worse.[27] Lowi depicted the Great Society era's federal legislative process as being typically dominated, policy domain by policy domain, by coalitions of self-interested citizens organized to exert political influence. Among the main protagonists in this political drama were the "1930s' left-wing liberals" who had "become the 1960s' interest-group liberals."[28] In Lowi's telling, Washington policymakers responded to demands by the interest groups and delegated authority for fashioning the programs favored by those groups to federal agencies. In due course, the agencies became captives of the interest groups. This factious pluralism resulted in ever longer but ever vaguer federal laws. Both in practice and "as a public philosophy," Lowi preached, interest-group liberalism "deranges and confuses expectations about democratic institutions . . . renders government impotent . . . demoralizes government," and "corrupts democratic government to the degree to which it weakens the capacity of governments to live by democratic formalisms."[29]

But in the book's concluding chapter, Lowi offered hope. He believed that interest-group liberalism could be contained or reversed by a move toward "juridical democracy" and that the first step in that direction would be "restoration of the *Schechter* rule."[30] In 1935, in *A.L.A. Schechter Poultry Corporation* v. *United States*, the U.S. Supreme Court declared that the National Industrial Recovery Act had gone too far in delegating lawmaking powers to an administrative agency. As Lowi acknowledged, the *Schechter* rule was "confirmed in a 1936 case but not seriously applied thereafter." But, writing more than three decades later, he nonetheless hung his hopes on the Court's "once again . . . declaring invalid and unconstitutional any delegation of power to an administrative agency that is not accompanied by *clear standards of implementation*."[31]

While waiting for the second coming of *Schechter*, Lowi counseled, we should warm up to Woodrow Wilson's old case "for *centralized administration* as a necessity for modern democracy."[32] Alas, Lowi's "juridical democracy" cure for interest-group liberalism was "a more formal and rule-bound administrative process." Rather than continue to "make a virtue of loose administration," he argued, we must instead create a new "administrative class"—"a Senior Civil Service."[33] Then he gives this sums-it-up sermon:

> If such a class were combined with court-imposed, Congress-imposed and administratively-imposed standards of law, the administrative process would inevitably be far more centralized without any loss of real pluralism in the larger system.[34]

In 1973, four years after Lowi penned his plea for Washington to covet "clear standards of implementation" and establish a more "centralized," direct public administration system for translating federal laws and policies into action, Jeffrey Pressman and Aaron Wildavsky published *Implementation*, the political science book with the best (or at least the longest) subtitle ever:

> *How Great Expectations in Washington Are Dashed in Oakland; Or, Why It's Amazing that Federal Programs Work at All, This Being a Saga of the Economic Development Administration as Told by Two Sympathetic Observers Who Seek to Build Morals on a Foundation of Ruined Hopes*[35]

As Pressman and Wildavsky made clear, the federal administrative process had been more *de*centralized than—and was becoming ever farther from—anything bearing the slightest resemblance to direct public administration (with or without senior civil servants in the mix). As they found, even in relation to a relatively tiny and low-budget federal project, federal policy implementation networks—federal, state, and local government agencies; private businesses; community groups; and others, each with their respective leaders, managers, workers, and members—were long, complicated, disjointed, and likely to become more, not less, so over time.

They were right. As I have elaborated elsewhere, America's post-1965 "big government" is BIG PAP: Big Inter-Government plus Private Administrative Proxies.[36] In addition to about 2 million full-time federal civil servants (not counting uniformed military personnel and postal workers), there are millions more citizens who function full-time or part-time as de facto federal government workers through state government agencies, local government agencies, for-profit firms, or nonprofit organizations.[37]

Today, what has been variously described as "government-by-proxy,"[38] "third-party government,"[39] and an "extended state,"[40] among other terms, involves politically entrenched, self-interested clientele networks of subnational public officials and employees, for-profit firms, and nonprofit organizations. Behind what passes today for federal "public administration" is what might be termed *implementation-group liberalism.* The federal government's assorted administrative proxies exert pressure both in the policymaking (lawmaking) process and in the policy implementation (legislative oversight) process against lawmakers (federal, state, or local) who might reduce their funding or change their programs in ways that they object to. They oppose any financial or administrative reforms that might threaten their grants or contracts.

For instance, in 2011, when a federal government shutdown was threatened but avoided and when the congressional "supercommittee" was searching for ways to rein in the federal budget, the CEO of the Aerospace Industry Association, speaking at the National Press Club, warned federal lawmakers that the "industry supports 2.9 million jobs across all 50 states" and urged them to "consider whether eliminating hundreds of thousands of jobs over the next decade" was "consistent with the national imperative to create jobs." Not to be outdone by the military-industrial complex, the entitlement-industrial complex also had its say. For instance, Independent Sector, an umbrella organization that advocates for nonprofits, sent a message to Pennsylvania's Republican senator and supercommittee member Pat Toomey, reminding him that more than 650,000 Pennsylvanians are employed by nonprofits.

You can lament this reality as reflecting an antidemocratic effort at "outsourcing sovereignty" and aspire to roll it back,[41] or you can make your peace with it and seek to make "collaborative governance" a virtue, while admitting that in health care and other areas it probably won't be.[42] Regardless, implementation-group liberalism makes for anemic to awful "public administration." Federal bureaucrats cannot "faithfully execute" even those few federal laws that do have something resembling Lowi's longed-for "clear standards of implementation." Even federal laws that do not embody multiple, vague, and contradictory objectives are not well administered: the Internal Revenue Service cannot collect all legally due federal income taxes; the U.S. Department of Defense cannot expeditiously trim or end payments to defense contractors that have violated procurement protocols; the Environmental Protection Agency cannot speedily clean up known toxic waste sites; the U.S. Department of Agriculture cannot supply meals to even a quarter of all eligible low-income children in the summer months; the Center for Medicare and Medicaid Services cannot stop improper payments to hospitals or facilitate development of functional IT systems for state health exchanges; and the list goes on and on.

MADISON'S NO. 10 . . . DOWNING

Despite the failures of public administration, the American politics scholars and analysts that I respect most remain acutely skeptical or flat-out opposed to any talk of far-reaching constitutional reforms. For instance, in this very volume, the great Pietro Nivola argues that often the Madisonian system still succeeds, even when it comes to hard financial choices, and the brilliant Jonathan Rauch argues that the U.S. system of government still fosters real compromises and delivers major policy shifts even on politically charged issues. They deny not a single hard fact about the nation's financial follies and administrative foibles. And they, too, spy few "enlightened statesmen" on the scene or over the horizon. Having stood where they stand for the last three decades—and being even more prone to Fourth-of-July feelings than they are with respect to the world-historic successes of the great compound republic bequeathed to its citizens by Madison and the other Framers—even now I am not sure that the case for considering far-reaching constitutional reforms is more right than not.

Just the same, let me be a one-handed political scientist: I believe that if Madison himself were here and knew the U.S. financial situation, BIG PAP, and implementation-group liberalism as they are, he would be prepared to ponder changes to the Constitution, and so the country should do no less. What, if any, specific constitutional reforms might ameliorate or fix the government's assorted financial, administrative, and democratic accountability dysfunctions? While waiting for Madison's ghost to arrive and tell me what to tell you, let's sample some reform proposals, starting with ones forged back in the 1980s by Brookings Institution scholar James L. Sundquist.

In 1981, Sundquist published *The Decline and Resurgence of Congress.* The book was Sundquist's maiden public motion for changing the Constitution in far-reaching ways. He credited the creation of the "modern era of the strong presidency" to a rational recognition by early twentieth-century leaders in Congress that the bicameral body has "two endemic weaknesses": it cannot plan, and it cannot act quickly.[43] In the book's concluding chapter, he endorsed a case for reframing the Constitution largely as a parliamentary democracy on the British model. But he quickly conceded that the "amendment process is so formidable that any basic structural change that arouses controversy and determined opposition is doomed from the start:"[44]

All the broad avenues toward fundamental reform to ameliorate the unending conflict between the branches seem, therefore, to be closed. Grafting some features of the parliamentary system to the American constitutional structure might help, but the issue is academic; basic change in the Constitution is impossible.[45]

Five years later, however, Sundquist flirted with the "impossible." In his 1986 book, *Constitutional Reform and Effective Government,* he contemplated changes that "might best be attempted, if one day a national consensus emerges that the United States government is indeed too congenitally divided, too prone to stalemate, too conflict-ridden to meet its immense responsibilities."[46] Putting aside questions of immediate political feasibility, he prescribed "an ideal series of amendments to the American Constitution" in the following "order of importance":[47]

1. Combining each party's candidates for president, vice president, Senate, and House on a "team ticket" that would be voted for as a unit
2. Four-year House terms and eight-year Senate terms

3. A method to call special elections to reconstitute a failed government
4. Permitting "dual office holding" so that members of Congress could serve in the executive branch
5. A limited line-item veto for the president
6. A limited legislative veto for Congress
7. A war powers amendment
8. Approval of treaties by a majority of the membership of both congressional chambers
9. A national referendum to break deadlocks.

Six years later, in 1992, Sundquist published a revised edition of *Constitutional Reform and Effective Government*. Therein he added examples of "failed government" from the preceding half-dozen years; noted how "the public attitude toward government" had grown only more "sour"; and dealt with two other proposals for constitutional reform, rebutting one (term limits for members of Congress) and provisionally embracing the other (altering or abolishing the electoral college).[48] In 1987, the year after the first edition of *Constitutional Reform and Effective Government* was published, the Committee on the Constitutional System—a blue-ribbon, bipartisan body composed of present and former legislators, governors, scholars, and others—had echoed Sundquist and issued a report on the need for far-reaching constitutional reforms. But despite the growing chorus of respectable opinion favoring such reforms, the 1992 edition ended word-for-word with the same counsel of despair that the 1986 edition did:

> All of the seemingly insurmountable obstacles to constitutional change could be overcome, of course, if the government were indeed to fail, palpably and for a sustained period. But the necessity to experience failure, in order to prepare for it, is not a happy prospect. This book must end, then, on a pessimistic note. Nothing is likely to happen short of a crisis.[49]

In 1993, Sundquist edited *Beyond Gridlock? Prospects for Governance in the Clinton Years—and After,* a volume produced in conjunction with the Committee on the Constitutional System.[50] With a return to unified party government, Sundquist and others considered the possibility that "effective government" might yet be possible even without major constitutional reforms. But just three years later, in 1996, they issued another volume, *Back to Gridlock? Governance in the Clinton Years*.[51] The political pitched battles between the first GOP-led House in four decades and the Democratic White House were enough to speed Sundquist and company back to the view that barring a catastrophe that might force fundamental changes, America's future prospects for good governance were mostly all bad.

In 2012, another Brookings scholar, Thomas E. Mann, and an American Enterprise Institute scholar, Norman J. Ornstein, coauthored *It's Even Worse Than It Looks: How the American Constitutional System Collided with the New Politics of Extremism*. The book became a bestseller. Echoing Sundquist, the two veteran Congress-watchers observed that "a Westminster-style parliamentary system provides a much cleaner form of democratic accountability than the American system does."[52] But they called instead for more minor reforms as well as for "creating a parallel or shadow Congress of former lawmakers from across the political spectrum that would periodically gather and debate key issues facing the country."[53]

Others, however, have gone farther than either Sundquist or Mann and Ornstein. For example, Sanford V. Levenson, a celebrated University of Texas political scientist, elaborates in his 2012 book, *Framed: America's 51 Constitutions and the Crisis of Governance*, on his earlier calls for a new Constitutional Convention to fashion a new Constitution.[54] And in his 2012 bestseller, *On Constitutional Disobedience*, Louis Michael Seidman, a leading constitutional law scholar–practitioner at Georgetown University, advocates that both elected leaders and the mass public begin disobeying (or simply ignoring) the Constitution and move quickly (and without regard to the amendment process specified in Article V) to do away with it.[55]

Of course, both in this volume and beyond it, the status-quo Congress and the unreformed Constitution still have armies of able defenders. For example, in his 2013 book, *Congress: A Performance Appraisal*, Andrew J. Taylor, a North Carolina State University political scientist, argues that "Congress's performance does not warrant the tremendous disdain in which it is currently held."[56] Taylor contends that Congress's failings are not rooted in the Constitution but in the unrealistic demands that people now make of Congress (like wanting ever more benefits with ever lower taxes). He suggests that "we should perhaps first look in the mirror" before criticizing Congress or pondering far-reaching constitutional reforms.[57]

MADISON'S NO. 14: CASE OPEN

Until recently, I would have ended by saying much the same thing as Taylor said. Despite impossible public demands, long-term debts, majority factions, government shutdowns, administrative meltdowns, partisan polarization, and all the rest, in the end the Madisonian system always seems to avert republic-wrecking failures while racking up some unexpected successes. It has kept the country's civic head pretty well above water. And it still allows (even if it does not facilitate) significant changes in law that either spark or reinforce positive changes in society.

All true, and yet the Constitution and the Bill of Rights were designed for a federal republic that was radically different from the federal republic that exists today. Today, the "federal" in federal republic is a vast, debt-financed system of *intergovernmental* relations that combines federal, state, and local governments in making policies, administering policies, and funding policies. The Constitution was fashioned to fit a strong and active but limited government. It was not designed to fit big government. And it most definitely was not devised with fifteen cabinet agencies; trillions of dollars a year in government spending, borrowing, and debt; and public administration by intergovernmental and other proxies in mind.

The country's ill-fitting constitutional machinery is now manipulated routinely by two types of factions. One is a persistent majority faction that is legally robbing future citizens in order to enjoy present benefits without having to pay for them itself. The other is a colossal coalition of special interests that includes subnational governments, for-profit firms, and nonprofit organizations that lobby for federal policies, programs, and regulations that they get paid to implement. And the U.S. incumbent-dominated, faction-empowering big government is not only politically polarized but administratively feckless, with epic program failures everywhere one looks and only rhetorical progress in improving "government performance and results." If an end to this fifty-plus-years-in-the-making tragedy is truly anywhere in sight, I do not see it.

There was substantial distance between the government needed for the "more perfect Union" and the government America had under the Articles of Confederation. The Constitution covered that distance and proved fitting for virtually all that Americans did at home and abroad well into the mid-twentieth century. And, even today, America's constitutional system is hardly inferior to the parliamentary regimes or unitary polities that govern most other contemporary democratic nations.

But there is today substantial distance between the government needed to do responsibly all or most of what Washington now is on the hook to do and the government that America has under the Constitution. The distance is arguably as great as the distance that Madison marked between the Articles and the Constitution. In phrases borrowed from *Federalist* No. 10, a new "republican remedy for the diseases most incident to republican government"—bigger, more expensive, and more complicated than any such government that Madison ever imagined—is needed. The nature, causes, and effects of "factions," including majority factions, have changed in ways that make the system more likely to reward than cure their "mischief." Thus, were Madison with us today, I think that he would make haste to dust off what he wrote in *Federalist* No. 14 about "the glory of the people of America":

[Americans] have not suffered a blind veneration for antiquity, for custom, or for names, to overrule the suggestions of their own good sense, the knowledge of their own situation, and the lessons of their own experience. To this manly spirit their posterity will be indebted for the possession, and the world for the example, of the numerous innovations displayed on the American theater in favor of private rights and public happiness.[58]

Given Americans' knowledge of their "own situation," Madison might not only give citizens a civic permission slip, but maybe even a sacred civic mandate, to consider the case for far-reaching constitutional reforms.

With Madison's blessing, a debate about the post-1965 lessons of American's "own experience" as it relates to far-reaching constitutional reform proposals should begin in earnest. Putting pure political feasibility questions to one side, I am more open than I have ever been to the case for moving from 1600 Pennsylvania Avenue toward 10 Downing Street. But I confess that I do not know how to think about whether or which quasi-parliamentary reforms might actually serve to mitigate posterity-be-damned majority factionalism or limit implementation-group liberalism. Having a new constitutional convention remains unthinkable to me, but allowing the status quo to persist into the next half-century has become equally unthinkable. Here is how Sandy Levenson weighs it:

> It is enough that you find yourself worrying . . . that your children and grandchildren will grow up in a far less attractive world . . . in part because of dysfunctionalities in our political systems that could be addressed, even if not wholly corrected. . . . Even if we are blasé about the consequences for ourselves, don't we owe our loved ones— and our fellow members of the American political community, if we take seriously the notion of being a part of "We the People"—at least some reflection about what those dysfunctionalities are and what in turn might be possible?[59]

As I said while still wearing my communion suit: "Amen."

Notes

1. In this section, I am reprising an argument that I first offered publicly at "Milestones in the History of a Free Society," a Princeton University conference cosponsored by Princeton's James Madison Program for American Ideals and Institutions and the University of Nebraska at Omaha's Association for the Study of Free Institutions, May 20, 2013.

2. For instance, see John J. DiIulio Jr., "Why I'm Still a Democrat," *Claremont Review of Books* (Winter 2012–13), pp. 71–72.

3. For instance, see John J. DiIulio Jr., "Are Conservative Republicans Now America's Ruling Class?," *Chronicle of Higher Education*, January 20, 2006, pp. 9–11; "Attacking Sinful Inequalities," *Perspectives on Politics* (December 2004), pp. 651, 667–70; "The Moral Compass of True Conservatism," in *The Fractious Nation? Unity and Division in Contemporary American Life*, edited by Jonathan Reider and Stephen Steinlight (University of California Press, 2003); and "Government by Proxy: A Faithful Overview," *Harvard Law Review* (March 2003), pp. 1271–84.

4. For instance, see John J. DiIulio Jr., "No Citizen Left Behind," *Sojourners* (November 2009), pp. 14–16; Frank J. Thompson and John J. DiIulio Jr., *Medicaid and Devolution* (Brookings Institution Press, 1998); and John J. DiIulio Jr. and Richard P. Nathan, *Making Health Reform Work: A View from the States* (Brookings, 1995).

5. For instance, see John J. DiIulio Jr., *Godly Republic: A Centrist Blueprint for America's Faith-Based Future* (University of California Press, 2007); John J. DiIulio Jr., *Deregulating the Public Service* (Brookings Institution Press, 1994); John J. DiIulio Jr., Gerald J. Garvey, and Donald F. Kettl, *Improving Government Performance: An Owner's Manual* (Brookings, 1993).

6. Office of Management and Budget, "Fiscal Year 2013: Historical Tables, Budget of the U.S. Government," table 3-1, "Outlays by Superfunction and Function, 1940–2017" (www.whitehouse.gov/sites/default/files/omb/budget/fy2013/assets/hist.pdf).

7. "Annual Report of the Boards of Trustees of the Federal Hospital Insurance and Federal Supplemental Medical Insurance Trust Funds" (Washington: 2013), pp. 28, 228–29, 278, and Appendix G.

8. James Q. Wilson, John J. DiIulio Jr., and Meena Bose, *American Government: Institutions and Policies*, 14th ed. (Cengage, 2015), p. 313.

9. Jeffrey H. Birnbaum and Alan S. Murray, *Showdown at Gucci Gulch: Lawyers, Lobbyists, and the Unlikely Triumph of Tax Reform* (New York: Random House, 1987).

10. R. Douglas Arnold, *The Logic of Congressional Action* (Yale University Press, 1992).

11. Office of U.S. Congressman Paul Ryan, "Wyden and Ryan Advance Bipartisan Plan to Strengthen Medicare and Expand Health Care Choices for All," December 15, 2011, pp. 2-3 (http://paulryan.house.gov/news/documentssingle.aspx?DocumentsID=272682).

12. Campaign for America's Future, "The American Majority Project Polling," Washington Post/ABC News Poll, March 10–13, 2011 (http://ourfuture.org/report/american-majority-project-polling); "The Public's Health Care Agenda for the 112th Congress," Kaiser Family Foundation/Harvard School of Public Health Poll, January 4–14, 2011; and "How America Would Deal with the Budget Deficit," University of Maryland, School of Public Policy, Center on Policy Attitudes, February 3, 2011, p. 49.

13. Erskine Bowles, quoted in David Broder, "Outside Washington, Feeling Hopeful on the Budget Crisis," *Washington Post*, July 15, 2010.

14. Paul N. Van de Water, "Federal Spending Target of 21 Percent of GDP Not Appropriate Benchmark for Deficit-Reduction Efforts" (Center on Budget and Policy Priorities, July 28, 2010).

15. Brian M. Riedel, "The Three Biggest Myths about Tax Cuts and the Budget Deficit" (Washington: Heritage Foundation, June 21, 2010).

16. Van de Water, "Federal Spending Target of 21 Percent of GDP Not Appropriate Benchmark," p. 1.
17. Ibid., p. 1.
18. Ibid., p. 8.
19. Report of the National Commission on Fiscal Responsibility and Reform, *The Moment of Truth*, December 2010, p. 14.
20. Statement by Richard Ravitch and Paul Volcker, *Report of the State Budget Crisis Task Force*, July 2012.
21. Statement by Richard Ravitch and Paul Volcker, *Report of the State Budget Crisis Task Force: Final Report*, January 2014.
22. Graham Allison, Robert D. Blackwill, and Ali Wyne, *Lee Kuan Yew: The Grand Master's Insights on China, the United States, and the World* (MIT Press, 2012), pp. 30, 153. Foreword by Henry A. Kissinger.
23. Ibid, pp. 25–26, 34–35.
24. Clinton Rossiter, *The Federalist Papers* (New York: Signet Classic Edition, 1999), p. 75.
25. Ibid., p. 382.
26. Thomas E. Mann and Norman J. Ornstein, *It's Even Worse Than It Looks: How the American Constitutional System Collided with the New Politics of Extremism* (New York: Basic Books, 2012).
27. Theodore J. Lowi, *The End of Liberalism: The Second Republic of the United States* (New York: W.W. Norton, 1969).
28. Ibid., p. 305.
29. Ibid., pp. 288–91.
30. Ibid., p. 298.
31. Ibid., pp. 126, 298 (emphasis added).
32. Ibid., p. 301 (emphasis added).
33. Ibid., pp. 303–04.
34. Ibid., pp. 304–05.
35. Jeffrey Pressman and Aaron Wildavsky, *Implementation* (University of California Press, 1973).
36. John J. DiIulio Jr., "Facing Up to Big Government," *National Affairs* (Spring 2012), pp. 22–41.
37. For a detailed account and analysis, see John J. DiIulio Jr., *Bring Back the Bureaucrats: Why More Federal Workers Will Result in Smaller (and Better!) Government* (West Conshohocken, Pa.: Templeton Press, 2014).
38. Donald F. Kettl, *Government by Proxy: (Mis?)Managing Federal Programs* (Washington: Congressional Quarterly Press, 1988).
39. Lester Salamon, *The Tools of Government: A Guide to the New Governance* (Oxford University Press, 2002).
40. Melvin J. Dubnick and George Frederickson, *Public Accountability: Performance*

Measurement, the Extended State, and the Search for Trust (Washington: National Academy of Public Administration and the Kettering Foundation, 2011).

41. Paul Verkuil, *Outsourcing Sovereignty: Why Privatization of Government Functions Threatens Democracy and What We Can Do about It* (Cambridge University Press, 2007).

42. Richard J. Zeckhauser and John D. Donahue, *Collaborative Governance: Private Roles for Public Goals in Turbulent Times* (Princeton University Press, 2010).

43. James L. Sundquist, *The Decline and Resurgence of Congress* (Brookings, 1981), pp. 30–36, 151–52.

44. Ibid., pp. 466–67.

45. Ibid., p. 478.

46. James L. Sundquist, *Constitutional Reform and Effective Government* (Brookings, 1986).

47. Ibid., pp. 240–41.

48. James L. Sundquist, *Constitutional Reform and Effective Government*, rev. ed. (Brookings, 1992), pp. 177, 187, 198.

49. Ibid., p. 334.

50. James L. Sundquist, *Beyond Gridlock? Prospects for Governance in the Clinton Years—and After* (Brookings Institution Press, 1993).

51. James L. Sundquist, *Back to Gridlock? Governance in the Clinton Years* (Brookings, 1996).

52. Mann and Ornstein, *It's Even Worse Than It Looks*, p. 198.

53. Ibid., p. 183.

54. Sanford Levenson, *Framed: America's 51 Constitutions and the Crisis of Governance* (Oxford University Press, 2012), p. 391.

55. Louis Michael Seidman, *On Constitutional Disobedience* (Oxford University Press, 2012).

56. Andrew J. Taylor, *Congress: A Performance Appraisal* (Boulder, Colo.: Westview Press, 2013), p. 18.

57. Ibid., p. 202.

58. Rossiter, *The Federalist Papers*, p. 99.

59. Levenson, *Framed*, p. 391.

Three

CONSTITUTIONAL SURPRISES

What James Madison Got Wrong

WILLIAM A. GALSTON

I yield to no one in my admiration for James Madison as a political thinker who brought theory to bear on practice as few had done before or have done since. By daring to disagree with "the celebrated Montesquieu" over the possible scope of republican government, he modernized republican theory and helped bring about a permanent advance in human liberty. He is rightly hailed as the progenitor of American pluralism and institutionalism. His reputation as the "father of the Constitution" is perhaps hyperbolic, but not wildly so. His debate with Alexander Hamilton over presidential executive powers under the Constitution has shaped interpretations of Article II from the 1790s to the present day.

Against that backdrop, it stands as a warning to pundits and political scientists alike that Madison should have so misjudged the dynamics of the national government that he helped set in motion. There are, of course, many developments that he could not have foreseen. He was certain, for example, that the influence of state revenue agents would always exceed those of the national government—as would have been the case had the 16th Amendment not constitutionalized the income tax in 1913. Nor can he be faulted for predicting that the election of senators by state legislators would make federal officials more dependent on the states than vice versa. That was in fact the case until the 17th Amendment—the second constitutional amendment of 1913—mandated the direct election of senators by the people.

Madison was sure that during peacetime, the federal military establishment would remain smaller and weaker than state militias, as it did until the decades-long mobilization during the cold war and, after a brief respite during the 1990s, following the terrorist attacks of September 11, 2001. More broadly, he believed that the federal government would be relatively weak except in times of war, which he thought would bear a "small proportion" to times of peace;[1] again, a reasonable expectation until the United States became a superpower with global reach. And even in the 1920s, few observers could have predicted the rise of the administrative state that has altered the balance among federal institutions without the formal authorization of constitutional change.

Executive versus Legislative Power

Somewhat harder to excuse was Madison's belief that legislative usurpation was a far greater threat to republican government than was executive power. To be sure, during his formative periods of service in the Continental Congress and the Virginia House of Delegates, he had directly experienced the vices of legislatures, and the arguments that he made during the Constitutional Convention and the debate over ratification reflected the influence of those years. Still, there is little evidence that he had thought through the relation between republican government and executive power with anything like his customary thoroughness. (Hamilton wrote all of the *Federalist Papers* that focused on that topic.)

Instead, Madison was content to repeat a proposition that he regarded as axiomatic: "In republican government, the legislative authority necessarily predominates."[2] The constitutions of the states, he said, had mistakenly relied on "parchment barriers" to restrain the growth of legislative power; as a result, "The legislative department is everywhere extending the sphere of its activity and drawing all power into its impetuous vortex." In a representative republic where the executive is limited "in both the extent and the duration of its power," it is the "enterprising ambition" of the legislature against which the people must take the greatest precautions.[3]

Barely six years after penning those words, in the wake of Washington's proclamation of neutrality between France and Great Britain, Madison found himself locked in pitched battle with Hamilton over the scope of executive power. Madison denied what Hamilton affirmed, that the first sentence of Article II was meant as a general grant of executive power. Madison affirmed what Hamilton denied, that the Neutrality Proclamation overstepped the constitutional boundaries of executive power by infringing on the Senate's treaty-making power. I have analyzed this debate in detail elsewhere.[4] For present purposes, suffice it to say that by successfully freeing the president from dependence on Congress, the drafters of the Constitution opened the door to a broader conception of executive power than Madison had understood in 1787. Washington's unassailable reputation allowed him to exercise that power. Future presidents with far less prestige used the structural features of their office—the ability to make decisions quickly and to speak with a single voice—to dominate Congress in the conduct of foreign policy and national defense.

The States versus the National Government

Even less prescient was Madison's thesis—articulated most fully in *Federalist* 45—that the principal threat to the Constitution would be state intrusion on federal power and authority rather than vice versa. It is not hard to understand why he made that argument. From a rhetorical standpoint, his principal challenge during the struggle over ratification was to persuade swing voters—many of them local notables—that the new government would not pose a threat to their interests and authority. It stands to reason that he would deploy every available argument in what amounted to a lawyer's brief to convince the local eminences that they had nothing to fear.

I do not mean to suggest that Madison was arguing in bad faith. In the months prior to the Constitutional Convention, he had been preoccupied with the incapacity of the Articles of Confederation, much of which he traced to state misconduct. In his remarkable memorandum of April 1787,

"Vices of the Political System of the U. States," he catalogued a dozen reasons why the confederal system was failing. The states not only refused to comply with the decisions of the Continental Congress but also engaged in constant "encroachments . . . on the federal authority." They refused to act in concert, even when the common interest clearly required it.[5] From Madison's perspective, a prime purpose of the new constitution was to strengthen national capacity against pervasive centrifugal forces. He found it hard to imagine that the opposite could be a problem.

Although scholars such as Lance Banning have characterized Madison as an ambivalent nationalist (which he may have been in the early 1780s), by 1787 any ambivalence was hard to detect.[6] Entering the Philadelphia convention, his ardent nationalism had crystallized into two objectives, neither of which he achieved. The first—representation proportional to population in the Senate as well as the House—is well known, while the second, which he regarded as equally important, has faded into obscurity. Put simply, Madison proposed that the national legislature have the power to review and veto all laws enacted by state legislatures. In a letter to George Washington prior to the convention, he argued that such a national power was "absolutely necessary, and . . . the least possible encroachment on the State jurisdictions" that would achieve his objective of protecting the rights of individuals and of the fledgling national government against the state governments. If the new central government lacked this "defensive power," it would be unable to protect itself against state encroachments and would fail to remedy one of the chief defects of the Articles.[7] In a convention speech featuring what Charles Hobson has described as a "burst of Newtonian imagery," Madison likened his proposed national legislative veto to gravity: it was "the great pervading principle that must control the centrifugal tendency of the States; which without it, will continually fly out of their proper orbits and destroy the order and harmony of the political System."[8]

Early in the Constitutional Convention, Madison seemed to be making progress. The delegates initially accepted a version of the legislative veto whose scope was narrowed to acts by the states that contravened the federal constitution, while simple policy disagreements were excluded. Madison subsequently tried but failed to restore the version that, in his formulation, would have authorized the veto "in all cases whatsoever." Five weeks later, the delegates changed their minds and rejected even the more limited version. Instead, they endorsed what became the Supremacy Clause and laid the foundation for judicial review.

Madison, who regarded these moves as an inadequate consolation prize, was bitterly disappointed. In a letter to Jefferson, he despaired that "the plan, should it be adopted, will neither effectually answer its national object nor prevent the local mischiefs which everywhere excite disgusts against the state governments."[9] In a post-convention letter to Jefferson, he continued to argue that the national veto was necessary both to protect the federal government against state encroachments and to protect the liberties of individuals against violations by local majorities—a significant protection. "It may be asked," Madison acknowledged, "how private rights will be more secure under the Guardianship of the General Government than under the State Governments, since they are both founded on the republican principle which refers the ultimate decision to the will of the majority." In the remainder of what he termed an "immoderate digression," he answered his own question by advancing an early version of the pluralist argument for the extended republic that attained mature formulation in *Federalist* No. 10.[10]

Without the legislative veto, Madison believed, the new constitution embodied the perhaps fatal mistake of allowing *imperia in imperio*. In the wake of the decision (on successive days) to reject both proportional representation in the Senate and the legislative veto, Connecticut's Oliver Ellsworth characterized the emerging constitutional structure as "partly federal and partly national." Madison adopted this formulation in *Federalist* No. 39 to argue that contrary to the claims of the Constitution's opponents, the proposed charter did not represent a consolidation of the states into a fully national government. To bolster his argument, he cited constitutional provisions, such as equal state representation in the Senate, against which he had fought during the convention.

The rejection of the most strongly nationalist provision of Madison's agenda may have influenced his belief that the states had little to fear from the new government. But he offered many other reasons as well. As we have seen, he thought that state-based procedures for electing senators and the president would give the states influence over those officials; that the states would predominate in times of peace, which would be the norm; that state militias would dwarf any standing army that the federal government could possibly maintain; and that the states' apparatus for revenue collection would outweigh that of the federal government. Constitutional amendments and foreseeable events have mooted all of those points.

But Madison's thesis rested on a more comprehensive and less mutable basis. He had spent months prior to the Constitutional Convention studying the history of ancient and modern federations. Centrifugal forces had weakened each of them, often fatally. Without the legislative veto, he wrote to Jefferson, there was a danger that the new constitution would suffer the same fate. "It may be said," he averred, "that the new Constitution is founded on different principles, and will have a different operation. I admit the difference to be material. It presents the aspect rather of a feudal system of republics, if such a phrase may be used, than of a Confederacy of independent States."[11] This analogy was the reverse of comforting, Madison continued: every such system had undergone a "continual struggle between the head and the inferior members, until a final victory had been gained in some instances by one, in others, by the other."[12] That is not a wholly inapt diagnosis of the epoch of U.S. history that ended only in 1865.

But there was another side to the story, as Madison knew well. Early in his public career, he had diagnosed the fundamental structural flaw of the Articles: Congress's writ, even when binding (and often it was not), applied to the states rather than to individuals. Madison arrived in Philadelphia determined to change that structure, and he succeeded. The Virginia Plan that kicked off the convention and shaped its proceedings embodied the principle that federal legislation should operate on individuals rather than the states. The small states' eventual riposte, the New Jersey Plan, would have retained the status quo. But as historian Jack Rakove observes, "This was a fatal weakness, and one reason why the delegates barely discussed the New Jersey Plan on its merits."[13] The small states were most interested in being equally represented in the Senate. Once they had prevailed on that issue, they did not seriously contest the direct link between national legislation and individuals, which became a key building block of the new constitution.

Arguing for its ratification, Madison acknowledged that shift. The Constitution's adversaries claimed that because the new government would exert its power on "individual citizens composing the nation in their individual capacities," it would be national rather than federal.[14] In that respect, Madison agreed, they were right. But he worked hard to deemphasize the significance of that point, embedding it in a litany of complex features of the Constitution pointing in different directions, which had the effect of obscuring just how fundamental the structural shift would prove. Madison had yet another arrow in his quiver. "The powers delegated by the proposed Constitution to the federal government are few and defined," he said. "Those which are to remain in the state governments are numerous and indefinite."[15] Section 8 of Article I gave that claim the appearance of plausibility, and the Tenth Amendment, drafted by Madison and ratified as part of the Bill of Rights in 1791, endorsed it.

But the matter was more complicated than Madison let on, perhaps more than he realized. It was by no means clear that enumerated powers would circumscribe the executive to the same extent as the legislature. Moreover, the extent of the limitation on the legislature was open to question. Late in the convention, the Necessary and Proper Clause was adopted unanimously. There is no evidence that the delegates saw it as a separate grant of legislative power or that Madison raised any objections. Writing in *Federalist* No. 44, Madison minimized its significance, even though, as he noted, "Few parts of the Constitution have been assailed with more intemperance."[16] If Congress exceeded its constitutional writ, the executive and the judiciary would push back. And if Congress invaded the prerogatives of the states, their officials would "sound the alarm to the people" and exert their influence to elect new representatives to the national legislature.

Madison persuaded many of his readers; he may even have persuaded himself. But his assessment was much too sanguine. Less than a decade after the Constitution's ratification, the Federalist-dominated Congress passed the Alien and Sedition Acts, and Madison felt compelled to resist. He drafted the Virginia Resolution, enacted by the Virginia state legislature in December 1798, which declared that the powers of the federal government rested on a "compact" to which "the states are parties." The Constitution enumerates those powers, which are to be construed according to the "plain sense and intention of the instrument." When the federal government exceeds the plain meaning of the powers granted to it, the states that are parties to the Constitution "have the right, and are in duty bound, to interpose for arresting the progress of the evil, and for maintaining within their respective limits, the authorities, rights, and liberties appertaining to them."

In the uproar that followed, Madison denied that any individual state could rightly declare a federal law to be null and void. His point was political, not constitutional: by vigorously objecting to *ultra vires* federal action, states could create a backlash that would compel the federal government to change course. But no state stood with Virginia except Kentucky, which had enacted a similar resolution, drafted by Jefferson. Fully ten states either rejected the Kentucky and Virginia Resolutions or passed resolutions of disapproval. It took the election of 1800 to end the immediate crisis.

But the episode had the effect of arming a ticking time bomb. From the Nullification Crisis to the Fugitive Slave Acts to the outbreak of the Civil War, aggrieved parties had recourse to the thesis that Madison had articulated in 1798. He had learned the hard way that the federal government could use its constitutional powers to threaten what many states regarded as their prerogatives under the Constitution. The document that Madison had successfully defended a decade earlier had opened the door to a government more national and less federal than he could comfortably accept.

DIRECT VERSUS REPRESENTATIVE DEMOCRACY

The new constitution set in motion a dynamic that led to a more directly democratic government than Madison had anticipated. The system of representation that he championed made the "extended republic" possible. But it was designed to perform other functions as well. Representation would act as a "filtration" process that advanced the most knowledgeable and public-spirited citizens to national office. It could help organize and moderate the clash of competing factions. And it could lean against the passions of the moment, giving added weight to cooler, longer-range considerations. All of that mattered because Madison's pluralism was more than procedural. To be sure, he questioned the classic republican reliance on virtue:

> It is vain [to say that] enlightened statesmen will be able to adjust . . . clashing interests and render them all subservient to the public good. Enlightened statesmen will not always be at the helm. Nor, in many cases, can such an adjustment be made at all without taking into view indirect and remote considerations, which will rarely prevail over the immediate interest which one party may find in disregarding the rights of another or the good of the whole.[17]

Artful institutional arrangements would have to fill the void that the scarcity of civic virtue inevitably creates.

Still, unlike many modern pluralists, Madison was unwilling to accept outcomes that represented only the vector-sum of contending interest groups. For Madison, the idea of the common good was more than a rhetorical device. It was real and definable, the polestar of republican politics: "the public good, the real welfare of the great body of the people, is the supreme object to be pursued."[18] Properly structured systems of representation would increase the odds that the policies of republican self-government more closely approximated the long-term good of the entire political community. As Madison summarized the case, the effect of a representative system is to

> refine and enlarge the public views by passing them through the medium of a chosen body of citizens, whose wisdom may best discern the true interest of their country and whose patriotism and love of justice will be least likely to sacrifice it to temporary or partial considerations. . . . It may well happen that the public voice, pronounced by the representatives of the people, will be more consonant to the public good than if pronounced by people themselves, convened for the purpose.[19]

Implicit in Madison's concept of filtration through representation (and also in Jefferson's understanding of elections as selecting the "natural aristoi") is the assumption that men with middling gifts would defer to those of superior capacity. As Gordon Wood shows in *The Radicalism of the American Revolution*, that expectation did not survive the founding generation. Democratizing social processes combined with egalitarian principles to eviscerate the culture of deference and empower people such as those who celebrated Andrew Jackson's inauguration by throwing what has been called "the wildest party in White House history."[20]

Later on, the ideal of direct democracy added to the pressures on Madisonian representation. Electing senators by popular vote rather than by state legislators was a step in that direction, as were the Progressive-era innovations of referendums and initiatives, which a number of states adopted as alternatives to rule by corrupt political insiders. Primary elections represented an additional move down that road. Rather than having political professionals select a party's candidates, the people would do it themselves. Egalitarianism meant mistrust of any institution that failed to give equal weight to individuals, a stance constitutionalized in the Supreme Court's *Baker* v. *Carr* decision.[21] So understood, political equality was bound to erode the legitimacy of institutions such as the Electoral College, at least to the extent that the outcomes that they generate deviate from one person, one vote. And then in the 1960s, direct or "participatory" democracy emerged from the shadows as the governing ideal for a new wave of radical reform. Insurgents on both the left and the right came to see face-to-face caucuses as the most legitimate way of selecting candidates. (Oddly, such caucuses replicated many features of the scorned "smoke-filled rooms," albeit with different occupants and—in the case of Democrats—without the smoke.)

Like many of his peers, Madison believed that the moral equality at the heart of the Declaration's revolutionary doctrine could coexist with political inequality and social hierarchy. That belief suffused his hopes for the constitutional institutions that he helped shape. But it turned out to be unfounded. Since the 1820s, when the culture of deference collapsed, the country has struggled without success to find functional substitutes for leaders with above-average capacities who take the long view and advance what Madison called the "real" public good, distinct from the desires of the moment.

PARTIES VERSUS INTEREST GROUPS

The controversies of the 1790s highlighted a key weakness in Madison's most famous contribution to political theory and practice—the argument that economic, social, and religious pluralism in an extended republic constituted sufficient protection against the tyranny of the majority. Madison not only opposed political parties in the modern sense of the term but also believed that the diversity of interests, beliefs, and faiths in a large population spread over a vast territory would prevent national parties from forming. At the worst, the single-front battle characteristic of party competition would arise in individual states, and it would stay there.

As Madison knew, there was an issue—slavery—that had the potential to override the fragmentation of interest groups and divide the new nation in two. During the Constitutional Convention, he did everything in his power to defuse the issue. But not long after the Constitution went into effect, he learned that there were others. The Franco-British conflict split the new nation, provoked a fundamental debate about executive power, and led to the Alien and Sedition Acts, which could have blown up the new republican experiment before it celebrated its tenth anniversary. By 1800, the U.S. two-party system had assumed the basic structure that it retains to this day—so much so that in his first inaugural speech Thomas Jefferson felt compelled to make a plea that reads like the template for the 2004 speech that elevated Barack Obama to national attention. "Every difference of opinion is not a difference of principle," Jefferson said. "We have called by different names brethren of the same principle." Then came the party-driven punch-line: "We are all Republicans, we are all Federalists."

"The accumulation of all powers, legislative, executive, and judiciary, in the same hands," Madison had declared, "may be pronounced the very definition of tyranny."[22] The Constitution was designed as a bulwark against tyranny, so understood. But the very structure that preserves liberty can also thwart the capacity to decide and act, essential attributes of any effective government. The party system has endured in part because it helps a system of divided powers and functions make decisions and carry them out. But as we have seen episodically throughout American history, in circumstances of deep division, the party system can prevent rather than facilitate effective governance. Quasi-parliamentary parties comport ill with the design of the U.S. constitutional system.

In sum, two failed predictions—one institutional, the other sociological—weakened the force of Madisonian pluralism. Madison failed to understand fully the logic of his own creation: to function effectively, a constitution of divided powers and functions would need a party system to organize and channel the multiplicity of interest groups. And he was too confident that this multiplicity would generate enough centrifugal force to prevent the formation of large agglomerations that could make possible the dreaded tyranny of the majority.

In the end, as Madison knew, there was only so much that institutions could do to solve perennial political problems. Even as he propounded a new science of politics in which clashes of interest and ambition were deployed in the service of liberty, he found himself compelled to reaffirm a portion of the older republican creed:

> As there is a degree of depravity in mankind which requires a certain degree of circumspection and distrust, so there are other qualities in human nature which justify a certain portion of esteem and confidence. *Republican government presupposes the existence of these qualities in a higher degree than any other form.* Were the pictures which have been drawn by the political jealousy of some among us faithful likenesses of the human character, the inference would be that there is not sufficient virtue among men for self-government; and that nothing less than the chains of despotism can restrain them from destroying and devouring one another [emphasis added].[23]

So the celebrated Montesquieu was not entirely wrong after all. And as civic republicans have long argued, "sufficient virtue" is not innate and spontaneous. The American system of education and structure of civil society must somehow nurture citizens' capacity for the kind of virtue that self-government requires. As the nation struggles to reduce today's debilitating polarization, it cannot safely ignore the classic question of how best to form the civic character that a republic needs to flourish.

Notes

1. *Federalist* No. 45, p. 293. All references in this chapter are to Clinton Rossiter, ed., *The Federalist Papers* (New York: New American Library, 1961).
2. *Federalist* No. 51, p. 322.
3. *Federalist* No. 48, pp. 308–09.
4. William A. Galston, "The Madisonian Understanding of Executive Power," in *Executive Power in Theory and Practice*, edited by Hugh Liebert, Gary L. McDowell, and Terry L. Price (New York: Palgrave Macmillan, 2012).
5. James Madison, "Vices of the Political System of the United States," in *James Madison: The Theory and Practice of Republican Government*, edited by Samuel Kernell (Stanford University Press, 2003), pp. 329–34.
6. Lance Banning, "James Madison and the Nationalists: 1780–1783," *William and Mary Quarterly*, 3rd Series, vol. 40, no. 2 (April 1983): 227–55.
7. Quoted and discussed in Charles F. Hobson, "The Negative on State Laws: James Madison, the Constitution, and the Crisis of Republican Government,"

William and Mary Quarterly, 3rd series, vol. 36, no. 2 (April 1979): 215–35, 219.

8. Ibid., p. 221.
9. Quoted in Jack Rakove, *Revolutionaries: A New History of the Invention of America* (Boston: Houghton Mifflin Harcourt, 2010), p. 381.
10. Letter to Jefferson, October 24, 1787, in Kernell, *James Madison,* pp. 343–50.
11. Ibid., p. 346.
12. Ibid.
13. Rakove, *Revolutionaries,* p. 370.
14. *Federalist* No. 39, p. 245.
15. *Federalist* No. 45, p. 292.
16. *Federalist* No. 44, p. 284.
17. *Federalist* No. 10, p. 80.
18. *Federalist* No. 45, p. 289.
19. *Federalist* No. 10, p. 82.
20. Scott Bomboy, "The Story of the Wildest Party in White House History," *Constitution Daily,* March 4, 2013 (http://blog.constitutioncenter.org/2014/03/the-story-of-the-wildest-party-in-white-house-history-2/).
21. *Baker* v. *Carr,* 369 U.S. 186 (1962).
22. *Federalist* No. 47, p. 301.
23. *Federalist* No. 55, p. 346.

Four

OVERCOMING THE GREAT RECESSION

How Madison's "Horse and Buggy" Managed

PIETRO S. NIVOLA

*I*n 2008, America and most of Europe plunged deeply into an economic crisis. In the United States, however, the economy hit bottom that fall and then began recovering, albeit little by little, and the recession was technically over by June 2009. Meanwhile, the Eurozone continued to sputter. Through 2012 and 2013 and well into 2014, prominent economies therein struggled to regain solid rates of growth.[1] The United States, by contrast, lowered its unemployment rate to less than 6 percent and has posted modest but notable economic growth over each of the past several years. The U.S. expansion may well pick up steam in 2015. The outlook for much of Europe, though improving, remains to be seen.[2]

Could it be that, for all the laments about the "broken," antiquated American political system, it actually did a better job of contending with the global recession and its aftermath than many other advanced democracies did? It looks that way. That comparatively favorable performance, moreover, may well have much to do with the actions that the American system *impeded*, not just the actions that it duly carried out.

Hence, this brief chapter ventures several rather unconventional observations. First, as is well known, a hallmark of this country's old Madisonian political order is its manifold opportunities to obstruct and delay. Less understood is that in dealing with the economic slump of recent years, obstructionism, ironically, often proved to be an advantage. Second, contrary to much received wisdom, the system in fact also has been suitably responsive and agile at the most critical junctures, when it was absolutely essential to act. Third, contrary to another widely held impression, Congress has effectively operated on a bipartisan basis at important times. Next, although the U.S. political process has admittedly faltered in at least one critical respect—failure to deal boldly with the fiscal problems of the more distant future—that particular shortcoming is scarcely unique among democracies. And this country may still be better positioned than most to meet those challenges when the moment of truth ultimately arrives. Finally, the chapter offers a few reflections on where the American constitutional order, so profoundly influenced by the thinking of James Madison, has enabled the outcomes described.

MADISONIAN VIRTUES

In its own quirky fashion, the U.S. government managed to avoid the trap that several European countries fell into as the Great Recession unfolded. In Europe, austerity measures were initiated in very frail economies. Granted, some of those countries had less choice in the matter; the bond market had already begun forcing their hand, whereas fortuitously the United States was able to continue financing its deficit-spending at rock-bottom interest rates. Yet that is not the whole story. Regime characteristics played a part. The U.S. system's separation of powers, with its sometimes frustrating checks and balances, blocked precipitous budget cutting and tax increases. That helped the U.S. economy turn up and then stay on track to regain firm footing. Eventually, some spending cuts and higher taxes were permitted here, too, but not before 2013, sufficiently long after the brunt of the recession was history.

Through three crucial years, 2010 to the end of 2012, when the economic recovery could easily have been derailed, the pattern of a great deal of U.S. fiscal policymaking was to kick the can down the road. In 2011 alone, for instance, unable to adopt an explicit budget, Congress passed instead no fewer than eleven stopgap spending bills—seven for fiscal year 2011 and four for fiscal year 2012. The lack of discipline appalled most commentators. But their scorn turns out to have been misplaced. Consider more closely what actually transpired following the dramatic 2010 midterm election, which ushered into the House of Representatives a large bloc of fiscal firebrands who were determined to curtail federal spending sharply and quickly. They began by attempting to slap a $1.03 trillion cap on discretionary spending for fiscal year 2011. The Senate, however, deemed that step too drastic. After two months of stalemate (and just minutes before the government would have had to shutter some of its basic operations for lack of funding) the two chambers finally agreed on an omnibus bill that capped spending at $1.05 trillion—higher than the House wanted, though still presumably $39 billion less than the previous year's level.

A reduction of $39 billion would have been relatively innocuous even if it had been real. But even that figure proved to be largely smoke and mirrors. As the *Washington Post's* David Fahrenthold reported in a penetrating exposé, the FY 2011 spending bill proved to be "an epic kind of Washington illusion. It was stuffed with gimmicks that made the cuts seem far bigger—and the politicians far bolder—than they actually were."[3] Outlays in fiscal year 2011 remained steady.

　　Then it was on to round two. Barely a day after Congress cleared that legislation, the House's deficit hawks went back on the attack. They proceeded to pass on April 15 a budget resolution proposing a $1.02 trillion cap on spending for the following fiscal year. Again, the Senate declined to go along. The impasse continued into the summer, when an additional battle was joined—a showdown between Congress and the White House over whether, or how much, to raise the federal debt limit. The debt ceiling fight in July of 2011 was widely perceived as a wretched low point in U.S. politics. The president and House speaker failed to agree on a long-term "grand bargain" that would finally put the nation's fiscal house in order, and the U.S. credit rating was downgraded. Not only that, but the negotiating parties went down to the wire, nearly triggering a Treasury default, before reaching an awkward limited compromise, the so-called Budget Control Act.

　　Less noted was that the Budget Control Act, for all its evident shortcomings, kept government spending essentially the same in fiscal year 2012 as in the previous year. Also, once the debt ceiling fight was over, Congress wisely extended a payroll tax reduction through 2012. John Maynard Keynes would have been pleased, for about the last thing the still shaky economy needed at the time was a jolt of fiscal frugality such as that contemplated by the House back in April or any sudden rise in the tax burden. A similarly useful stasis had occurred during 2010. Congress's annual budget process had fallen to pieces earlier in the year, thanks to that biennial American peculiarity, the upcoming midterm election. No budget resolution for fiscal 2011 emerged. What's more, no regular appropriations bills were enacted. What a mess, right? Wrong. The upshot was that then, too, federal spending largely continued at nearly the level of the previous fiscal year—enough space for the fragile economy to dodge the bullet of any ill-timed budget reductions.

GRIDLOCKED?

Paradoxically, America's *immobilisme* was an advantage much of the time. But at the outset, when the crisis struck with full force in the latter part of 2008, immediate government intervention had been required to avert a depression. The first order of business was to arrest the free fall of financial markets. Next, aggregate demand was in need of a lift through a combination of monetary easing and fiscal stimulus. In addition, specific parts of the "real" economy—most notably, the automobile industry, on which so much of the nation's employment depended—had to be bolstered directly. The United States, moving at times more nimbly than any other democracy, managed to accomplish all those tasks in relatively short order.

Let us begin with the saga of the Troubled Assets Relief Program (TARP). On September 29, 2008—"Black Monday"—the House of Representatives temporarily rejected a colossal financial rescue plan that had been hastily crafted by George W. Bush's treasury secretary, Henry Paulson. In terms shrill and unsparing, many editorial writers viewed this seemingly infamous episode—which precipitated a meltdown in the stock market—as a poster child of "dysfunctional" Washington.

But was the House vote on September 29 really little more than a hissy fit of "pique and polarization" thrown by partisan ideologues, as a *Washington Post* editorial on the following day implied ?[4] The purpose of the biennially elected House of Representatives is, as the Framers intended, to reflect the people's will—and to do so as faithfully as possible or face retribution at the polls within a matter of months. At the outset, Paulson's scheme, which proposed to put nearly unprecedented peacetime power in the hands of the Treasury, had met with much public doubt. In the face of it, Congress was not just going to rubber-stamp his plan overnight. Fear that its enormous costs might not actually achieve the desired result was intense and extraordinarily broad. A Pew survey taken at the end of September found that 63 percent of the public was profoundly worried that "government action won't fix things that caused the problem" in the first place.[5] Significantly, clear majorities of all stripes—Republicans, Democrats, and independents—expressed skepticism. There was little chance that the House could simply have ignored so widespread a sentiment, especially with an election barely a month off and, no less important, with too little time to deliberate.

It is true that about three-quarters of Republican conservatives voted against the original bill and were joined by many of the most liberal House Democrats—an example of *les extremes se touchent*. Ideological effects were involved, and not just among members with safe seats. The far right saw the specter of "socialism." The far left seemed to prefer bailing out over-leveraged homeowners instead of Wall Street. Yet the main story was less about the stubborn stance of partisan zealots than about straightforward electoral imperatives—that is, elected representatives doing their job, which is to listen to their constituents. So, for example, in the fifty-some House districts with seats that were likely to be closely contested in November, the current occupants voted overwhelmingly against the bailout bill. The only sure pro-bailout votes on September 29 came from the two dozen or so members who had announced their retirement.[6] The House, in short, was mostly in step with popular preferences.

Of course, popular preferences can be mercurial and not always judicious, so in times of national peril, the initial impulses of "the people's house" (prone, as it sometimes could be, to "sudden and violent passions") should not necessarily represent the last word.[7] Mercifully, in the great TARP debate, it wasn't. Matters were satisfactorily resolved in the end. The House was encouraged to reverse itself a few days later, enabling Congress to adopt the controversial legislation in almost record time—and thereby to pull the economy back from the abyss. How, exactly, did this swift course correction occur? After the initial popular backlash, there was bound to be a second wave of constituent and interest group reactions, this time pressing for passage. Those powerful voices—which included the Chamber of Commerce, the Business Roundtable, the AARP, Main Street banks, and thousands of local car dealerships—needed a few days to mobilize and weigh in. When they finally did, the effect was felt.

Perhaps even more important, Madisonian institutions played their intended part. To keep the House's hypersensitivity to public opinion in check, the Constitution had summoned a uniquely intricate form of bicameralism. The Senate—a smaller deliberative assembly composed of members mostly representing larger, hence more internally diverse, polities and chosen to serve longer, staggered terms—was deliberately designed to be less receptive to impulsive popular moods. Senators, as Madison had hoped, could be more statesmanlike under pressure. The dramatic debates of September and October 2008 followed that script almost to a fault. Immediately following Black Monday, the Senate took charge. Stepping over the rubble left by the House, the upper chamber forged ahead with a revised bill and adopted it by a wide margin, thereby applying an additional inducement to the other body to perform an about-face. Senate rules, as everyone knows, can facilitate procrastination. But in this instance, the same institution offered its members extraordinary opportunities to lead—and lead they did.

The endgame was remarkable. Democracies do not always deliberate prudently, if at all, in a matter of hours or days. Legislatures ordinarily need longer to think through momentous decisions, even when time is obviously running short. When Congress was called upon to fix another sizable banking problem, the collapse of the savings and loan industry in 1989, the lawmakers had spent six months writing remedial legislation. To address the financial debacle of 2008, six months or even six weeks would have been out of the question. What was accomplished on Capitol Hill in a mere five days was therefore quite startling.

The much-maligned TARP was the single most crucial step that the U.S. government took to forestall a calamity at the worst phase of the economic upheaval. It was soon supplemented by another important measure, an $800 billion stimulus bill enacted promptly in 2009. The effectiveness of that particular remedy, too, would be endlessly disputed. True, substantial portions seemed too encumbered by red tape and hence by protracted lead times to have had much near-term impact.[8] Yet, all told, the American Recovery and Reinvestment Act may well have been among the interventions that at least helped prevent the recession from worsening. Similarly, the mega-bailout of the auto industry, although bitterly controversial at the outset in December 2008, subsequently proved more successful than its detractors had predicted.[9] Last but hardly least, America's mighty central bank played a decisive role in securing an ongoing recovery. Unlike, for instance, the European Central Bank, which struggled for many crucial months to produce effective countercyclical measures, the Federal Reserve pumped liquidity into the U.S. economy, promptly, consistently, and on a vast scale.

One can argue about whether some of the projects undertaken amid the tumult of the past several years (including, besides the activities already noted, the sweeping regulatory reform of the banking system, the remedies for the federally sponsored mortgage giants Fannie Mae and Freddie Mac, and more) will prove durable and efficacious over the long term. What *cannot* be concluded, contrary to a common misperception, is that U.S. policymakers were passive or paralytic in the face of an emergency. Instead, the record was generally sound. It combined at times reasonably constructive action when urgently required—and at other stages, healthy hesitation when the advisable course was "Don't just do something. Stand there!"

2013: A YEAR OF RECKONING?

The accommodating mix of policies finally came to an end in 2013. The reduced marginal tax rates that had been enacted during the presidency of George W. Bush were set to expire at the end of 2012, as was a payroll tax holiday that had been repeatedly extended for anti-recessionary purposes. No one—certainly no Republicans or President Obama—was prepared to allow *all* of the Bush tax cuts to terminate. Well short of permitting that to happen, however, the White House and most Democrats in Congress were determined to compel enough House Republicans to accept at least a portion of the scheduled revenue increases so as not to be boxed into relying exclusively on reduced spending to shrink projected deficits.

Further, the Budget Control Act (BCA) of 2011 had imposed a new, apparently stiff constraint: it charged a special joint congressional committee with presenting a plan for some $1.2 trillion in budget cuts over a decade, starting in 2013. If the committee failed to reach agreement, the BCA authorized at least $900 billion in cuts to take effect automatically over the same period. The Obama administration had a hand in crafting the scheme: the negotiators had calculated that because it would trigger indiscriminate, across-the-board reductions (including deep ones at the Pentagon), Congress, if and when the time came, would not have the stomach to let this "sequestration" actually happen. Instead, however, the unforeseen *did* happen: the Republicans were duly forced to capitulate to a significant tax hike (aimed at high-income households) beginning in 2013—but then unexpectedly, they simply allowed the sequester to go forward. In sum, although the GOP had been bested in the tax contest, the party's fiscal hardliners managed to come away with a pound of flesh from the spending side of the ledger.

On the face of it, the assortment of changes commencing in 2013 amounted to a notable retreat from the expansionary policies that had characterized the government's de facto agenda throughout the economic downturn. Adding together the spending cuts mandated by the BCA, the higher income tax rate to be paid by affluent households, and the re-set of the payroll tax (plus an additional tax imposed to implement aspects of Obama's big health care law, the Affordable Care Act), Americans would receive around $300 billion less stimulus in 2013 than in 2012. While that was nothing like the vertiginous "fiscal cliff" over which the country would have tumbled if the full extent of the pre-Bush tax rates had been allowed to snap back, some critics worried nonetheless that the economy would be dealt a major setback. They noted, for example, that on paper the lower level of U.S. spending as a percentage of GDP now resembled some European reductions.

What has to be taken into account, however, is the timing of belt-tightening and also of stimulus (such as "quantitative easing"). U.S. policymakers extended copious financial relief early, and did not start administering a significant dose of austerity while the economy was still flat on its back. Instead, the "gridlocked" Americans defaulted to some fiscal stringency only later in the game—in 2013. By then, signs pointed to a steady upturn, sufficiently robust and secure to be able to take the hit. Moreover, when the blow finally came, though it was not trivial, it was just not forceful enough to be of grave consequence. We can certainly take issue with the arbitrary *composition* of the BCA's budget sequester, for instance, but we cannot easily stipulate that an overall fiscal trim so modest—one half of 1 percent of GDP—was now too much to absorb.

Nor was the economy seriously bruised by another political spectacle that transfixed Washington later in the year. In a last-ditch attempt to vent their distaste for "Obamacare," Republicans in Congress forced the federal government to partially shut down for approximately two weeks in October, and then, as in the summer of 2011, they threatened not to raise the debt ceiling. Never mind that similar antics had predictably backfired in the past; a bloc of right-wing Republicans insisted on testing the tactics again anyway. Sensing that now a prolonged shutdown, let alone renewed threats of a U.S. default, would not pose a credible stratagem, the president called the GOP's bluff. Before long, the Republican gamble collapsed—and foreseeably, the fabricated crisis blew over.

Once again, Senate leaders had come to the rescue, writing a last-minute measure that temporarily funded the government and lifted the debt limit. The dynamics resembled those of the TARP tussle in 2008. When the Senate passed its bill (overwhelmingly, 81 to 18), the House had little choice but to follow suit, acquiescing 285 to 198 (with 87 Republicans joining all 198 Democrats in favor). Following that bipartisan activity, at the end of the year, House and Senate negotiators brokered a full budget accord for fiscal years 2014 and 2015. Not only was a cease-fire reached in the running dispute over the government's borrowing power; about half of the BCA's automatic sequestration was called off.

In the end, any adverse economic impact of the theatrics in October 2013 proved minimal. This time, the nation's credit rating remained entirely intact. True, the sixteen-day disruption of certain government operations was estimated to have subtracted perhaps as much as $12 billion from fourth-quarter growth. That toll, however, amounted to briefly nicking, at worst, a mere 0.3 percentage point off the country's colossal economy's growth rate.[10]

Bipartisanship

James Madison, like the rest of the Founders, had feared that organized political parties might subvert the public interest. In his famous words, mischievous parties could often be so "inflamed" by "mutual animosity" as to become "more disposed to vex and oppress each other than to co-operate for the common good."[11] Today, the "mischief" of partisan politics has certainly made the government's fiscal decisions frequently contentious, at times even ugly. Polarization of the parties helps explain the brinkmanship that led to ill-designed formulas, like the Budget Control Act (with its blunt instrument, sequestration), and to tense negotiations between Congress and the White House that barely kept the country from hurtling down the fiscal cliff in the final hours of 2012. Partisan politics seemingly renewed the possibility of a debt default in the fall of 2014. At the root of these ordeals, no doubt, was unwillingness among most Republicans to countenance tax increases, even strictly for the purpose of deficit reduction—and the penchant of many Democrats to keep taxing (selectively) and spending (less selectively).

But there is also a tendency among pundits to overstate the extent of the partisan divide where concurrence mattered most. Think, for instance, about what did *not* occur as part of the fiscal cliff drama. In the end, among other key outcomes, income taxes, which were scheduled to jump for all taxpayers, did not budge for 99 percent of them. That was not a perverse result, given the state of the economy. On the contrary, it was the right answer (at least for the time being). The interesting question is how did it come about?

The oft-overlooked fact is that *both* of the political parties feel duty bound to promise tax relief for an overwhelming majority of people. Granted, the GOP eschews higher taxes of virtually any kind for anybody, whereas the Democrats mostly object to any increased burden on the middle class. But their definition of "middle class" is so expansive that it includes everyone except for the wealthiest 1 or 2 percent of households. In sum, in large part, *bipartisan*—not polarized—preferences have prevailed for U.S. tax policy. This consensus may be far from optimal for the long term (as I suggest later in the chapter), but in the tense final days of 2012, it had the salutary effect of all but ruling out a sudden, sweeping income tax increase, the most damaging prospect of the looming fiscal cliff.

The point bears elaborating from another angle. Casual observers often seem to impute just about all U.S. countercyclical policies in recent years only to the handiwork of a Keynesian president and Democratic senators who thwarted the House's many Republican skeptics of Keynes. But that perspective is an oversimplification. The GOP tends to be skeptical that heightened public spending can yield an effective fiscal stimulus, but the party waxes far less anti-Keynesian where *tax relief* is concerned. Almost every Republican insists that additional taxation would be a pro-cyclical "job killer." As noted, leading Democrats share a good deal of that concern. Let us recall that as a presidential candidate in 2008, Barack Obama campaigned explicitly to perpetuate most of the Bush-era tax cuts. And indeed, the president favored extending *all* of them at the end of 2010 as well as a payroll tax break to keep boosting the economy. Republicans were so committed to lightening the tax load at almost any cost that they also acquiesced to a continuation of unemployment benefits through the end of 2011. The serendipitous fruit of that meeting of the partisan minds was a countercyclical twofer, one that came along at just the right moment.

Consensual ground rules covered other areas as well. Like the TARP, the lifeline to the automobile industry was a combined effort of the Obama and Bush administrations. The latter initiated the bailout by committing $17.4 billion at the end of 2008, and Obama completed the job with an additional $60 billion in 2009. Alongside such joint operations was the overarching presence of another powerful player: the independent Federal Reserve System. The Fed consistently pursued its own program of macroeconomic stimulus through massive bond-buying interventions. The resulting near-zero interest rates continued to pour money into the economy, partially offsetting the contractive impacts of other policies—such as sequestration at the federal level and cutbacks in spending by state and local governments. It is not too much to say, as Senator Charles E. Schumer (D–N.Y.) remarked not too long ago, that "Ben Bernanke, along with George Bush and Barack Obama, saved us from another Great Depression."[12] On the fringe of the Republican Party, a few politicians murmured misgivings about the Fed's autonomous initiatives. But unlike in the early nineteenth century, when debates raged about the proper function or even legitimacy of a national bank, no party has mounted a serious challenge to the formidable Federal Reserve, which operates more or less unfettered today.

Would Madison have been surprised by these examples of partisan convergence? Probably not. For he had foreseen that a suitably large republic, equipped with effective representative institutions and "auxiliary precautions," would ultimately provide a measure of "relief" from the divisive machinations of parties (or "factions").[13] Today's Democrats and Republicans may not act like perfectly "proper guardians of the public weal," but at the end of the day, both have to govern with public consent. And on certain central questions—such as the limits of federal taxation and even the independence of the Federal Reserve—a national consensus continues to prevail.[14]

WHAT ABOUT THE LONG RUN?

Over five turbulent years—from the frightful financial collapse in the fall of 2008 to the end of 2013—American politics, for all the disharmony and seeming disarray, had managed to muddle through constructively. Truly ill-conceived policies were largely avoided, postponed, or modified. When, in 2013, certain taxes were finally due to rise and significant budget cuts were no longer put off, the economy was sturdy enough to begin its new, leaner fiscal diet. Moreover, by then, the combination of additional budget restraints, a modicum of new revenues, and modest but continuing economic growth (plus an unexpected slowdown in the growth rate of health care costs) brightened the nation's fiscal prospects for the near term. The Congressional Budget Office predicted that the actions to which Congress had defaulted at the end of 2012 would yield an appreciable deficit reduction over the next five years.[15]

Beyond that, however, nagging questions remain. Barring a recession-proof future and uninterrupted moderation of health care expenses (both of which are heroic assumptions), out-year deficits and debt will almost certainly return, possibly with a vengeance, because of basic demographic trends.[16] The U.S. political process weathered an immediate tempest, but it has done too little to prepare for an arguably foreseeable fiscal tsunami. Isn't that a serious indictment? Yes and no. In a perfect world (or, paraphrasing Madison, if elected officials were angels), the government would not only have deferred tax hikes and tighter budgets through the worst of the economic bust but *also* addressed the great long-term imperative of gradually introducing binding reforms of the big-ticket items in public spending—the welfare state's major entitlement programs. These, after all, are the eventual budget busters, not the assortment of discretionary expenditures shaved by measures like the sequester.

The failure to initiate reform of entitlements, however, has less to do with polarized parties, craven political calculations, or basic defects attributed to the eighteenth-century institutions of American governance (the usual explanations wheeled out in commentary on the subject) than with something simpler: the public's unrelenting resistance. The stark reality confronting U.S. politicians is that 65 percent of the public prefers traditional Medicare over a proposed change that instead would give people a specific amount of money to spend on either private or government health insurance.[17] Upward of 57 percent oppose raising the amount that Medicare recipients contribute to their health care. Around 60 percent want to keep Social Security in its current form, as opposed to, say, allowing workers to invest the equivalent of their payroll taxes themselves. And at least 56 percent disapprove of gradually raising the Social Security retirement age. In Congress, even the fiercest deficit hawks have trouble maintaining the courage of their convictions in the face of such attitudes.

It is easy to deplore this deference to the electorate's will as feckless and irresponsible. Shouldn't elected representatives shape or "lead," instead of almost always slavishly following popular desires? Most of the Founders— and surely, not least, James Madison—recognized a need to strike a balance between a purely representative role for politicians in a democracy and a place for statesmanship. But when it comes to demanding fiscal sacrifice from current voters strictly for principled reasons—to ensure the well-being of future generations—precious few, if any, democracies have manifested very impressive profiles in courage. Yes, various governments abroad had moved to impose greater fiscal discipline on their countries while America debated and delayed. But how much of the policy agenda in Europe has been optional—and, more fundamental, how much has been *genuinely structural*—remains open to question.

In some countries (Greece, Portugal, Spain), the day of reckoning had arrived: financial markets left officials little choice but to slash spending or accept insolvency. In most cases (certainly in France and Italy, two of the

Eurozone's biggest economies), the measures adopted to date do not yet look structurally transformative.[18] Germany and more recently Britain have made more progress toward restructuring, though it is still well short of what their aging societies, too, will need going forward. True, Germany managed to raise the retirement age for pensioners from 65 to 67. Nevertheless, with Europe's oldest population, Germany faces a woeful shortfall of working-age people by mid-century to support its generous pension system.[19]

Parenthetically, it also is worth noting that the examples of consequential reform in Europe have not been necessarily more significant than those in the United States. The British government in 2013 planned to increase the full retirement age to 67 as of 2028. A divided U.S. Congress had mandated a similar change thirty-two years ago, to take effect in 2022. The British economy in 2012 had one of the industrial world's weaker rates of investment—a problem that, if it were to persist, would have potentially dire implications for the long run. Aggravating Britain's investment lag was a credit squeeze that the banking system, as of 2013, was still laboring to relieve.[20] Early on, U.S. policymakers had moved methodically to regenerate the country's battered capital markets so that they could resume lending. Comparatively soon, that effort had proven promising. And America's demographic trends, though hardly optimal, are less disturbing than those in Europe and Japan. Birth rates are higher, and vigorous immigration here feeds more young workers into the labor force. The latter asset may eventually be further strengthened if Congress can revisit sensible immigration reform, along the lines of a bipartisan bill that had been pending not long ago.

In sum, systemic architecture does not appear to determine which regimes facing *long-range* fiscal predicaments are most inclined to plan ahead or to punt. At least with regard to the conundrum of preparing for the distant future, the conclusions of *Do Institutions Matter? Government Capabilities in the United States and Abroad,* a Brookings study published two decades ago, largely still seem to hold true: "Problems with balancing budgets are ubiquitous. All elected (and most unelected) governments are reluctant to impose losses [on powerful lobbies, such as pensioners]. Particular institutional arrangements do not cause these governance problems; they are inherent in complex societies and in democratic government."[21]

CONCLUSIONS

Madison was aware that the representative government that he helped frame would not be immune to what he called the "errors and delusions" of the people—including a proclivity not to give up present gratification (or "illicit advantage") for future gain.[22] Such flaws would remain a risk in a polity in which an elected legislature "necessarily predominates" (or, more to the point, where politicians must perpetually campaign).[23] The Framers did not overcome every vice of popular governance. The short time horizon of voters, in particular, continues to be a vulnerability endemic in this democracy as in others. (Naturally, Madison and his peers could not have anticipated the intergenerational inequities and political impasses that would one day result from the modern welfare state's massive transfer programs.) But the Founders did build an institutional structure that at least could often stall or slacken pressures to pursue "intemperate," precipitous policies that might wreak havoc not only over time but here and now. Not least among the Constitution's helpful brakes in this regard is its separation of the legislative branch into two differently constituted but equally powerful bodies as well as its check on legislators by way of the executive veto. Those features proved useful when the nation confronted especially treacherous economic circumstances in recent years. The U.S. Senate, in particular, sometimes did indeed provide "a defence to the people" against their temporary "follies."[24] Thanks in part to such designs—attributes that reflect the Madisonian legacy, broadly construed—the United States fared better than many other countries.

Notes

1. As of midsummer 2013, output in the seventeen nations that form the Eurozone was 3 percent lower than at its pre-crisis peak in 2007–08 while in America it was 4 percent higher. *The Economist*, August 17, 2013, p. 60.
2. The Eurozone's unemployment rate still stood at 11.5 percent in November 2014. *Eurostat News Release: Euro Indicators*, January 7, 2015.
3. David A. Fahrenthold, "Many 2011 Budget Cuts Had Little Real Effect," *Washington Post*, February 10, 2013, pp. A1, A16.
4. "Congressional Neroes," *Washington Post*, September 30, 2008.
5. Pew Research Center, "Small Plurality Backs Bailout Plan," September 30, 2008 (www.people-press.org/2008/09/30/small-plurality-backs-bailout-plan/).

6. Sarah Binder, "The Failed Bailout Vote: Channeling Tip O'Neill?" *The Monkey Cage*, October 1, 2008.

7. *Federalist* No. 62, in *The Federalist*, edited by Edward Mead Earle (New York: Modern Library, 1937), p. 403.

8. See James Q. Wilson and Pietro S. Nivola, *Lessons of the Stimulus* (Hoover Institution, October 14, 2010).

9. Nevertheless, half of the public continued to disapprove of the auto bailout several years later. A Gallup poll in February 2012, for instance, reported that 51 percent remained skeptical while 44 percent approved (www.gallup.com/poll/152936/republicans-democrats-differ-automaker-bailout.aspx).

10. Annie Lowrey, Nathaniel Popper, and Nelson D. Schwartz, "Gridlock Has Cost U.S. Billions," *New York Times*, October 17, 2013, p. A1.

11. *Federalist* No. 10, in *The Federalist*, edited by Earle, p. 56.

12. Quoted in John Harwood, "Fed Chairman's Departure Casts a New Light on the Bush Legacy," *New York Times*, July 27, 2013, p. A12.

13. *Federalist* Nos. 51 and 10, in *The Federalist*, edited by Earle, pp. 337, 54–56.

14. It is true that Americans sometimes appeared to be divided on the merits of the Federal Reserve's role during the economic crisis. In 2008, for instance, an ABC/Washington Post poll in Virginia found that 46 percent approved of the Fed's policies but 42 percent disapproved; see ABC News/Washington Post Poll: The Race in Virginia, September 22, 2008 (http://abcnews.go.com/images/PollingUnit/1072a1TheRaceinVirginia.pdf). Further, some surveys detected a demand for greater accountability. A Bloomberg poll dated December 9, 2010, noted that while 37 percent were apparently comfortable with the status quo, 39 percent felt that the Federal Reserve should be rendered "more accountable to Congress." A fringe—16 percent—said that it would favor abolishing the Fed, and the remainder had no opinion (www.bloomberg.com/news/articles/2010-12-09/more-than-half-of-americans-want-fed-reined-in-or-abolished). On the other hand, by a clear plurality, public confidence in the Fed's leadership has held fairly steady: it stood at 41 percent in 2006 and 42 percent in 2013, according to Gallup polls reported on April 10, 2013 (www.gallup.com/poll/161723/americans-trust-obama-economy.aspx).

15. Congressional Budget Office, *The Budget and Economic Outlook: Fiscal Years 2013 to 2023* (CBO: February 2013), pp. 1, 7.

16. By 2023, according to Congressional Budget Office, public debt will reach 77 percent of GDP, if current laws governing federal taxes and spending do not change. Even forecasters who question the urgency of restraining outlays for Medicare and Social Security acknowledge that, barring changes, the debt-to-GDP ratio could near a distressing 100 percent by the year 2040. See, for instance, Richard Kogan, Kathy A. Ruffing, and Paul N. Van de Water, "Long-Term Budget Outlook Remains Challenging, but Recent Legislation

Has Made It More Manageable" (Center on Budget and Policy Priorities, June 27, 2013), p. 1.

17. See, for instance, National Opinion Research Center (NORC), "Americans' Views on Entitlement Reform and Health Care" (NORC at the University of Chicago, 2013), p. 2. The Pew Research Center's polls in October 2012 and mid-2011 cover some of the same ground and are pretty much consistent with findings such as the NORC survey's (www.people-press.org/2011/07/07/section-3-views-of-medicare/). See Pietro S. Nivola, "To Fathom the Fiscal Fix, Look in the Mirror," January, 2013 (www.brookings.edu/blogs/up-front/posts/2013/01/07-fiscal-fix-nivola).

18. The retirement age in France was raised from 60 to 62, for instance, but there appears to be little prospect of raising it any further. See *The Economist*, June 22, 2013, p. 56.

19. See the excellent special report on Germany in *The Economist*, June 15, 2013, especially pages 12–13. See also Suzanne Daley and Nicholas Kulish, "Germany Fights Population Drop," *New York Times*, August 14, 2013, p. A1. Projections indicate that the percentage of persons sixty-five or older in Germany will increase from one-fourth to one-third by 2060.

20. See "How Is Britain's Economy Really Doing?" *The Economist*, August 10, 2013, pp. 10, 49.

21. R. Kent Weaver and Bert A. Rockman, *Do Institutions Matter? Government Capabilities in the United States and Abroad* (Brookings, 1993). I am indebted to R. Shep Melnick of Boston College for reminding us of this insight.

22. *Federalist* No. 63, in *The Federalist*, edited by Earle, pp. 409–10.

23. *Federalist* No. 51, in *The Federalist*, edited by Earle, p. 338.

24. *Federalist* No. 63, in *The Federalist*, edited by Earle, p. 409.

five

GRIDLOCK AND
THE MADISONIAN CONSTITUTION

R. SHEP MELNICK

To no one's surprise, the last two Congresses proved to be the least productive of the past sixty years. Not only did they fail to address such pressing issues as immigration, climate change, and the looming Social Security deficit, but they made little effort to fix programs (such as No Child Left Behind) that everyone acknowledges are badly in need of repair. The congressional budget process lies a shambles: emergency continuing resolutions have replaced regular appropriations bills, and no budget resolution has been enacted since 2010.

In recent years, the U.S. government has stumbled from one crisis to another, avoiding the "fiscal cliff" and default on the federal debt only at the last minute. In October 2013, all non-essential government workers were sent home because Congress could not agree on appropriations bills. In December 2014, Congress avoided another shutdown by passing a 1,600-page omnibus continuing resolution—ominously referred to as the "cromnibus"—that almost no one had read. Each immediate crisis was resolved without tackling the more difficult choices necessary to address the country's long-term fiscal plight. Not surprisingly, the public's confidence in its governing institutions continues to plummet. By 2013 two-thirds of the public was "dissatisfied with the way the nation is being governed," the highest percentage in forty years.[1] A Pew poll found that 75 percent of respondents want to see current members of Congress defeated for reelection.[2]

The current political predicament gives renewed prominence and credibility to the venerable argument that the "Madisonian" constitutional system has become outmoded, no longer capable of meeting the demands of twenty-first-century America. For well over a hundred years, the most persistent complaint about the U.S. Constitution has been that by making legislation so hard to pass, it invites political stalemate. Its distinctive combination of separation of powers, bicameralism, and federalism creates so many veto points in the legislative process that intensely committed minorities can often thumb their noses at popular majorities and at times produce government paralysis. Many distinguished students of American politics—ranging from Woodrow Wilson and other Progressives at the turn of the twentieth century to James McGregor Burns, Lloyd Cutler, Robert Dahl, James Sundquist, and Sanford Levinson in more recent years—have agreed.[3] Seldom has this argument seemed more compelling than it does now.

The present discontents have driven even John DiIulio, heretofore a vigorous defender of the Madisonian Constitution, to conclude that the current level of government dysfunction calls for serious consideration of major constitutional change. DiIulio's main concern is not the standard complaint that the constitutional system stifles innovation or prevents the people from building an energetic government, but the opposite: having built a large, convoluted regulatory and welfare state, Americans are no longer able to run those multitudinous programs effectively or to stop passing on their ever-growing costs to future generations.

Pietro Nivola is no less alarmed by the country's steadily worsening fiscal plight but doubts that it can be attributed to—or fixed by—constitutional arrangements. Almost all advanced industrial democracies are struggling to cope with the consequences of a combination of generous entitlements and an aging population. In fact, the United States has fared comparatively well in that regard. Nivola notes that the federal government responded quickly and effectively to the 2008 economic crisis. Moreover, the frequently decried congressional "gridlock" that followed the 2010 elections actually had beneficial fiscal consequences, preventing the United States from imposing the sort of austerity measures that have prolonged the recession and slowed recovery in most European nations. One might conclude that in an era of hard political choices, familiarity breeds undeserved contempt.

Jonathan Rauch urges us to consider not just the Constitution's immediate effect on public policies but its long-term effect on the nation's political culture. The greatest contribution of the Madisonian constitution, he argues, is the spirit of compromise and moderation that it cultivates and reinforces. Conversely, the biggest threat to the country's political health comes not from government inaction or overspending but the "anti-compromise movement" currently exemplified by the Tea Party faction within the Republican Party. Constitutional revision not only would fail to address current problems but most likely would also strengthen the political forces that have prevented the nation from dealing effectively with them in the recent past.

These are subtle arguments that take us beyond the standard argument that lazy, corrupt, and excessively partisan leaders simply "can't get anything done." Nor are the arguments of DiIulio, Nivola, and Rauch as far apart as they might seem. Since the turn of the twenty-first century, the spirit of compromise championed by Rauch has helped Americans deal rather successfully with at least two major challenges: terrorism and the financial meltdown of 2008. At the same time, efforts to resolve long-term fiscal problems have been stymied not only by the inherent reluctance of democratically elected officials to impose costs on current voters but also by the anti-compromise ethos that Rauch rightly decries.

This chapter attempts to shed light on the diverse features of the Madisonian constitution by looking back at the major policy developments of the past decade and a half. Its first aim is to lay to rest the "gridlock" meme that has so dominated contemporary political analysis. Its second is to emphasize that the Madisonian system not only creates multiple "veto points" but also provides policy entrepreneurs with innumerable "opportunity points" from which to initiate and expand government programs. That flexibility makes American government far more energetic than its critics recognize. But it also contributes to the problems of coordination and governability highlighted by DiIulio. The central difficulty is not that government "can't get anything done" or that American public institutions have become insulated from public opinion; it is that those institutions are doing so many things and responding to so many political demands that they are incapable of resolving the serious conflicts among them. Washington, we do have a problem. But it is not the one that most critics of the Madisonian constitution have identified.

FROM STALEMATE TO GRIDLOCK

For most of the twentieth century, criticism of the U.S. constitutional structure came almost exclusively from the left. Progressives and New Dealers argued that the country's "horse and buggy" institutions prevented the people from building a modern state, by which they meant constructing a generous welfare state and a national government capable of moderating swings in the business cycle and regulating large corporations. Although Progressives and most New Dealers showed little interest in civil rights, their successors could see that the same features of the Constitution also prevented the federal government from dislodging the racial caste system in the South. Their strategy was to use a combination of presidential leadership and party government to overcome all the veto points in the legislative process. With the policy "breakthroughs" of 1933–35 and 1964–65, they largely succeeded. After landmark legislation was enacted in those years, it became much easier for the president, Congress, administrative agencies, and the states to engage in incremental expansion of welfare, regulatory, and civil rights programs. Despite divided government, the scope of federal authority grew substantially in the 1970s. "Stalemate" and "deadlock," terms so frequently used to describe congressional politics in previous decades, were briefly out of fashion.

In the Reagan years the old critique reappeared with a new twist and a new title: "gridlock." The term was invented in 1980 to describe traffic congestion so severe that cars would block multiple intersections, preventing movement in any direction. It quickly became the leading metaphor to describe congressional politics after Ronald Reagan's initial legislative victories in 1981. Hugh Heclo has aptly described one of the chief consequences of the expansion of the government agenda in the 1960s and 1970s as "policy congestion."[4] As the government does more and more, policies intersect with one another with greater frequency, often pushing in different directions. "Energy policy" is a motley collection of hundreds of conflicting policies and programs, some decades old, that seek to promote and discourage, subsidize and tax, various forms of energy use and production. "Welfare policy" is an array of programs run by many different agencies under the jurisdiction of scores of congressional committees that is notorious for creating inconsistent rules and conflicting incentives for recipients. Much the same could be said for "health care policy," which in turn is inextricably linked to welfare policy. Federal "budget policy" is the sum of the millions of decisions on spending and taxing that hundreds of governments—local, state, and national—make every year.

"Gridlock" captured the sense that the government could no longer manage or coordinate all the intersecting programs that it had created in the preceding decades. That was true for budget policy in particular during the Reagan years. The Reagan tax cuts and military buildup created massive deficits (by pre-2001 standards), and the "obstacle course on Capitol Hill" seemed incapable of putting much of a dent in them. No longer was the complaint that Congress and the president could not build an extensive modern state. Now the complaint was that Congress and the president could not govern the massive state that they had created. Especially with entitlement spending growing automatically due to cost-of-living adjustments, rapidly escalating health care costs, and the aging of the population, inaction by Congress now meant an ever-larger federal budget. Now conservatives and good-government technocrats complain as much about "gridlock" as liberals had complained of "stalemate" in years gone by.

The liberals who complained about "stalemate" in the 1950s and 1960s thought that they knew what to do about it: develop a "responsible" two-party system and change the rules of the legislative process to allow the majority party to govern. Decades later they got their wish but not the results that they expected. In the 1980s—just as political scientists and pundits declared "The party's over"—the country began to develop unified, national, programmatic political parties. The fierce partisan polarization that became so evident in early twenty-first-century American politics had first appeared in Congress two decades before. By the time that the Republicans took control of Congress in 1995, party leadership in the House rivaled that of the powerful speakers last seen nearly a century earlier. Within the House, most of the veto points so frequently criticized for promoting stalemate were eliminated. The speaker now controls the Rules Committee, tells committees which bills to report, and determines when and how bills come to the floor. Roll call votes on important issues almost always follow party lines.

During the presidency of George W. Bush, Republicans briefly gained control of both the House and the Senate and rammed through Congress a series of tax cuts and a major expansion of Medicare with virtually no support from Democrats.[5] In 2009–10 Democrats enacted the Affordable Care Act and the stimulus bill in a similar fashion. Although partisan polarization is almost always listed as a primary cause of gridlock, it is undeniable that it has also contributed to dramatic policy change.

Advocates of party government assumed that stronger, more ideological parties would allow one dominant party to give coherent direction to the government as a whole. Over the long run, the public has not been enamored of either party, and the result has been years of divided government. As soon as one party seems to be gaining effective control of government, the voters revoke its mandate. The 2010 and 2012 elections were just the latest manifestation of this recurring pattern, which has led some analysts to conclude that American voters are "cognitive Madisonians" who wish to prevent either party from dominating. It may be more accurate to say that voters are seriously divided and deeply ambivalent. A majority wants to retain and even extend the entitlements, services, and protections offered by the welfare state, but they do not want to bear the taxation, regulation, and limitations on individual choice that such a state requires.

Once seen as a way to overcome the problems associated with the separation of powers, parties in practice often magnify its effects. In 1978, Anthony King noted that American politics seemed to imitate the behavior of large crowds: it oscillates between moving "either very sluggishly or with extreme speed."[6] Partisan polarization has exaggerated both phases of the American political system's manic-depressive behavior. During the rare periods of unified government, the majority party's program moves through Congress at a speed unimaginable in the days of the "committee barons." When the country returns to divided government, congressional activity on important legislation grinds to a halt until a crisis of some sort forces the parties to reach a short-term compromise. The gridlock metaphor captures only one phase of the political system's mood swings.

Today gridlock is like the weather; every elected official complains about it, but no one knows what to do—other than clobber the other party in the next election. Not surprisingly, attacking and blaming the other party has become the main activity of members of Congress. Ever eager to blame "out of touch" politicians for the nation's woes, voters have continued to elect fierce partisans while fiercely condemning partisanship. Casting and avoiding blame have become as common among average citizens as among politicians.

What makes this situation especially ominous, of course, is the long-term fiscal condition of the federal government. Not only does the United States face a large deficit in the short run, but the red ink will rise further as the population ages and health care costs escalate. Many state governments are in even worse fiscal shape than the federal government. These are problems faced by all advanced industrial democracies. Democracies find it especially hard to impose losses—either in terms of greater taxation or entitlement reductions—on their citizens. But imposing losses becomes all the more difficult when neither party is firmly in control and casting blame is the most effective tactic for each.

What Gridlock? A Look Back at 2001–12

It is hard not to become exasperated by a Congress that cannot enact appropriations bills or adjust the debt limit to the levels of spending and taxing that it has endorsed. But is it true that the combination of the Madisonian system and partisan polarization has created a situation in which, as we so frequently hear, "government can't get anything done"? In a word, no. Consider, for example, some of the steps that the federal government took in response to the financial crisis of 2008:

—That fall, Congress passed a $700 billion financial rescue package. The Bush administration managed to push its proposal through Congress despite massive Republican defections. Not only was the banking system quickly stabilized, but most of the money has been repaid.

—With only tepid support from the White House, Congress bailed out Fannie Mae and Freddie Mac, adding several hundred billion dollars to the total bailout.

—A few months later, the Treasury Department and the Federal Reserve announced a plan to pump an additional $1 *trillion* into the banking

system. That was done by the Fed, the Treasury, and the Federal Deposit
Insurance Corporation without additional congressional authorization.

—After providing billions of dollars to keep General Motors and Chrysler
afloat, the federal government played a central role in managing their
bankruptcy and downsizing. The government temporarily became the
largest stockholder in two of the nation's biggest companies.

—In the fall of 2008, Congress passed a $150 billion stimulus package—
large by historical standards, although small in comparison with the
$800 billion stimulus package enacted a few months later.

As Nivola emphasizes, the United States has responded to the Great Recession more prudently and more effectively than have parliamentary governments in Europe.

One could respond to these remarkable events by saying that the American political system is capable of responding to emergencies but not so good
at fashioning policies that prevent such emergencies from striking in the
first place. So let's look back at the first seven years of the Bush administration. Here was a recipe for stalemate. The electorate was divided 50-50 in
both the 2000 and 2004 elections, with George W. Bush losing the popular
vote in 2000 and eking out a narrow victory in 2004. The Senate, too, was
divided 50-50 in 2001, but control soon shifted to the Democrats with Vermont senator Jim Jeffords's defection from the Republican Party. The Republican margin in the House after the 2000 election was only nine votes,
producing the slimmest partisan margin in both houses in seventy years.[7]
In the 2006 elections the Democrats regained control of the House and
Senate, returning the country to divided government. Animosity between
the parties and against the president ran unusually high. But consider what
Congress accomplished during those years:

—It enacted No Child Left Behind (NCLB), the biggest change in federal
education policy since 1965 and the most prescriptive federal education
legislation ever enacted.

—It created Medicare Part D, the largest entitlement expansion since the
passage of Medicare and Medicaid in 1965.

—It passed the Bush administration's tax cuts in 2001, 2003, and 2004.
Together, they constituted the largest tax cuts in American history.

—Despite substantial opposition from Republicans, Congress approved the McCain-Feingold campaign finance reform law, which rivals the 1974 campaign finance statute for being the most important piece of legislation ever passed on the subject.

—It passed the Sarbanes-Oxley Act of 2002, which *CQ Weekly* at the time described as "the biggest increase in the regulation of publicly traded companies since the Depression."[8]

Some of these laws (NCLB and Sarbanes-Oxley) received bipartisan support; passage of others relied almost entirely on Republican votes (the tax cuts and Medicare Part D).

Foreign and defense policy rarely come up in discussions of stalemate and gridlock. Like partisanship in days gone by, the gridlock conceit stops at the water's edge. But the ability of the world's most powerful nation to act decisively is of no little import. Since 2001, the United States has fought two very long wars, both authorized by Congress. Congress created the Department of Homeland Security, enacted the USA Patriot Act in 2001, and passed legislation banning torture, establishing military commissions to try detainees, and denying detainees held outside the United States the right to file habeas corpus petitions. Those were all highly controversial measures. But the most common criticism is that the United States has been *too aggressive* in using military force and gathering intelligence and that there have been *insufficient checks* on executive power. According to Sanford Levinson, the Constitution created an "unconstrained" president who "can all too easily engage in dramatic exertions of power, especially in the realm of foreign policy."[9]

This highlights the fact that one of the most important characteristics of the presidential system—one emphasized by the Founders, particularly Hamilton—is that it *reduces* the prospects of stalemate and instability in foreign affairs. Any serious discussion of the Constitution's tendency to create stalemate or gridlock needs to pay at least as much attention to foreign policy as domestic. When one looks at the sweep of U.S. foreign policy over the past hundred years—the most important example being the pivotal role that the United States played in defeating Nazi Germany and the Soviet Union and also its post-9/11 success in preventing further attacks on American soil—it is hard to deny that the structure of the Constitution has served the country pretty well.

The greatest challenge to the gridlock argument came from the 111th Congress (2009–11), which compiled a record that rivals the famed 89th Congress of 1965–66. While many of the enactments of the 111th Congress are well known, it is worth recounting them to indicate the sweep of congressional action:

—Most important, Congress passed a massive and controversial overhaul of the American health care system, extending coverage to 30 million Americans; imposing extensive mandates on insurance carriers, employers, and state governments; creating new insurance exchanges; imposing an array of new taxes, fees, and penalties; extending drug benefits; and making significant cuts in the current Medicare program.

—Later in 2010,Congress enacted a 1,500-page law to create a new regulatory structure for the entire financial services sector and to establish a mechanism for "winding down" failing banks and brokerage houses. According to *CQ Weekly*, the Dodd-Frank Wall Street Reform and Consumer Protection Act "touches just about every major piece of financial regulatory law of the 20th century, from the New Deal–era banking and securities acts to the post–savings and loan crisis legislation of the late 1980s and early 1990s."[10] The law requires regulatory agencies, including the new Consumer Financial Protection Bureau and the Financial Stability Oversight Council, to produce 250 additional sets of regulations to govern the financial sector.

—Soon after convening, Congress passed the American Recovery and Reinvestment Act, a.k.a. the stimulus package, to pump an additional $800 billion into the slowing economy. The act included a diverse mix of tax cuts, an extension of unemployment benefits, grants to the states for infrastructure and health care, and measures to encourage the development of clean energy. It also provided more than $4.5 billion for the Obama administration's "Race to the Top" initiative to encourage innovation in elementary and secondary education.

—Congress passed legislation authorizing the Food and Drug Administration (FDA) to regulate the content and marketing of tobacco products. It later expanded the authority of the FDA to regulate food safety.

—Shortly before adjourning, the lame-duck Congress passed a compromise engineered by President Obama and Republican leaders to extend both unemployment benefits and the Bush tax cuts, to renew the estate tax, and to reduce temporarily the Social Security tax on employees.

—The Senate confirmed two new Supreme Court justices, Sonia Soto-mayor and Elena Kagan, both by wide margins and without the threat of a filibuster. That brought to four the number of justices approved by the Senate since 2001 without significant delay or opposition.

In addition, the Obama administration substantially increased the U.S. military commitment in Afghanistan, the second major American war zone "surge" in recent years. The years 2009–10 were certainly years of partisan animosity, but hardly of gridlock.

To be sure, Congress failed to pass immigration legislation (or even the stripped-down "Dream Act"), and the jerry-built climate change bill passed by the House died quietly in the Senate. It is also undeniable that Obamacare passed only by the skin of its teeth. When Scott Brown won the Senate seat that had long been held by Edward Kennedy, the Democrats lost the crucial sixtieth vote for cloture. Health care legislation passed only because the Democrats were both lucky—the Massachusetts election came after the Senate had approved its version of the bill—and willing to employ the budget reconciliation process in a novel manner. That reminds us that while partisan polarization often leads one party to engage in obstruction-ism, it also compels the other party to revise the rules to counteract such obstructionism.

The Perils-of-Pauline health care story points to another shortcoming of the conventional narrative. "Gridlock" is almost always used to imply that an obstinate minority is frustrating the will of the majority. But in 2010 Obamacare was in grave danger because public opinion was turning against it. Democrats from "purple" districts feared that a vote for the bill might end their tenure in Washington. In many instances they proved to be correct. The 2010 Massachusetts Senate race became a referendum on the administration's health care bill. It would have been hard for Democrats to pick a more favorable forum for such a referendum: one of the most liberal and reliably Democratic states in the nation; one in which a similar pro-gram had already been enacted; a seat formerly held by a popular senator who had made universal health care his life's work; and a contest between an experienced Democrat and an unknown Republican. But Scott Brown won anyway, providing the first tangible evidence of the degree of public dissatisfaction with the Democrats' plan. The next one came in 2010, when the Democratic Party experienced what President Obama described as a "shellacking." If anything, the health care battle shows that the federal government is capable of taking dramatic action even when the public support for such action is shallow.

Since the 2010 elections, the Republicans have controlled the House and an extraordinarily combative anti-Obama minority has dominated the Republican caucus. As a result, in early 2013 the country stood at the edge of the "fiscal cliff." But then the president and Congress agreed on a deal that raised taxes (a bitter pill for Republicans), cut spending (in ways that neither party liked), and, according to the Congressional Budget Office, stabilized the national debt as a percentage of GDP.[11] It is true that the process was ugly and the budget cuts arbitrary. At the same time, though, the fiscal cliff deal followed the contours of public opinion.[12] Perhaps the country's success in muddling through is further proof that "God looks out for little children, drunkards, fools, and the United States of America." More likely it is evidence that the Madisonian system works better in the long run than the contemporary instant-analysis political culture appreciates.

From Veto Points to Opportunity Points

If the Constitution creates so many "veto points," how has the United States managed to build such a large welfare, regulatory, civil rights, penal, and national security apparatus? Part of the answer is that a combination of presidential leadership, party loyalty, and crisis (especially war and economic depression) have frequently created the supermajorities necessary to overcome the hurdles established by the Constitution. But that is not the whole picture. One of the most serious weaknesses of the gridlock argument is that it focuses so intently on one small part of domestic policy, namely passage of major pieces of legislation at the national level. Commonly ignored are the daily decisions of administrators, judges, and subnational officials as well as members of Congress engaged in the quotidian business of passing appropriations, reauthorizations, and budget reconciliation bills. Taken individually, those decisions might seem like small potatoes, but collectively they can produce major policy change. Critics of the Constitution overlook the enormously important fact that a political system that creates multiple "veto points" simultaneously creates multiple points of access for policy entrepreneurs and assorted claimants. Every "veto point" that can be used to block action is also an "opportunity point" that can be used to initiate or augment government action. As a result, American government is both more extensive and more innovative than its critics recognize.[13]

Consider the problem of global warming, widely considered a prime example of gridlock in (in)action. Congress has repeatedly been condemned for failing to take action to reduce carbon emissions. In 2009 the House passed a bill that combined a mishmash of regulatory requirements with a cap-and-trade program that would have had little bite for many years. By the time it emerged from the House, even environmental groups questioned its merits. Mercifully, it died in the Senate. Meanwhile, though, a number of state governments have taken steps to reduce emissions of greenhouse gases. A decade ago Barry Rabe reported that several states "have addressed the climate change issue with vigor, developing a series of reduction policies and demonstrating a level of policy sophistication that may rival the staunchest European nations supporting the Kyoto Protocol."[14] Seven northeastern states reached an accord promising to reduce power plant emissions by 10 percent by the year 2020. In 2006 California governor Arnold Schwarzenegger signed an agreement with British prime minister Tony Blair to curb global warming by promoting clean-burning fuels. The governor claimed that California had a responsibility "to be a world leader on this issue" and therefore would not "wait for our federal government to take strong action on global warming."[15]

More important, in 2007 the Supreme Court ordered the federal Environmental Protection Agency to regulate greenhouse gases.[16] As an interpretation of the Clean Air Act, the Court's decision was bizarre: the act is clearly designed to improve *local* air quality, not reduce the U.S. contribution to a global environmental problem unrelated to the quality of the air that we breathe. There can be little doubt but that five justices on the Court had decided that since Congress was not addressing this pressing problem, the judicial and executive branches should.

EPA's first response to *Massachusetts* v. *EPA* was to issue new emissions and fuel-efficiency standards for motor vehicles. Those rules were even stricter than the rules considered but rejected during the congressional debate over the 1990 Clean Air Act amendments. The Obama administration then started work on new rules that limit carbon dioxide emissions from new and modified industrial sources, an especially tricky task given the lack of fit between the greenhouse gas problem and the law's regulatory structure. But the worse the EPA proposal, the better the prospect for congressional action: if Congress failed to act, EPA's flawed plan became the default position. An early 2009 *New York Times* article on climate change legislation noted that President Obama was "holding in reserve a powerful club to regulate carbon dioxide emissions through executive order." Although "Administration officials consistently say they would much prefer that Congress write new legislation," they held the Supreme Court decision and the prospect of imminent EPA rulemaking "in reserve as a prod to reluctant lawmakers."[17]

Once Republicans retook the House in 2010 and any hope for congressional action evaporated, the EPA and the White House set to work crafting regulations for coal- and gas-fired power plants that would substantially reduce greenhouse gases without becoming administratively unmanageable. In the fall of 2013, the EPA announced new limits on greenhouse gas emissions from new stationary sources that would make it virtually impossible to build new coal-burning power plants. In 2014 the EPA proposed a "Clean Power Plan" designed to reduce carbon emissions 30 percent by 2030. This plan sets emission quotas for each state and requires them to make major changes in the way that energy is produced and consumed within their borders. The greenhouse gas agreement announced by President Obama and China's President Xi Jinping later in 2014 commits the United States to achieving these substantial reductions.[18] Everyone recognizes that compliance with the rules will be very expensive. Whether it will be economically, technically, administratively, or politically feasible for states and utility companies to comply with EPA's extensive requirements remains to be seen. Meanwhile, the European Union, once held up as a model of environmental stewardship, has begun to backtrack on regulation of greenhouse gases, fearing it will slow economic recovery.[19]

Shortly after the 2014 election, President Obama announced his controversial plan to protect an estimated 4 million undocumented immigrants from the threat of deportation. He argued that this unusual systematic use of prosecutorial discretion was justified by Congress's failure to pass legislation to fix a broken system—or even to allow a vote on the House floor. Republicans have vowed to roll back this exercise of unilateral presidential power but at present have no clear strategy for doing so.

In 2011 the Office for Civil Rights (OCR) in the federal Department of Education launched an aggressive attack on colleges' handling of sexual assault allegations. OCR not only issued lengthy guidelines on how colleges must structure investigations and disciplinary proceedings but also required them to provide a variety of services to those subject to sexual harassment and extensive training to all students, faculty, and administrators. The most controversial element of these rules requires schools to use the lenient "preponderance of the evidence" ("more likely than not") standard to determine whether a student is guilty of sexual assault. OCR initiated nearly a hundred well-publicized investigations of colleges, including some of the best-known institutions in the country. The sole statutory basis for this regulatory effort is Title IX of the Education Amendments of 1972, which prohibits gender discrimination in educational institutions receiving federal funds.[20]

That was hardly the only example of OCR expanding its reach in recent years. In October 2014 it issued a thirty-five-page "Dear Colleague" letter explaining how it planned to investigate complaints of racial disparities in school funding. It announced its intention to examine how local school districts spend money on everything from teachers' salaries to paint and carpeting.[21] Relying on a provision in the 1964 Civil Rights Act that prohibits discrimination on the basis of "national origin," OCR and the Department of Justice have negotiated legally binding agreements with large school districts throughout the country on how they teach English language learners.[22] In all of these cases, OCR has dispensed with standard rulemaking procedures, instead issuing "significant guidance" documents and "Dear Colleague" letters backed by the threat of lengthy investigations.

By the time that President Obama took office, it was clear that the signature domestic initiative of the Bush administration, No Child Left Behind, needed to be substantially revised. (Shockingly, after seven years of new federal mandates, not every student in the country was at or above the national average.) Thousands of schools across the nation faced serious sanctions for failing to meet standards no longer considered to be feasible or sensible. Nonetheless, for over a decade Congress failed to amend the law. That did not mean that a federal education policy that everyone conceded to be outmoded remained intact. Congress included nearly $5 billion for the Obama administration's "Race to the Top" initiative in the 2009 stimulus bill. Later, the administration offered to grant states waivers from the onerous requirements of NCLB if they would accept the school reform "principles" announced by Secretary of Education Arne Duncan.[23] NCLB makes no provision for such conditional waivers, which in effect allowed the secretary of education to rewrite the law. Here again, inaction by Congress did not produce policy *stasis* but further experimentation by the executive branch.

Secretary Duncan also used the stimulus money to encourage states to adopt the emerging Common Core curriculum and to develop tests based on it. To date, forty-four states have done so. This is an example of an increasingly common but seldom noted phenomenon: the development of national policy without an explicit mandate from Congress, the executive, or the federal judiciary. The most significant example of this strange form of policymaking is the multistate tobacco settlement of 1998. Those looking for evidence of gridlock in Washington might point to the Senate's last-minute failure to agree to legislation that imposed a large tax on tobacco products and limited tobacco advertising and marketing. But soon after that legislation died at the hands of a Senate filibuster, state attorneys general throughout the country negotiated an agreement with tobacco companies that established a $250 billion tax on tobacco products—to be dispersed to state treasuries—together with unprecedented limits on advertising, sponsorships, and lobbying by tobacco companies. After it became clear that they would lose novel "unjust enrichment" suits in a few state courts, the tobacco companies looked for a way to settle the rapidly multiplying legal claims. Once a few states had hammered out an agreement that would raise tobacco prices nationwide, all the others joined in. None wanted to see their citizens taxed and have the proceeds go elsewhere. Having lost narrowly in one arena, anti-tobacco activists prevailed in another.[24] Multistate litigation by state attorneys general has also left its mark on policies dealing with environmental and consumer protection, pharmaceutical regulation, and Medicaid reimbursement.[25]

We usually think of federalism as a barrier to the expansion of national programs, but in many instances the opposite is true. When the Securities and Exchange Commission was criticized for being too lax in regulating Wall Street, another state attorney general, the now infamous Eliot Spitzer, stepped into what he perceived to be a policy void. Given the concentration of the financial sector in his state, he could in effect establish national standards on the basis of an exceptionally vague state law. When the Obama administration appeared too tolerant of AIG's bonuses, Spitzer's successor as Attorney General, the equally ambitious Andrew Cuomo, took steps to expose the miscreants. The U.S. Supreme Court has ruled that state tort law can add a level of regulation of pharmaceuticals on top of that established by the FDA.[26] Companies that serve a national market must follow the most restrictive state rules or face huge potential damages in state court suits. California, an especially large domestic market, has frequently imposed environmental standards more stringent than those of the federal government, and many other states have followed its lead.

Over the past several decades, the politically unpopular, means-tested Medicaid program grew faster than the supposedly sacrosanct Medicare program. Why? After all, the former serves the poor, while the latter provides benefits to one of the most potent political forces in American politics, the elderly. According to Lawrence Brown and Michael Sparer of the Columbia School of Public Health, part of the explanation is the shrewd incrementalism of congressional entrepreneurs such as Henry Waxman, who steadily added federal Medicaid mandates to budget reconciliation bills in the late 1980s.[27] Even more important, Brown and Sparer argue, is the fact that "fiscal federalism" had the dual effect of "prompting coverage expansions during good times (the Feds paid most of the bill) and deterring cutbacks even in bad times (every state dollar saved meant two or three federal dollars lost.)"[28] Instead of promoting a "race to the bottom," post–New Deal "cooperative federalism" has stimulated expansion of the welfare state. After studying federalism for years, Richard Nathan has concluded that "U.S. federalism's dominant effect has been to expand the scope and spending of the social sector."[29]

One could easily add example after example of federal administrators, federal judges, and state officials engaging in substantial policymaking independent of Congress. Each month the Federal Reserve buys $85 billion worth of bonds to stimulate the economy and promote job growth. The Dodd-Frank Act requires various federal regulatory agencies to undertake

nearly 250 rulemaking proceedings in the coming years, but it offers virtually no legislative standards to guide them. How did affirmative action—
highly unpopular with the American public—become embedded in so many
federal programs? Slowly, subtly, and at times surreptitiously, a long series
of court decisions, agency rules, and complex legislative provisions inserted
the presumption of proportional representation into federal civil rights programs.[30] How did the federal government come to set national standards for
state mental institutions, schools for the developmentally disabled, nursing
homes, and prisons? Largely through litigation and consent decrees negotiated by the Department of Justice. How did the Obama administration
manage to set up a $20 billion fund to compensate those injured by the BP
oil spill? By convincing BP that it would fare much worse if it tried to defend
tort suits in state courts, federal courts, and the court of public opinion. How
did the Department of Education develop rules regarding bullying on elementary school playgrounds, sexual relations between college students, and
the definition of competitive intercollegiate sports? Through a long series of
court decisions, "Dear Colleague" letters, and administrative guidelines, in
which each institution built on the work of others.[31] As a result, the United
States has more extensive prohibitions against discrimination based on race,
gender, and disability than any other Western democracy, and those rules
are vigorously enforced.

Over the past two decades, the United States has witnessed a remarkable
social transformation. In the 1990s the government ended the ban on gays
serving in the military, and in the early years of the Obama administration it ended the "Don't ask, don't tell" policy. Within the past ten years,
the number of states recognizing same-sex marriage has gone from zero
to thirty-six. In some states the changes came through court decisions, in
others through legislation, in a few others through referendums. In 2013,
the Supreme Court struck down part of the Defense of Marriage Act and
required the federal government to recognize same-sex marriages performed
in those states. It seems quite likely that by June 2015, the Supreme Court
will prohibit all states from limiting marriage to heterosexual couples. Considering how long civil marriage has been assumed to be "between one man
and one woman," one can only marvel at how quickly public policy in the
United States has changed.

What most arguments about gridlock miss is not just the opportunities created by a constitution that disperses authority but also the extent to which a wide variety of U.S. government institutions have developed both the capacity and taste for policy innovation. More federal administrative agencies exist now than ever before, and American administrators are notable for their entrepreneurial spirit, born of the necessity of building their own constituencies.[32] Judges hire energetic clerks eager to apply the theories that they learned in elite law schools. Tort lawyers likewise ply the judiciary with new legal theories and countless expert witnesses. Judges can call on special masters and compliance review committees to carry out detailed structural injunctions. Congressional staff has swelled since the late 1960s, helping to produce statutes of remarkable length and detail. As the example of state attorneys general indicates, state governments have become much more sophisticated, in part because they have been handed so many jobs and so much grant money by the federal government. The proliferation of interest groups and think tanks has added to the array of policy proposals and constituencies primed for mobilization. As the agenda of the national government has grown inexorably, the American system of "separated institutions sharing power" has adapted to new demands and new opportunities. Those who focus exclusively on large-scale legislative change miss most of the action in contemporary American politics.

Back to Madison

It is, of course, more than a little unfair to James Madison to describe the current American constitutional arrangements as "Madisonian." Madison was not happy with several features of the original Constitution, most notably equal representation in the Senate and the national government's limited control over legislation enacted at the state level. As Martha Derthick suggests in her chapter, Madison would be disturbed not only by the vast expansion of the responsibilities of the national government but also by the nearly impenetrable interweaving of national and state authority that we call "cooperative federalism." As Jack Rakove demonstrates in his chapter, Madison would strenuously disapprove of the Senate's routine use of filibusters and unilateral "holds." As Lynn Uzzell's chapter shows, he would also object to the contemporary proclivity to view the Supreme Court as the ultimate interpreter of the Constitution. If, as William Galston's chapter indicates, Madison was alarmed about the growth of executive power during his own lifetime, imagine what he would think of the modern presidency.

We cannot look to Madison for specific guidance on how to devise a constitution for popular government. In *Federalist* No. 37, he warned that when we "pass from the works of nature" to the "institutions of man," we must moderate "our expectations and hope from the efforts of human sagacity." He cautioned, "Experience has instructed us that no skill in the science of government has yet been able to discriminate and define, with sufficient certainty, its three great provinces—the legislative, executive, and judiciary; or even the privileges and powers of the different legislative branches."[33] The work of thousands of members of the American Political Science Association has done little to bring us closer to that goal. We can, however, look to Madison to inoculate us against the powerful prejudices of our own time and to help us think more clearly about the purposes of constitutional revision and institutional reform.

One of those dangerous prejudices is the notion that today's world is changing with unprecedented speed and that governments and constitutions should constantly be modernized to keep up with technological, economic, and cultural revolutions. To succeed in curbing temporary public passions and channeling the ambitions of those drawn to politics, Madison argued, it is essential that a constitution be the object of that *"veneration* which time bestows on every thing, and without which perhaps the wisest and freest governments would not possess the requisite stability."[34] A constitution that is easy to amend and subject to frequent change, he politely suggested to Jefferson, fails to inculcate "those prejudices in its favor which antiquity inspires, and which are perhaps a salutary aid to the most rational Government in the most enlightened age."[35] Without such continuity and veneration, a constitution is in constant danger of being reduced to a mere "parchment barrier" that can be ignored whenever it becomes inconvenient.

Frequent constitutional revision is dangerous for another reason as well: wise constitution writing requires an unusual level of insulation from the ordinary preoccupations and demands of democratic government.[36] The Constitutional Convention of 1787 was certainly subject to competing sectional demands, but meeting behind closed doors hundreds of miles from their constituencies allowed its members to engage in deliberations over the long-term interests of the country as a whole and to accept compromise when necessary. It is hard to believe that similar insulation, deliberation, and compromise can take place in the era of Twitter and Facebook, Fox and MSNBC, Ted Cruz and Edward Snowden. Why should we believe that voters who are unable to elect members of Congress capable of agreeing on a one-year budget can somehow select delegates to a constitutional convention tasked with producing a framework for governing for a century?

The "mutability" of ordinary law is no less dangerous for popular government. Before we condemn the complexity of the U.S. legislative process, with its attendant opportunities for delay and sabotage, we would do well to remember Madison's argument that "public instability" not only undermines public confidence and weakens the country internationally but also gives an "unreasonable advantage" to "the sagacious, the enterprising, and the moneyed few over the industrious and uninformed mass of the people."[37] When the tax code, campaign finance legislation, or banking and securities regulation are revised, who are the first to take advantage of the shift? Today we would most likely use the all-purpose political curse word, "special interests," but the point remains the same. We have more than enough examples to confirm Madison's generalization.

Contemporary critics of the Constitution not only ignore Madison's warning about the mutability of the law but also insist that the dangers created by government inaction are far greater than those created by rash, premature, or intemperate action. They assume—contrary to overwhelming political science evidence—that government mistakes can be easily remedied. We know that most government programs create constituencies that are highly organized, acutely aware of the benefits that they receive from government, and strategically positioned to block substantial change. As Paul Pierson has written, "The well-documented imbalance between the way that voters react to losses and gains further enhances the political position of retrenchment opponents."[38] In short, delays are temporary, but mistakes last nearly forever.

A second powerful prejudice that Madison's thought can inoculate us against is the dogma that constitutions should be judged primarily by how readily they allow popular sentiments to be converted into public policy. The signal advantage of representative government over direct democracy, Madison argued, is that if properly designed, the former is able to "refine and enlarge the public views by passing them through the medium of a chosen body of citizens" who will be "least likely" to sacrifice "the true interest of their country" to "temporary or partial considerations." As he famously argued in *Federalist* No. 10, providing representatives with the insulation that they need will be easier in a diverse "extended republic" than in a small, homogeneous polity. Moreover, by providing an opportunity for a "sober second thought," bicameralism reduces the possibility that legislation will be the product of momentary public passions.[39]

As Greg Weiner has convincingly argued, Madison was committed to majority rule, but he insisted that the majorities needed to enact legislation be more than temporary.[40] Because time usually cures intemperate political passions, the wheels of the legislative process should grind slowly. For critics of the Constitution, from Woodrow Wilson to Sanford Levinson, majority faction and intense public passions are to be embraced, not thwarted. (At least in the legislative process. Contemporary advocates of majoritarianism generally leave such thwarting to the unelected judiciary.) What Madison described as "a rage for paper money, for an abolition of debts, for an equal division of property, or for any other improper or wicked project," they would no doubt celebrate as the authentic and long-submerged voice of "the people."[41]

Recent history provides us with many examples of the fickleness of public opinion. As crime rose, so did public fear of crime, producing draconian criminal laws that filled American prisons and led to equally impassioned attacks on the racist "carceral state" and reckless spending on the prison-industrial complex. Since 9/11, the public has swung from approving ambitious military actions to remake the entire politics of the Middle East to overwhelmingly opposing a modest effort to punish a regime that used chemical weapons against its own people; now it has swung back to supporting air attacks against a group that opposes that very regime. In 2008, the electorate gave control of the presidency and Congress to Democrats committed to universal health insurance. Two years later, voters punished the Democrats for enacting a law that bore a very close resemblance to universal health insurance. Then they reelected the president, whose principal legislative legacy is Obamacare. While we might excuse politicians for their craven flattery of voters, those of us who are not dependent on voters' whims should be willing to admit that Madison's reservations about the short-term judgment of the average citizen were well founded.

If there is anything that prevents us from thinking seriously about how to increase the capacity of American political institutions to reconcile the competing demands placed on government, it is the democratic insistence that "the people" are unified, sensible, and selfless while politicians are fractious, scheming, and interested only in preserving their own power and perks. This is where Madison can be of most help. In *Federalist* No. 10, an essay frequently read and frequently ignored, Madison emphasized that the "latent causes of faction" are "sown in the nature of man." Our "reason" will forever be corrupted by our "self-love." The "diversity of the faculties of men" is both the primary cause of faction and "an insuperable obstacle to a uniformity of interests." Madison noted that "the most common and durable source of factions has been the various and unequal distribution of property." Those with property and those without; creditors and debtors; a landed interest, a manufacturing interest, a mercantile interest, and a moneyed interest, all "grow up of necessity in civilized nations and divide" into "different classes, actuated by different sentiments and views."[42] Today we could add to the list of diverse types of property not just collateralized debt obligations and patents on genetic patterns but the "new property" of Social Security, Medicare, and Medicaid benefits; food stamps; and myriad other entitlements. The nation has developed a huge "nonprofit" sector as well as a Title VII bar, an Americans with Disabilities Act bar, a tort bar with its own venture capitalists, and even a GITMO bar devoted to expanding the rights of prisoners held at Guantánamo Bay.[43]

Just as important, a "zeal for different opinions concerning religion, concerning government, and many other points as well of speculation as of practice" and "an attachment to different leaders ambitiously contending for preeminence and power" have "divided mankind into parties, inflamed them with mutual animosity, and rendered them much more disposed to vex and oppress each other than to co-operate for the common good."[44] Technological innovation has made it easier for those who share political passions and temporary rages to join together and make their strident voices heard. Pro-choice and pro-life groups exemplify this religious zeal. Today American politics is animated by both resentment at the "1 percent" and disdain for the "47 percent," scapegoating of immigrants, and condescension to those who "cling to their guns and religion," not to mention visceral hatred of both Republican and Democratic presidents. Madison reminds us that such features of democratic politics are not merely the unpleasant product of the Internet, cable news, or pliable campaign finance laws. Thinking about the proper design of democratic institutions require us to face the inherent dilemmas of governing and some of the less than edifying aspects of human nature.

For better or for worse, American political institutions are constantly evolving. The partisan standoffs of recent years recently led the Senate to curtail the use of filibusters and unilateral "holds" on presidential nominations. With Congress enacting fewer laws, both the president and the courts have devised new ways to amend statutes without going through Congress. State officials are inventing new methods for establishing national policies without the aid of the federal government. Given the difficulty of amending the formal Constitution, the nation will almost certainly need to rely on these more modest and subtle shifts to address the serious problems that lie before it. Madison teaches us that in evaluating these institutional adjustments, we should focus not on how well they respond to popular demands and problems of the moment, but whether in the long run they produce public policies whose costs and consequences national majorities will be able to understand and willing to accept.

Notes

1. Karlyn Bowman and Andrew Rugg, "Deeply Troubling Trends on Attitudes toward Government: What You May Have Missed in the Poll," October 10, 2013 (www.aei-ideas.org/2013/10/deeply-troubling-trends-on-attitudes-toward-government-what-you-may-have-missed-in-the-polls/).
2. Pew Research Center, "Record Anti-Incumbent Sentiment Ahead of 2014 Elections," October 15, 2013 (www.people-press.org/2013/10/15/record-anti-incumbent-sentiment-ahead-of-2014-elections/).
3. Stanford Levinson, *Our Undemocratic Constitution: Where the Constitution Goes Wrong (and How We the People Can Correct It)* (Oxford, 2006); James McGregor Burns, *The Deadlock of Democracy* (Prentice-Hall, 1963); Lloyd Cutler, "To Form a Government, *Foreign Affairs* (Fall 1980); James Sundquist, *Constitutional Reform and Effective Government* (Brookings, 1992); Robert Dahl, *How Democratic Is the American Constitution?* (Yale, 2002).
4. Hugh Heclo, "One Executive Branch or Many?," in *Both Ends of the Avenue*, edited by Anthony King (AEI Press, 1983).
5. Barbara Sinclair, *Party Wars: Polarization and the Politics of National Policy Making* (University of Oklahoma Press, 2006), especially chapter 4; and

Thomas Mann and Norman Ornstein, *The Broken Branch: How Congress Is Failing America and How to Get It Back on Track* (Oxford, 2006).

6. "The American Polity in the Late 1970s: Building Coalitions in the Sand," in *The New American Political System*, edited by Anthony King (AEI, 1978).

7. Mann and Ornstein, *The Broken Branch*, p. 123.

8. "Highlights: 107 Congress, Second Session," *CQ Weekly*, December 7, 2002, p. 3176.

9. Levinson, *Our Undemocratic Constitution*, p. 108.

10. Steven Sloan and Charlene Carter, "Historic Overhaul in Final Stretch," *CQ Weekly*, June 28, 2010, p. 1572.

11. See Jonathan Rauch, "Rescuing Compromise," *National Affairs* (Fall 2013) (www.nationalaffairs.com/publications/detail/rescuing-compromise).

12. Pietro Nivola, "To Fathom the Fiscal Fix, Look in the Mirror," Brookings, January 7, 2013 (www.brookings.edu/blogs/up-front/posts/2013/01/07-fiscal-fix-nivola).

13. For an especially convincing argument on this point, see Christopher Howard, *The Welfare State Nobody Knows: Debunking Myths about U.S. Social Policy* (Princeton, 2007).

14. Barry Rabe, *Statehouse and Greenhouse: The Emerging Politics of American Climate Change Policy* (Brookings, 2004), p. xii.

15. Quoted in Deborah Schoch and Janet Wilson, "Governor, Blair Reach Environmental Accord," *Los Angeles Times*, August 1, 2006.

16. *Massachusetts v. EPA* 549 U.S. 497 (2007).

17. John M. Broder, "Obama, Who Vowed Rapid Action on Climate Change, Turns More Cautious," *New York Times*, April 11, 2009, p. A10. We have seen this pattern play out before: this is how the large air pollution control program called Prevention of Significant Deterioration came into being over thirty years ago. R. Shep Melnick, *Regulation and the Courts: The Case of the Clean Air Act* (Brookings, 1983), chapter 4.

18. See Philip Wallach, "U.S. Regulation of Greenhouse Gas Emissions," Brookings, October 2012 (www.brookings.edu/~/media/research/files/papers/2012/10/26%20climate%20change%20wallach/26%20climate%20change%20wallach.pdf); and Philip A. Wallach, "Debating the EPA's Clean Power Plant Proposal: The Big Picture for EPA's Clean Power Plan," Brookings, August 27, 2014 (www.brookings.edu/blogs/planetpolicy/posts/2014/08/27-big-picture-epa-clean-power-plan-wallach).

19. Stephen Castle, "Europe, Facing Economic Pain, May Ease Climate Rules," *New York Times*, January 22, 2014.

20. 2011 Dear Colleague Letter (http://www2.ed.gov/about/offices/list/ocr/letters/colleague-201104.pdf); and 2014 "Questions and Answers on Title IX and Sexual Violence" (http://www2.ed.gov/about/offices/list/ocr/docs/qa-201404-

title-ix.pdf). For a list of the more than ninety schools being investigated, see Tara Culp-Ressler, "These Are the Colleges and Universities Now under Federal Investigation for Botching Rape Cases," January 13, 2015 (http://thinkprogress. org/health/2015/01/13/3610865/title-ix-investigations/).

21. On racial disparity in funding, see Dear Colleague letter of October 1, 2014 (http:// www2.ed.gov/about/offices/list/ocr/letters/colleague-resourcecomp-201410. pdf).

22. For a list of these agreements, see Department of Justice, "Educational Opportunities Cases" (www.justice.gov/crt/about/edu/documents/classlist.php).

23. Martha Derthick and Andy Rotherham, "Obama's NCLB Waivers: Are They Necessary or Illegal?," *Education Next* (Spring 2012).

24. Martha Derthick, *Up in Smoke* (CQ Press, 2002), chapter 9.

25. Paul Nolette, *Federalism on Trial: State Attorneys General and National Policy Making in Contemporary America* (University of Kansas Press, 2015).

26. *Wyeth* v. *Levine*, 555 U.S. (2009).

27. Lawrence Brown and Michael Sparer, "Poor Program's Progress: The Unanticipated Politics of Medicaid Policy," *Health Affairs* (January 2003), pp. 31–44. They quote Waxman as explaining, "Incrementalism may not get much press, but it does work."

28. Ibid. Others have reached the same conclusion: see Aaron Wildavsky, *New Politics of the Budgetary Process* (Scott, Foresman and Company, 1988), pp. 303–08; and Michael Greve, "Washington and the States," AEI *Federalism Outlook* No. 13 (May 2003).

29. Richard Nathan, "Federalism and Health Policy," *Health Affairs* (November 2005), p. 1.

30. Hugh Davis Graham, *The Civil Rights Era: Origins and Development of National Policy* (Oxford, 1990); John Skrentny, *The Ironies of Affirmative Action* (University of Chicago Press, 1996).

31. R. Shep Melnick, "The Odd Evolution of the Civil Rights State," *Harvard Journal on Law and Public Policy*, vol. 37, no. 1 (2014), p. 113.

32. Joel Aberbach, Robert Putnam, and Bert Rockman, *Bureaucrats and Politicians in Western Democracies* (Harvard, 1981).

33. *The Federalist Papers*, edited by Clinton Rossiter (New York: Mentor, 1961), p. 226. All references to *Federalist* essays in this chapter are to this edition.

34. *Federalist* No. 49, page 314, emphasis added.

35. Letter from Madison to Jefferson, February 4, 1790, quoted in Greg Weiner, *Madison's Metronome: The Constitution, Majority Rule, and the Tempo of American Politics* (University of Kansas Press, 2012), p. 59.

36. For an especially compelling explanation of Madison and Hamilton's thinking in this regard, see Michael Greve, *The Upside Down Constitution* (Harvard, 2012), chapter 1.

37. *Federalist* No. 62, p. 381.
38. *Dismantling the Welfare State? Reagan, Thatcher, and the Politics of Retrenchment* (Cambridge University Press, 1994), p. 18.
39. *Federalist* No. 10, p. 82.
40. See generally, Weiner, *Madison's Metronome*, n. 34.
41. *Federalist* No.10, p. 84.
42. Ibid., p. 79.
43. Jack Goldsmith, *Power and Constraint: The Accountable Presidency after 9/11* (W.W. Norton, 2012), chapter 6.
44. *Federalist* No. 10, p. 79.

Six

Rescuing Compromise

Jonathan Rauch

A funny thing happened, as they say in the Borscht Belt, on the way to legislative gridlock and fiscal meltdown. Over the past few years in paralyzed, polarized Washington—where Democrats refuse to reduce spending without revenue increases, which Republicans peremptorily reject—Democrats accepted spending cuts and Republicans accepted tax increases, with the result that legislative gridlock and fiscal meltdown were avoided.

True, it all happened in an ugly, piecemeal fashion, with the two parties lurching from one self-created crisis to another. At one stage, Republicans seemed willing to default on the national debt rather than compromise; at another, an automatic "sequestration" cut spending in what everyone agreed was a nonsensical fashion. Instead of joining hands in the grand bargain so ardently desired by pundits and much of the public, Congress and President Obama fought their way through a series of kludges, each of them greeted as disappointing, if not appalling. Yet the results bear pondering. According to Congressional Budget Office projections, the cumulative effect of Washington's serial muddling was to stabilize the national debt as a share of gross domestic product over the coming decade.[1] The resulting level, by many accounts, is still too high, and more remains to be done about long-term increases in health care spending and other entitlement costs. But the debt emergency is over.

To get there, Congress cut spending by about $2.6 trillion over ten years and raised taxes by about $700 billion (according to the Center on Budget and Policy Priorities). After adjusting for padding and assorted gimmicks on the spending side, that ratio of spending cuts to tax increases looks remarkably close to the ratio of between 2:1 and 3:1 recommended by many of the mainstream economists and pundits who called for a grand bargain.[2] At least as important, all of that fiscal tightening happened at a pace that slowed but did not abort a delicate economic recovery. Too much deficit reduction would have caused a recession, aggravating the debt problem; too little would have left the underlying crisis untended. Having accomplished several years of risky fiscal tightening, the government then, in late 2013 and into 2014, eased up on the austerity measures, providing what many economists believe was a well-timed breather that helped the economy reestablish momentum. Unlike Europe, America seemed to have gotten both the pace and the magnitude of the fiscal adjustment about right. One might add that, in 2013, budget negotiations curtailed some of the sequestration's worst excesses and that Republicans, stung by a resounding defeat when they shut down the government and achieved nothing, backed away from their most extreme tactics. All in all, the system acquitted itself remarkably well, steering a course between hostile political factions and dangerous economic outcomes. Somewhere, James Madison is smiling.

Madison understood something that many contemporary political commentators forget: politicians, like other people, compromise because they have to, not because they want to. So he designed a system that would compel them to bargain. Looking at the budget battles of the past few years, he would not be surprised to see stubbornness, partisanship, and rancor. He saw his share of those in the scorching political strife of the 1790s. But he might have been surprised—rather pleasantly surprised—to see that, more than 200 years on, the system that he helped design to force compromise was still working.

That cheerful narrative, however, is not the only way to look at the events of the past few years. There is an alternative story, one in which Madison and the Constitution are not vindicated but betrayed. In this story, compromise has led to a triumph not *of* the Constitution but *over* it: a victory for self-serving politicians eager to expand the federal government and their own power far beyond the bounds that Madison and the other Founders imagined. Compromise, in this story, undermines, rather than underlies, the constitutional order, and the results of the budget debates of the past few years traduce rather than transmit the Founders' vision. Neither of these stories is by any means new: both reach back to the Founders' era. But the second story, the one that would have patriots draw a line against compromise when the size of government is at issue, has lately enjoyed a major resurgence—advanced by a prominent political insurgency, namely the Tea Party and its kin.

This argument, which has claimed for itself the mantles of conservatism and constitutionalism, demands an answer in the form of a vigorous conservative and constitutionalist case for compromise. Compromise is not merely a political expedient but a republican virtue—indeed, a cardinal virtue, according to no less a conservative luminary than Edmund Burke: "All government, indeed every human benefit and enjoyment, every virtue, and every prudent act, is founded on compromise and barter." Compromise is not, in the U.S. constitutional system, merely a necessary evil but a positive good: an indispensable source of political discipline, competition, and stability—all of which are conservative values. There is, in short, nothing unprincipled about it.

COMPELLING COMPROMISE

The Constitution was designed to do many things at once. Modern conservatives who say that it sets limits on the power of government are correct. Modern progressives who say that it creates a flexible framework to promote the general welfare also are correct. Those who say that it establishes federal supremacy are as correct as those who say that it safeguards the sovereignty of the states.

The foremost thing that it does, however, is embodied in its structure rather than its text. It forces politicians to compromise, by creating competing power centers and depriving any of them of the power to impose its will on the others. The resulting system is often referred to as one of checks and balances, but that phrase, as William F. Connelly Jr. notes in his 2010 book *James Madison Rules America*, fails to do justice to both the intricacy and the dynamism of the constitutional order. The Constitution forces compromise not merely between the branches of the federal government (legislature versus executive versus judiciary), nor merely between levels of government (federal versus state), but also *within* each of them and within each of the parties that populate them. Members of the majority party in each chamber of Congress must negotiate with one another to garner votes, and members of the minority party must negotiate with one another about whether to cooperate with the majority or obstruct it. "Factions within each party constantly fight over whether they are part of the government or part of the opposition," writes Connelly.[3] "The majority party in Congress is not the government, nor is the minority party merely the opposition, whether under conditions of divided government or even under conditions of so-called united party government. Neither Democrats nor Republicans govern; rather, the Constitution governs."[4]

For its part, the executive, though more unitary than Congress, must slalom between cooperation and conflict with the opposition party and between solidarity and "triangulation" with its own allies. And all the participants must dance with an ever-shifting congeries of interest groups. Even individual politicians balance competing roles, playing the loyal partisan foot soldier one day and the self-interested political entrepreneur the next. Politics in Madison's system is a constant struggle for balance. Case-by-case compromise generally supersedes durable coalitions. Absent a rare (and usually unsustainable) supermajority, there is simply not much that any single faction, interest, or branch of government can do. Effective action, in this system, depends on nothing *but* a series of forced compromises.

Why arrange things in such a seemingly chaotic and unstable way? Why should every little thing require negotiation and coalition building? The architects of the Constitution had two reasons in mind, only one of which is well appreciated. The better-known reason was famously explained by Madison himself: Setting faction against faction, ambition against ambition, and interest against interest can help contain the excesses to which unopposed faction, ambition, and self-interest will run. Madison's greatest insight was the counterintuitive proposition that the remedy for political predation is not less politics but more. No "mere demarcation on parchment," as he says in *Federalist* No. 48, could contain ambition; the only effective container is ambition itself.[5] As markets enlist competition and exchange to direct and harness the energy of greed, so Madisonian politics enlists competition and compromise to direct and harness the energy of ambition.[6] The "checking and balancing" of power is the negative advantage, so to speak, of forcing compromise. It guards against tyranny. Less widely appreciated but just as important is a positive advantage: Compromise forces adaptation.

The Founders had no way to know what sorts of problems their new government might be called upon to cope with decades (and now centuries) into the future. They faced an apparently impossible conundrum: how to provide enough stability to make the system durable while also ensuring enough flexibility to allow it to adjust to changing circumstances. Their ingenious solution is the core of the U.S. system of government. Periodic elections, of course, are an essential element. But they are only part of the story. What happens between elections, in the day-to-day ebb and flow of policymaking, when there is no opportunity to consult the voters? What happens when electoral results are ambiguous or produce deadlock? The Madisonian answer was to build constant adjustment into the system itself, by requiring constant negotiation between shifting constellations of actors. As Connelly notes, the idea that Madison and the Founders sought to bias the system against change is only a half-truth; after the trauma of the Articles of Confederation, they were also interested in ensuring that the government would be sufficiently energetic. "They designed the constitutional separation of powers to promote stability *and* energy—to impede change *and* advance innovation."[7] They wanted to discourage undue haste while encouraging essential reform.

Compromise was the mechanism that they believed would allow for that difficult combination. Forcing actors to bargain and collaborate slows precipitous change while constantly making negotiators adjust their positions. Except over short intervals, stasis of the kind that had afflicted so many monarchies and empires in the past is impossible in Madison's government. The requirement to bargain and find allies provides new ideas and new entrants with avenues to enter politics and shake up the status quo. But that same requirement prevents upheaval by ensuring that no one actor can seize control, at least not for long.

Ingenious though it was, the two-edged constitutional system supports two quite different interpretations of its purpose. How was the country to understand it: as a brake on change or as an engine of innovation? Jeffersonians, Hamiltonians, and their successors have been arguing over that question since the first Congress. But neither Jefferson nor Hamilton played an important role at the Constitutional Convention. And the man who played the most critical role, Madison, wanted it both ways.

Madison was first and foremost a practical politician, and a very skillful one. He saw the Constitution as a dynamic political mechanism, whereas today many Americans tend to see it as a substantive ideological statement. In Madison's dynamic framework, it matters less whether Hamiltonians or Jeffersonians have the right idea about government than that neither side ever finally prevails. Compromise, then, is not merely a necessary evil; it is a positive good, a balance wheel that keeps government moving forward instead of toppling. Of course, that does not mean that compromise is admirable in every instance or person. The old cliché is true: whether a compromise is good or bad depends on the compromise. But there is a crucial difference between virtue at the *individual* level and at the *systemic* level. What individuals may dislike (often rightly) in particular cases may nonetheless be good for the system—and for the country—in repeated instances over time. The Madisonian system neither requires nor desires that every individual should be a deal-cutting moderate. It assumes that people have every entitlement to strong beliefs and every reason to enter negotiations reluctant to budge. Hard bargaining and adamantine opinion provide much of the energy that invigorates politics and forces new ideas into the system— provided, crucially, that the energy can be contained, mixed, and channeled through compromise.

At the end of the day, the Madisonian framework asks not that participants *like* compromising but that they *do* it—and, above all, that they recognize the legitimacy of a system that makes them do it. It asks them to acknowledge that the compromise-forcing constitutional structure is principled and admirable, even if some compromises are not.

The Anti-Compromise Movement

Poll after poll has shown that most Americans do in fact acknowledge the virtue of compromise as a general principle. The level of public support depends on how the question is asked, but the overall sentiment is not in doubt. For example, when people were asked in 2013 by the Pew Research

Center whether they preferred elected officials who stick to their positions or those who make compromises with people that they disagree with, respondents favored compromise by a margin of 50 percent to 44 percent.[8] In 2011, when Gallup asked (using less neutral wording) whether it is more important for political leaders "to compromise in order to get things done" or "stick to their beliefs even if little gets done," compromise prevailed by 51 percent to 28 percent.[9] If anything, the culture of compromise has strengthened in recent years. According to Pew, the preference for compromise has risen slightly since 1987 but markedly since 2010.[10]

There is, however, a counter-trend. Many polls find that today's Republicans differ from both Democrats and independents in their attitude toward compromise. Depending on how the question is asked, they are either significantly less supportive of it (they were split down the middle in the 2011 Gallup poll, with its compromise-friendly wording) or downright hostile to it (as with Pew's more neutral 2013 wording, which found Republicans preferring "stick to positions" over "make compromises" by a strong margin of 55 percent to 36 percent). Significantly, the Tea Party movement is several notches more hostile to compromise than are Republicans as a whole. In 2010, Pew found Republicans preferring "stick to positions" over "make compromises" by 59 percent to 36 percent. Among Tea Party sympathizers, however, the margin was an even more lopsided 71 percent to 22 percent.[11]

I have interviewed many Tea Party supporters and leaders in the last few years. What comes across when they discuss their concerns is not just fiscal libertarianism and hostility to big government, although those certainly are defining predilections. Nor did I find extremism or radicalism as conventionally thought of. They are smart, successful people who have no interest in upending the social order as we know it; in fact, they tend to think of themselves as seeking to preserve the social order from government's efforts to usurp it. They are not temperamentally opposed to compromise; in their daily lives, they do it all the time. Rather, they are *ideologically* opposed to compromise. They have made a reasoned judgment that compromise has served the country and the Constitution poorly.

It has served the country poorly, they say, by corrupting politicians who promise one thing and then go to Washington and do the opposite after being absorbed by the deal-making, log-rolling culture of politics as usual. Leaders who show up swearing to master big government wind up serving it instead. Pushed to defend themselves, such craven politicians say "We didn't have the votes" or "At the end of the day, we had to get something done." This kind of realpolitik, whatever its tactical merits, is a one-way ratchet toward ever bigger government. And it can hardly be rational to continue to support a counterproductive strategy, the very strategy that got the country into the current mess. When you are in a hole, the first thing to do is stop digging; therefore compromisers should just *stop*. That is the only way that they can act as a restraint on the system today.

Underpinning that strategic judgment, and strengthening the conviction on which it rests, is a particular view of the Constitution. Compromise, in this view, has sold the Constitution down the river. The Constitution was never fixed in stone, of course, but its essence—a small federal government with limited and enumerated powers—has been compromised out of existence in the course of the past century. It is fine, continues this argument, to compromise up to a point—but not to the point where the Constitution itself is swallowed up by the compromises made in its name. Anything Madison, Jefferson, or even Hamilton might have recognized as a reasonably bounded federal government has vanished beneath layer upon layer of federal self-aggrandizement. By now, politicians are just compromising on how much more of the Constitution to whittle away. Today, when compromise has become the enemy of the constitutional order, the first injunction is, once again: just stop.

Of course, Tea Partiers are hardly the first to argue that compromise has undermined or distorted the Constitution. Barry Goldwater inspired millions (though he alarmed millions more) with his declaration that "extremism in the defense of liberty is no vice" and his claim that much of what the government did was unconstitutional. The antebellum South developed an elaborate ideology holding that any compromise on slavery would sabotage the Constitution, while many abolitionists believed that a compromise allowing slavery to persist in any form was anathema to America's constitutional ideals. The Tea Party argument, however, stands apart by being strategically focused in a way that its predecessors were not. Instead of aiming mainly to defeat liberals or moderates in general elections, it aims to defeat conservatives in primary elections if they compromise on fiscal matters. In that way, it deters a specific behavior (compromise) rather than merely promoting a general ideology (fiscal conservatism). Although many

Tea Partiers would certainly like to build a constructive national majority and hope someday to do so, they are more than willing to begin by building an obstructive congressional minority.

Even those who disapprove of the Tea Party's goals may grudgingly admire the canniness of its asymmetrical political warfare. A firm anti-compromise minority, if willing to play the spoiler, can exert leverage far disproportionate to its numbers. The Tea Party Republicans have sought to use that leverage to change the basic calculus of compromise in American politics. If Madison's premise was that politicians don't compromise because they want to but because they have to, the Tea Party's premise is that politicians can and should be deterred from compromising even when they want to. As hard-edged and ideological as Barry Goldwater and Ronald Reagan could be rhetorically, both were accomplished legislative dealmakers. And both could get away with cutting deals because their conservative base trusted them to bargain in pursuit of conservative goals. For anti-compromisers, by contrast, the very fact that a deal is a deal makes it suspect, never mind who presents it. If the other side would agree to it, after all, something important must have been given away, and that is the kind of horse trading that got the country into today's mess. As Richard Mourdock, a Tea Party–backed candidate who beat a more moderate incumbent, Richard Lugar, in Indiana's 2012 Republican Senate primary race, put it, "We are at that point where one side or the other has to win this argument. One side or the other will dominate."[12] He averred that he was for compromise and bipartisanship, provided "compromise" and "bipartisanship" meant that Democrats capitulate to Republicans in rolling back the size of government.[13]

THE SPOILERS' DILEMMA

To some extent, anti-compromise ideology may be self-defeating, or at least self-limiting. Much of what it gives insurgents by way of leverage in particular races it takes back by way of unpopularity among the broader public. In the 2012 general election, Mourdock himself lost what should have been a safe Republican Senate seat to a Democrat—a stinging defeat that did not go unnoticed among Tea Partiers. In April 2013, when, in an open-ended question, Gallup asked respondents to "tell me one or two specific things you dislike about the Republican Party," 21 percent cited the party's inflexibility and unwillingness to compromise—swamping all the other responses. In fact, an even more dominant share of Republicans themselves, 26 percent, cited unwillingness to compromise as their party's biggest flaw.[14]

As with any insurgency, so with the Tea Party: the same hardball tactics that amplify its influence also restrict its reach. Punishing compromisers may work tactically for a while, but as a longer-term strategy it may so damage the Republican brand as to marginalize itself in all but a hard core of congressional redoubts. And even at its peak in the early 2010s, the Tea Party and its allies were able to make compromising harder but could not make it impossible, as the fiscal deals of the Obama years show. If Madison were around today and writing a *Federalist* No. 86 about anti-compromise movements, he might argue that they may enjoy some success for a while but sooner or later will burn out.

Even so, there are reasons to be concerned. "A while" can be a long time, especially in a House of Representatives where congressional districts are so thoroughly gerrymandered that incumbents can effectively ignore the views of all but their most hard-line constituents. Worse, the feedback loops on which self-correction depends have been weakened by today's primary system, with its vulnerability to small, ideologically committed groups. Moreover, even if the Madisonian system can ultimately digest even a pretty big helping of anti-compromise ideology, it will suffer from indigestion along the way. Elected officials who put protest ahead of governing have their place, but the more of them there are, the more friction the system will encounter. A minority of spoilers on either side of a prominent debate can increase by an order of magnitude the political danger and difficulty of transactional politics, even when majorities on both sides want to cut a deal and would gain by achieving one.

In particular, spoilers have three pernicious effects. First, they make it difficult for leaders to lead. If any deal that a leader brings back from negotiations is suspect precisely because it *is* a deal—and if any leader who brings back such a deal is likely to be accused of treason by a significant share of his base—then it will be hard for a leader either to accept a compromise or deliver on one. That is exactly the kind of problem that has weakened House Speaker John Boehner in recent years. Second, the presence of a knot of spoilers on one side increases polarization by hardening opinion on the other side. Why compromise, after all, if you think that the other side will put any concessions in its pocket and then demand more? "We won't compromise because they won't" is not an unreasonable attitude. As opposing positions harden and polarize, the substantive ground for compromise shrinks and the trust necessary to find it erodes. That, in turn, makes it harder, not easier, to make painful but important reforms such as long-term budget and entitlement changes. Third, either party's isolation from the political mainstream—and from the mainstream's acceptance of the give-and-take of transactional politics—is undesirable in its own right. At some point, when insurgent voices within a party become dominant (or at least disproportionately influential), that party will begin behaving less like a party and more like an interest group.

Parties traditionally combine disparate factions under a single political tent; they gather diverse ideologies and interests together and forge durable coalitions for political gain. Interest groups, by contrast, pitch separate tents. They pursue narrow agendas and form only temporary, goal-oriented coalitions; they distill rather than blend their identity; and they focus on one aim or just a few to the virtual exclusion of all others. Republicans' recent emphasis on ideological purity and their obsession with fiscal policy to the near exclusion of other priorities suggest that they have veered in the direction of becoming a conservative interest group, when what the country needs is a conservative *party*.

A Patriot's Case for Compromise

So now what? Various structural reforms might help restore the internal feedback loops on which the Madisonian compromise-forcing system relies. Thoughtful observers have made cases for changing the primary election process, or adjusting congressional rules, or reforming the redistricting process to reduce gerrymandering. But to concentrate on narrow technical changes is to miss the forest for the trees. Tinkering with filibusters and gerrymanders and the like may be worthwhile, but wholesale change requires an injection of *ideas*. Small-bore change will not work without an intellectual effort to advance a principled, positive, patriotic case for compromise, especially on the right.

The Tea Party's critique of compromise has merit, at least from the point of view of someone who believes that modern government is far too big. The problem is not that the anti-compromise view is present in the conservative movement but that it is inadequately opposed. It encounters nothing like the sort of robust ideological critique that it deserves. Fighting something with nothing is always hard. When one prominent strand of conservative thought vigorously propounds a thought-through ideology opposed to compromise while proponents of transactional politics twiddle their thumbs in embarrassed silence, no one should be surprised that the vocal, ideologically coherent group becomes dominant. As long as conservatives perceive and portray compromise as at best a negative virtue—and more often as a violation of conservative principles—its reputation will be diminished and its legitimacy shadowed.

Playing hardball in politics is not unhealthy. Hardball is often necessary and important, and many who complain about it should pay more attention to getting better at it. To reemphasize: Madison's framework does not require or desire that all individuals should be moderates. But to valorize hardball for its own sake *is* unhealthy, and even more unhealthy is to veto a compromise because it is a compromise. There is no contradiction between compromise and political principle—or at least no necessary contradiction. Nor is compromise at odds with constitutional principle. Just the reverse: compromise is the most essential principle of the U.S. constitutional system. Those who hammer out painful deals perform the hardest and often the highest work of politics. They deserve, in general, respect for their willingness to advance their ideals constructively, not condemnation for their treachery. No one is saying, of course, that anyone should support anything only because it is a compromise, any more than that he or she should oppose something only because it is a compromise. The point, rather, is that compromise is a republican virtue. It endows the constitutional order with stability and dynamism; it not only tempers the worst in the nation but often brings out the best. It is patriotic, not pathetic, and it deserves to be trumpeted as such.

An encouraging, if still embryonic, development on the right is the emergence of some prominent conservative defenders of compromise. Peter Wehner, a former George W. Bush administration official, has written critically of the knee-jerk rejection of compromise and supportively of the willingness of politicians like Madison and Lincoln to reject the "seductive appeal of the absolute."[15] He defends moderation as a conservative virtue and praises a conservatism "disposed toward compromise, incremental progress and taking into account shifting circumstances."[16] Peter Berkowitz, of the Hoover Institution, recently published a superb book that makes a case for a conservative politics that weighs and interweaves many values and seeks a balanced public life. Constitutional conservatism, he writes, "stresses that balancing worthy but conflicting political principles depends on cultivating the spirit of political moderation institutionalized by the Constitution."[17] This is the politics, Berkowitz notes, of the first and greatest modern conservative, Edmund Burke.

Berkowitz and Wehner and a handful of others do not represent a sea change, but they are a start toward rebuilding an intellectual foundation on the right for a multivalent politics, and that is important. If conservatism is to regain its rightful place in the American mainstream, it needs to restore compromise to respectability in the conservative movement. Burke, Henry Clay, Lincoln, Reagan, Margaret Thatcher, and, of course, Madison himself were not just imposing conservatives and committed patriots but deft compromisers, too. They understood in their various ways what American conservatism urgently needs to rediscover: patriotism, principle, and compromise, though sometimes in tension, stand or fall together in the constitutional pantheon—and compromise is in no respect the least of the three.

Notes

1. See, most recently, Congressional Budget Office, *Updated Budget Projections: 2015 to 2025* (March 2015), table 1.
2. Estimates are from data provided to the author by Paul Van de Water of the Center on Budget and Policy Priorities, whose help is gratefully acknowledged.
3. William F. Connelly Jr., *James Madison Rules America: The Constitutional Origins of Congressional Partisanship* (Lanham, Md.: Rowman and Littlefield, 2010), p. 164.
4. Ibid., p. 83.
5. James Madison, *Federalist* No. 48, in *The Federalist Papers* (New York: Barnes and Noble Classics, 2006), pp. 279.
6. Madison, *Federalist* No. 51, pp. 288.
7. Connelly, *James Madison Rules America*, p. 5.
8. Pew Research Center, "Obama in Strong Position at Start of Second Term," Pew Research Center Poll, January 2013, question 22 (www.people-press. org/2013/01/17/section-2-views-of-congress-and-the-parties/#).

9. "Americans Again Call for Compromise in Washington," Gallup Poll, September 2011, question 36 (www.gallup.com/poll/149699/Americans-Again-Call-for-Compromise-Washington.aspx).

10. Pew Research Center, "Partisan Polarization Surges in Bush, Obama Years," Pew Research Center Poll, June 2012, question 40h (www.people-press.org/values-questions/q40h/like-politicians-who-make-compromises-to-get-the-job-done/#total).

11. Pew Research Center. "Little Compromise on Compromising," Pew Research Center Poll, September 2010, question 5 (www.pewresearch.org/2010/09/20/little-compromise-on-compromising/).

12. Mackenzie Weinger, "Richard Mourdock Dismisses Dick Lugar Attack," *Politico*, May 9, 2012 (www.politico.com/news/stories/0512/76094_Page2.html).

13. Ibid.

14. Gallup, "Americans' Top Critique of GOP: 'Unwilling to Compromise,'" Gallup poll, March 2013, question 2 (www.gallup.com/poll/161573/americans-top-critique-gop-unwilling-compromise.aspx).

15. Peter Wehner, "The Different Interpretations of 'Compromise,'" *Commentary*, June 30, 2011 (www.commentarymagazine.com/2011/06/30/the-different-interpretations-of-compromise/).

16. Peter Wehner, "What Is True Conservatism?," *Commentary*, May 24, 2013 (www.commentarymagazine.com/2013/05/24/what-is-true-conservatism/).

17. Peter Berkowitz, *Constitutional Conservatism: Liberty, Self-Government, and Political Moderation* (Stanford, Calif.: Hoover Institution Press, 2013), p. 117.

Part II

WHAT MIGHT MADISON SAY?

Seven

A MODEL FOR DELIBERATION
OR OBSTRUCTION

Madison's Thoughts about the Senate

JACK N. RAKOVE

*A*mong the current "vices of the political system of the U. States"—to borrow a famous phrase from James Madison—none ranks higher than the working rules and habits that have turned the U.S. Senate into a paradigmatic example of legislative incapacity.[1] The juxtaposition of this evil with the Madisonian notion of political vice becomes even more striking when one realizes how much of Madison's constitutional thinking in the 1780s was inspired by and devoted to the misdeeds of American legislatures. By experience and principle, Madison was first and foremost a deliberative legislator. The preparation of his agenda of constitutional reform in the mid-1780s was shaped largely by his analysis of the defects of legislative assemblies and the procedural aspects of framing legislation. Within that assessment, Madison had high aspirations for the role that the upper legislative house should play in restoring "wisdom and stability" to republican government. Some of those aspirations were quickly frustrated by the actions of the Constitutional Convention, particularly its decisions giving each state an equal vote in the Senate and allowing the state legislatures to elect senators. Yet Madison's conviction that a well-constructed upper house had an essential republican role to play in tempering impulsive legislation and improving the quality of legislative deliberation survived those setbacks.

How one should reconcile Madison's aspirations for improvement and deliberation with the mechanisms of obstruction and impasse that now dominate the Senate is a fair question. Madison was never an enthusiast for thoughtless or impulsive legislation. There was indeed a quasi-libertarian strain in the criticisms of state lawmaking that he voiced in his 1787 memorandum on the "Vices of the Political System of the U. States": "As far as laws are necessary, to mark with precision the duties of those who are to obey them, and to take from those who administer them a discretion, which might be abused, their number is the price of liberty," he wrote. "As far as the laws exceed this limit, they are a nuisance," he added, "a nuisance of the most pestilent kind." Yet Madison did not approach the task of lawmaking simply as a project to discourage legislatures from acting or to multiply the number of veto points within government. He also cared deeply about improving the quality of legislative deliberation and the technical aspects of framing legislation. Equally important, his opposition to the equal state vote in the Senate rested on the conviction that the equal vote—which he never defended on its merits and which he treated as a "compromise" only in retrospect—was unjust in principle. The idea that it needed further elaboration and reinforcement through the adoption of additional anti-majoritarian procedures was a position he was most unlikely to champion.

The various charges that constitute the current indictment of the Senate are easily stated. One obvious line of complaint pertains to the mess in the appointment process, which has now moved beyond judicial nominations, the original site of infection, to contaminate appointments to other administrative positions. In some cases, delays in filling vacancies in executive agencies have effectively paralyzed their operations. More important are the basic rules that threaten the completion of any legislation. One device, arguably the most important, is the quorum call requirement that permits any senator, under any pretext, to halt the work of the Senate as members abandon their committees and hike or ride the Capitol subway to the floor in order to register their presence. Given the shortness of the senatorial work week—which could generously be described as a three-day cycle that might embarrass even the French with its brevity—this threat acts as a powerful deterrent against any responsible floor leader who is aware of what absolutely needs to be done and wants to keep the Senate functioning at some minimal level of efficiency.[2] More controversial and constitutionally far more significant is the escalating use of the threat of filibuster to retard and obstruct legislation. This threat is often deployed to delay decisions that are entirely noncontroversial, not because there is any need for further deliberation on the issue at hand but simply to retard other Senate business.[3] But beyond this further impediment to serious deliberation, the current use of the threat of filibuster raises a far more disturbing question: whether the Senate has effectively added a new supermajoritarian rule to the Constitution, supplementing the specific occasions on which supermajorities are textually required with a procedural rule that has the same result.

The question of the constitutional legitimacy of the filibuster *cum* cloture procedures of the Senate deserves more attention—one might say stricter scrutiny—than it has received. There are, of course, other ways to approach this issue. One can readily identify a short list of substantive reforms that would preserve the general existence of the filibuster while eliminating its worst abuses—for example, by limiting the opportunity to filibuster to one attempt per bill instead of allowing it on amendments and procedural motions as well.[4] But rather than elaborate on the nuances of senatorial rules, it might be helpful to consider the filibuster from the vantage point of 1787 and the underlying norms of constitutional design. Here two significant objections immediately emerge, one textual, the other historical. Whatever power either house of Congress derives from its authority under Article 1, section 5, to "determine the Rules of its Proceedings," the collapse of the distinction between a preparatory rule of deliberation and a final rule of decision, allowing the former to supplant the latter, effectively destroys the principle of majority rule in the Senate. But the Constitution is quite explicit about the circumstances when simple majorities are insufficient (treaty ratification, veto overrides, constitutional amendments, and impeachment decisions). Under *expressio unius est exclusio alterius*, the conventional legal doctrine (which was well known to the Founders), an attempt to create an effective supermajoritarian rule for ordinary legislation or appointments to office is presumptively unconstitutional. Second, the idea that the rulemaking authority of either house of Congress could trump the rules laid down in the text plainly defies the tenor and substance of the constitutional debates of 1787–88. It would come as a remarkable surprise to the framers of the Constitution, who knowingly debated when supermajorities should and should not apply, that they had left a back door open for creation of a supermajoritarian rule through procedural rules of debate. No one, I believe, would be more surprised by this outcome than James Madison, who had very different expectations for the role that the Senate should play.

The construction of a proper senate—of a deliberative chamber capable of acting truly senatorially—was an early subject of interest in the development of Madison's constitutional thinking. In fact, it was the original point that he raised in the letter that scholars regard as the first sustained expression of his ideas about republican institutions: his August 23, 1785, letter to his college classmate Caleb Wallace, who had written him to solicit advice about the constitution that Kentucky should write when it separated from Virginia. Wallace had wondered whether the initial constitution for under-populated Kentucky should even include a senate.[5] Madison replied that it should: "*The Legislative department* ought by all means, as I think to include a Senate constituted on such principles as will give *wisdom* and steadiness to legislation. The want of these qualities is the grievance complained of in all our republics." The original cause of that grievance, Madison suggested, lay in the colonists' natural tendency in 1776 to react against the misuse of *executive* power that they had suffered under the British crown and therefore to fail to anticipate that the proper regulation of *legislative* power would pose the problems that they would face thereafter.[6]

Madison's approach to bicameralism was deeply fortified by his experience in the Virginia House of Delegates in the mid-1780s. "Not a single Session passes," he observed, "without instances of sudden resolutions by the latter [the lower house] of which they repent in time to intercede privately with the Senate for their negative." His abiding fear was that a numerous body composed of amateur lawmakers would often act impulsively. A smaller, more deliberate upper house was needed to check their impulses, even if that body was as badly designed as the Virginia senate. ("[A] worse could hardly have been substituted," he grumbled, "& yet bad as it is, it is often a useful bitt in the mouth of the house of Delegates.") Although Madison was increasingly concerned with protecting property rights, he did not regard the upper house as a bastion of a propertied elite. There were different schemes for selecting an upper house, and Madison liked the model adopted in neighboring Maryland. But he did not regard the mode of election or the class status of senators as providing an adequate basis for enabling the upper house to check the behavior of the lower house. In Madison's view, the decisive fact of republican politics was that paramount advantage would fall to whichever branch of government enjoyed the closest connection with the people. That would clearly work to the benefit of the lower house. Unlike John Adams, Madison was not looking for some American version of mixed government, in which an elite could be recruited to offset the people's immediate representatives. Whatever advantage a senate enjoyed would derive from its institutional qualities and the character of its deliberations, not from its social standing.

This concern with improving the quality of legislative deliberation formed a crucial element in Madison's thinking in the period leading up to the Constitutional Convention. It was manifested, for example, in other points that he developed in his 1785 letter to Wallace. Madison liked the novel institution established in the New York constitution of 1777, the joint executive-judicial council of revision, which was armed with a limited negative (limited veto) over legislation. The advantage of joining judges in the enterprise of framing legislation outweighed whatever injury might be done to a strict principle of separated powers. It was a trade-off in which the prevention of improper legislation would be far more valuable than the later correction of the difficulties that it produced. Madison also favored creating "a standing comm[it]tee composed of a few select & skilful individuals" with the dual power "to prepare bills on all subjects which they may judge proper to be submitted to the Legislature at their meetings & to draw bills for them during their Sessions." To compensate for the additional power that this committee would enjoy, its members might be barred from "holding any other Office" in any department of government. The greater influence that they would gain would thus be limited by a check on their ambitions. They would act, in a sense, as professional lawgivers, not on the Enlightenment model, which worshiped the wisdom of Solon or Lycurgus or Moses, but as experienced lawmakers trained in the task of drawing legislation. Madison's desire to give legislators terms longer than a single year similarly rested less on a desire to insulate them from their constituents than on the recognition that the newcomers who stocked most assemblies and regularly served only a term or two would need time in office to learn their trade.

It is not scholarly news, of course, that Madison believed deeply in the idea that a sound process of republican elections should operate "to refine and enlarge the public views," helping to recruit a class of legislators who would be better able to recognize the public good than "the people themselves." Some of that superiority would arise, he hypothesized, through elections that would weed out "unworthy candidates," those cunning adepts at "the vicious arts, by which elections are too often carried." Somehow the electoral process would operate to identify and favor "men who possess the most attractive merit."[7] But to Madison's way of thinking, that merit was not limited to visible marks of personal "character," a word that resonated deeply in the revolutionary vocabulary. Nearly four years of service in the Continental Congress (1780–83) and another three in the Virginia House of Delegates (1784–86) had taught Madison practical lessons about the nature of collective debate and deliberation. Experience as well as character had turned Madison into a legislative statesman, someone who prepared for discussion by thinking through the issues, recording notes of previous debates, grasping the importance of seizing the agenda, and demonstrating the mastery that others necessarily respected, even if his earnestness sometimes exhausted his colleagues.

These points merit emphasis to establish what might otherwise seem an obvious point. Madison grasped what few if any of his contemporaries saw as fully as he did. With the effective evisceration of executive power in the republican constitutions of 1776, the locus of political decisionmaking had effectively shifted to the legislature. In the British model of statehood, the confirmation of legislative supremacy by the Glorious Revolution did not erode the crown's leading role in governance. Policies still emanated from the crown and its ministries, although active parliamentary review of the workings of government contributed significantly to the public confidence that made the British state so effective.[8]

In the American situation after 1776, however, the executive largely lost its political influence and the capacity to influence legislative deliberations. The notable exceptions were New York and Massachusetts, the two states that drafted constitutions after 1776 and started the revival of executive power by allowing governors to be elected by the people, not the assemblies. It was not by chance that George Clinton and John Hancock became the two most potent governors of the states. In Virginia, by contrast, electing

Patrick Henry to the governorship was the best way to minimize, not enhance, his influence over the legislature. A legislator by experience, Madison expected American governance to develop along another vector: in his view, as a matter of both principle and politics, the legislature should and would be the dominant branch of government. The institution that spoke most directly for the people—or more specifically, for the dominant interests into which the people would form and divide—would exert the greatest influence on politics. The legislature would be the forum where those interests were resolved. Its capacity to achieve the two main objectives of Madison's political philosophy, pursuing the public good and securing private rights, would depend on the deliberative qualities of its members.

The shortcomings of legislative deliberation and enactments at the *state* level formed the final three (or putatively four) items in Madison's pre-convention analysis of the "Vices of the Political System of the U. States." Here he indicted and assessed the "multiplicity," "mutability," and worst, the "injustice" of state legislation, while leaving unexamined a final heading on the "impotence of the laws of the states." Madison's indictment assumed that impulsive legislation could not be explained wholly in terms of wartime pressures to mobilize for the struggle against Britain. Laws were "repealed or superseded" before the population even knew of their existence and "before any trial can have been made of their merits." More important, Madison worried that this impulsive and mutable legislation had called "into question the fundamental principle of republican Government, that the majority who rule in such Governments, are the safest Guardians both of public Good and of private rights." Madison's answer to this challenge, however, was not to question the republican premise—not to impugn the principle of majority rule per se—but to ask how majorities could be properly formed.[9]

Madison located the *causes* of these vices "1. in the Representative bodies. 2. in the people themselves." His ensuing analysis paid much more attention to the second factor, and it was there that he articulated his first exposition of the popular sources of faction as the great evil threatening republics. His treatment of the shortcomings of legislators was much more concise. Yet it still identified basic elements of Madison's concern. "Ambition" and "private interest," he noted, rather than concern for the "public good," were the prevalent motives driving legislators into office. The lawmakers who felt those motives, "particularly, the second," proved "the most industrious, and most successful in pursuing their object." The voters might be expected to reject these faithless servants. But in fact, the miscreants could use crass appeals to the "pretexts of public good and apparent expediency" to mask their motives. So, too, "the honest but unenlightened representative"—presumably the type of lawmaker that Madison desired—would often fall sway to "the sophistical arguments" of "a favorite leader."

Madison hoped that the large electoral districts necessary for a national legislature would produce a better quality of lawmaker. Local demagogues would somehow cancel each other out, allowing a superior class of representatives to be chosen. Still, he understood that this was more a hypothesis than a concrete prediction. Nor did it abate his concern that a popularly elected house in the national legislature would still be prey to interested pressures from below—that is, from constituents. Going into the convention, therefore, Madison's great institutional concern continued to lie with the upper house. And that, of course, was the one institution that proved most controversial during the first half of the convention and the one whose authority declined moderately afterward. By contrast, the character of the lower house did not perplex the Framers very much. True, there was some early disagreement over whether the people or the state legislatures should elect members of the lower house. But that disagreement ended quickly, and the Framers generally agreed with the proposition, laid down by John Adams in *Thoughts on Government* (1776), that the popular house of a legislature should be "in miniature an exact portrait of the people at large."[10] That diverged significantly from the practice in Britain. There the popular fiction that the whole British people were somehow represented in the House of Commons was belied by conditions that led critics to denounce the "rotten" character of the British constitution, with its pocket boroughs easily controlled by some dominant interest, rotten boroughs with bare handfuls of voters, and a limited national electorate that did not accurately capture the social complexity of the nation at large.

While Adams's proposition had become an American orthodoxy, the exact composition of the portrait of the people remained in dispute, as did the question of whether or how slaves—who were never citizens—would figure in apportioning seats among the states. But even that difficult question was settled with a few days of active debate that juxtaposed broad statements of principle both for and against slavery with a candid recognition that, in the end, it was a matter for an expedient compromise.

It was altogether different with the upper house. Its character was the subject of bitter debate from the opening week down to the misnamed "compromise" of July 16 that gave each state an equal vote in the Senate. That decision passed only because the Massachusetts delegation split, effectively costing the state its vote and enabling the critical decision to squeak by on a vote of five states to four. Once that decision was taken, the Senate remained a source of controversy. In the closing weeks of the convention, a set of decisions that were in part a reaction to the vote of July 16 worked to the net advantage of the presidency, the one institution that the Framers collectively found most puzzling.

Madison wanted the Senate to be constituted on some rule that would conform to the principle of proportional representation rather than the equal state vote used under the Articles of Confederation. His formula for how that would be done was not fully articulated. Article 5 of the Virginia Plan provided "that the members of the second branch of the National Legislature ought to be elected by those of the first, out of a proper number of persons nominated by the individual Legislatures." The article did *not* require each state to receive a senator. State legislatures would nominate candidates, without the assurance that one of their nominees must be elected, while the principle of proportional representation would be respected by having the lower house make the choice. Convention delegates from the small states might naturally surmise that their nominees would be less likely to be elected than candidates from the more populous states, but that begged the question of the basis on which members of the lower house would actually vote. As Madison and his allies repeatedly argued, the size (or more specifically, the populousness) of a state would never provide an adequate or useful explanation of how its representatives would behave. Size was an interest worthy of recognition only when one was voting on rules of voting. If, for example, regional interests came to the fore as the decisive variable influencing election to the Senate, nominees from small states could presumably gain seats, regardless of the size of the state that they represented.

The key point for Madison was that the Senate should not follow the precedents set by the Articles of Confederation. Eliminating the equal state

vote was essential. Not only was the rule unjust in itself; its adoption would
also risk dooming a completed constitution to rejection in the large states,
whose preferences, he believed, must ultimately prevail. It was equally desirable to deprive the state legislatures of the authority to elect senators. Their
deficiencies, particularly on matters relating to the national public good,
were a recurring motif in Madison's analysis of "the vices of the political
system." But the decisive consideration in establishing the Senate, Madison thought, was that it should be not a representative institution but a deliberative one. That became evident in the critical debate of June 7, when
John Dickinson introduced a motion to have the state legislatures elect the
Senate. Madison roundly rejected that idea. "If the motion should be agreed
to," Madison recorded himself saying,

> we must either depart from the doctrine of proportional representa-
> tion; or admit into the Senate a very large number of members. The
> first is inadmissible, being evidently unjust. The second is inexpedi-
> ent. The use of the Senate is to consist in its proceeding with more
> coolness, with more system, & with more wisdom, than the popular
> branch. Enlarge their number and you communicate to them the
> vices which they are meant to correct.[11]

Strictly speaking, election by the state legislatures did not preclude a
proportional scheme. But all legislatures were institutionally equal to each
other, and Madison worried that the endorsement of this rule would imply
equality among the states as well. But the "inexpediency" of Dickinson's
motion lay closer to Madison's substantive concern. Dickinson alleged that
the Senate would gain weight with numbers. Make it more numerous, and
it would somehow prove better able to counteract the impulsive lower house.
Madison disagreed. He reasoned arithmetically about the deliberative character of institutions. Larger bodies were more impulsive, more vulnerable to
being swept away by the passions of the moment as each member felt less
responsible for the outcome. A smaller body would increase the sense of
responsibility that each member would feel, while facilitating the capacity
for serious deliberation. The strength of the Senate would derive from the
quality of its debates. Madison was equally skeptical that the Senate would
gain authority if it could be constituted, as Dickinson proposed, to represent

great families. There could be no surety that the legislatures would act on that principle. More important, Madison reasoned, "If an election by the people, or thro' any other channel than the State Legislatures [,] promised as uncorrupt & impartial a preference of merit, there could surely be no necessity for an appointment by those Legislatures."[12]

Madison and James Wilson, his closest ally on this point, lost this contest decisively right away, when the committee of the whole approved Dickinson's motion, ten states to none, on June 7. That was an adverse development, but it did not stop Madison from thinking that the Senate remained a vital institution. The next day, when Madison's proposed negative on state laws was under discussion, he suggested that it "might be very properly lodged in the senate alone."[13] On June 11, Madison declared that a seven-year term for senators was "by no means too long." His main goal "was to give to the Govt. that stability which was every where called for, and which the enemies of the Republican form alleged to be inconsistent with its nature."[14] This comment was wholly apposite to his letter to Caleb Wallace two years earlier. Madison coupled that concern with the Senate with a corresponding desire to improve the deliberative quality of members of the lower house, the institution that he still worried "would be too great an overmatch" for the upper house. A three-year term for ordinary representatives would be essential, he noted on June 12, simply for members "to form any knowledge of the various interests" of other states.[15] That point was reinforced by the likelihood that successive congresses would bring "a large proportion" of newcomers, who would need "to acquire that knowledge of the affairs of the States in general without which their trust could not be usefully discharged."[16]

Comments like these illustrate how deeply his legislative experience had shaped Madison's perception of good governance. Yet Madison never converted his concern with improving the quality of deliberation—including conceiving the Senate as a check to an impulsive lower house—into a formula for obstruction. Madison at the convention was a majoritarian, not an advocate for special interests deserving extra recognition, including the capacity to clog decisionmaking by additional procedural hurdles.

His critical remark on this subject came on June 30, as the convention was moving toward the impasse on the rule of voting in the Senate. The occasion for this debate was the motion of Connecticut delegate Oliver

Ellsworth to balance the acceptance of proportional representation in the lower house with an equal state vote in the Senate. The lower house would represent the people as individual citizens of one nation; the Senate would represent the states "as equal political Societies."[17] Ellsworth necessarily stumbled in explaining exactly when or how states with interests as diverse as those of Virginia, Pennsylvania, and Massachusetts would conspire against their respective near-neighbors Maryland, New Jersey, and Rhode Island or Connecticut. "Altho' no particular abuses could be foreseen by him, the possibility of them would be sufficient to alarm him." That was as low a threshold as one could set, when the concern was to ensure that "the power is given to the few to save them from being destroyed by the many" without having to specify what plausible motive would produce that result or what form the destruction would take.[18] Madison and his allies had argued that the large states had divergent interests and unless they formed some utterly corrupt bargain, they could never coalesce into one coherent interest. But Ellsworth's position, at bottom, was simply that the small states could not allow themselves to be governed by rules of proportional voting in both houses of the new congress.

Madison answered this claim directly on June 30, after his ally James Wilson and his opponent Oliver Ellsworth had both spoken at length. His remarks (in his own summary, of course) are worth citing:

It was urged, he said, continually that an equality of votes in the 2d. branch was not only necessary to secure the small, but would be perfectly safe to the large ones whose majority in the 1st. branch was an effectual bulwark. But notwithstanding this apparent defence, the majority of States might still injure the majority of people. 1. they could *obstruct* the wishes and interests of the majority. 2. they could *extort* measures repugnant to the wishes & interest of the Majority. 3. they could *impose* measures adverse thereto; as the 2d. branch will probably exercise some great powers, in which the 1st. will not participate.

Obstruction, extortion, and imposition were not markers of the improved deliberation that Madison desired, but prices and penalties to be paid for contributing to the unwarranted demands of a numerical minority.

Madison did concede that "every particular interest whether in any class of citizens, or any description of States, ought to be secured as far as possible." But that goal had to be connected to some real, existing social interests, not to the artificial claims of the small states that being in a numerical minority was a true interest in itself. The best way to balance those claims, Madison then noted, was to realize that the true difference of interest within the Union "did not lie between the large & small States: it lay between the Northern & Southern," and it arose "principally from the effects of their having or not having slaves."[19] In theory, one might substitute two rules of representation tied to that difference, counting total population (slaves included) in one house and free people alone in the other. That remained problematic, however, because the two houses would possess somewhat different powers, thereby destroying any symmetry between the two rules.

Madison's position remained majoritarian in both cases. It only conceived that majorities could be constituted in two different ways, one predicated on counting slaves as a major source of property, the other on denying slaves political existence because they lacked any claims to the rights of citizenship. Yet both kinds of majorities still represented real, definable interests, not the imaginary fears that Madison believed the delegates from the small states were evoking. Madison saw the debate over the Senate as a test of the basic principle of majority rule. If "the Convention was reduced to the alternative of either departing from justice in order to conciliate the smaller States, and the minority of the people of the U.S. or of displeasing these by justly gratifying the larger states and the majority of the people," he declared on July 5, after the compromise committee had reported, "he could not himself hesitate as to the option he ought to make."[20] On July 7, according to Rufus King, Madison again complained that the equal state vote "will enable *a minority* to hold the Majority—they will compel the majority to submit to their particular Interest or they will withhold their assent to essential & necessary measures."[21] And in his final speech of July 14, Madison reiterated his fundamental objections against the equal state vote on the same majoritarian grounds, adding only one new point: "the evil instead of being cured by time, would increase with every new State that should be admitted, as they must all be admitted on the principle of equality."[22] Visions of Idaho and North Dakota danced in his head.

Two days later, by the narrowest margin possible, the equal state vote in the Senate carried the day. Over the next two months, the delegates learned to think of it as a compromise, not in its political origin but in rhetorical retrospect. Two days before it adjourned, the convention locked the equal state vote into the Constitution as the one rule not subject to Article V amendment. Originally the delegates had *rejected* Roger Sherman's motion prohibiting any state, without its consent, from being "affected in its internal police, or deprived of its equal suffrage in the Senate." "Begin with these special provisos," Madison had warned, "and every State will insist upon them." But after the motion failed, "the circulating murmurs of the small States" led Gouverneur Morris to rescue the second part of Sherman's motion.[23] The rest is history, and the modern Senate, in some distant fashion, is its result.

Of course, it would be absurd to trace the stagnant rules of the modern Senate solely to the fateful error of July 16. The key inference to be made about Madison's views is different. The grudging acceptance of the equal state vote and its rewarding of the claims of an arbitrary minority of states whose real interests would never correspond to their size was a sufficient departure from the majoritarian principles that Madison favored. It is difficult or indeed (in my view) impossible to imagine Madison the Framer ever endorsing the development of an institutional culture that would treat the decision of July 16 as a legitimating starting point for the further elaboration of the array of procedures that now bedevil the Senate. The perceived necessity of accepting the equal state vote was as far as he was willing to go. The alternative, after all, was the potential breakup of the convention if either the large states or small states decided to bolt, a risk that Madison finally proved unwilling to take. But the idea that the equal state vote was only a foundation or threshold for elaborating rules designed not to improve deliberation but to obstruct decisionmaking was a lesson that Madison would never have drawn. He had had experiences of that kind in the Continental Congress, particularly when David Howell doggedly represented Rhode Island during the debates over the impost. The idea of allowing lone individuals to obstruct action was not his model of senatorial deliberation, as comments recorded by Rufus King on July 7 make clear.[24]

Madison's lack of enthusiasm for the convention's key decisions on the Senate were well illustrated in the two essays of *The Federalist* that he dedicated to the upper house. *Federalist* No. 62 devoted all of three perfunctory

sentences to the legislative election of senators. The next point, the equal
state vote, received lengthier treatment—three paragraphs rather than three
sentences—yet one hardly needs to be a votary of the esoteric reading techniques of high Straussians to detect Madison's persisting qualms. It would
not have been very difficult, after all, for Madison to borrow the arguments
made by delegates like William Paterson, Oliver Ellsworth, and John Dickinson to justify the equal state vote in far more robust terms than he managed to muster. Instead, Madison simply noted that "it is superfluous to try,
by the standard of theory, a part of the Constitution which is allowed on all
hands to be the result, not of theory, but 'of a spirit of amity, and that mutual
deference and concession which the peculiarity of our political situation rendered indispensable.'" Similarly, Madison could not mention the dual security that Americans would receive from requiring successful legislation to
represent a majority of the people and the states without insinuating other
doubts about the rationality of this norm. There would be times, he noted,
when "this complicated check on legislation" might prove "injurious as well
as beneficial." More important, "the peculiar deference which it involves in
favor of the smaller States, would be more rational, if any interests common
to them, and distinct from those of the other States, would otherwise be exposed to peculiar danger." But of course Madison's whole theory of faction
presupposed that the size of a state would never define its interests. Thus,
he concluded, "It is not impossible that this part of the Constitution may
be more convenient in practice than it appears to many in contemplation."[25]

"More rational" and "not impossible" were hardly the words of a committed advocate. Yet when Madison moved past the decisions that he still
resented to consider the "purposes" of the institution, his comments remained faithful to the concerns that he had been expressing since at least
1785. The remaining paragraphs of *Federalist* No. 62 and *Federalist* No. 63
strongly echo, in terms readily recognizable to Madison scholars, dominant
themes of his constitutional analysis. Madison expresses familiar concerns:
with the impulsive nature of popular legislatures; with the lack of acquain-
tance amateur lawmakers have with public affairs; with the embarrassing
task of "repealing, explaining, and amending laws, which fill and disgrace
our voluminous codes"; with the harmful effects of "a mutable government"
and "a mutable policy." Within this situation, Madison observes at the close
of *Federalist* No. 62, it is possible that an "unreasonable advantage" will fall

"to the sagacious, the enterprising, and the moneyed few over the industrious and uninformed mass of the people." The task of establishing "a due sense of national character," which will be so essential to relations with foreign nations, can never be discharged "by a numerous and changeable body." It could only be done by a small durable chamber, one composed of individual members who might expect to gather personal credit for the success of national measures and who would feel as well a sense of "pride and consequence" tied to the "reputation and prosperity of the community." Such a body would also feel a connection to "a succession of well-chosen and well-connected measures," the cumulative effects of which could be felt only over time. Members who came and went with every new congress, as Madison rightly expected would be the case, would rarely acquire that ambition, but senators might.[26] Madison closed *Federalist* No. 63 by moving beyond the role that the Senate would play in balancing the misdeeds of the people's representatives to argue that it would also provide "a defence to the people against their own temporary errors and delusions."[27]

A Madisonian constitution thus required a bicameral legislature. Even with the vices of an equal state vote and the legislative election of senators, Madison remained firmly committed to the value of a sober and prudently deliberative upper house. The same concern appears in his October 1788 comments on the revised constitution that Jefferson had drafted for Virginia back in the early 1780s. As in his 1785 letter to Caleb Wallace, Madison made the senate's character his point of departure. Madison opened his comments by criticizing Jefferson's proposal to give senators a mere two-year term. More revealingly, he disliked the idea of having senators elected by districts, preferring a statewide electoral system "making them the choice of the whole Society, each citizen voting for every Senator."[28] Once again, the representative basis of an upper house was secondary to its deliberative duties.

Yet Madison's continued attachment to the institutional value of the Senate rested on his recognition that it would necessarily be the weaker of the two houses. "Against the force of the immediate representatives," he wrote in his last sentence as Publius, "nothing will be able to maintain even the constitutional authority of the senate, but such a display of enlightened policy, and attachment to the public good, as will divide with that branch of the legislature, the affections and support of the entire body of the people themselves."[29] At first glance, this sentence corroborates the image of the Senate as a checkpoint against the impulsive temptations and tendencies of the lower house, the true "impetuous vortex" of the Constitution. But that check would not be provided by parliamentary devices that took the unjust principle of the equal state vote as a foundation for additional procedural rules that would further enlarge the ways in which minorities of senators or individual members could thwart the conduct of business. Madison's constitutional theory conceived the Senate not as the bulwark of obstruction that it has become but as a superior model of deliberation. Its political strength would rest on the manifest evidence of the quality of its deliberations, not on its maddening and inane anti-majoritarian rules.

Notes

1. One should distinguish the political impulses on which either House or Senate may act from the procedural constraints that impair any action. The former may provide countless cases of misjudgment, but the latter deal with institutional impairments to action, which is a better example of incapacity.
2. My understanding of this issue was much improved by a lunchtime conversation with former senator Jeff Bingaman and a public discussion at Stanford Law School in which he participated along with former senator Russ Feingold and Burt Neuborne of the New York University School of Law.
3. See the brief account in Thomas E. Mann and Norman J. Ornstein, *It's Even Worse than It Looks: How the American Constitutional System Collided with the New Politics of Extremism* (New York: Basic Books, 2012), pp. 89–91.
4. See the proposals discussed in Mann and Ornstein, *It's Even Worse than It Looks*, pp. 166–72.
5. Letter from Caleb Wallace to Madison, July 12, 1785, in *The Papers of James Madison: Congressional Series*, vol. 8, edited by William T. Hutchinson and others (University of Chicago Press and University of Virginia Press, 1962–91), pp. 322–23.
6. Letter from Madison to Wallace, August 23, 1785, in *Papers of Madison*, vol. 8, pp. 350–51.
7. *Federalist* No. 10, in Jack N. Rakove, *James Madison: Writings* (New York: Library of America, 1999), p. 165.
8. See, for example, the influential work of John Brewer, *The Sinews of Power: War, Money, and the English State, 1689–1783* (Harvard University Press, 1990).
9. Quotations in this and the following paragraph come from Madison's preconvention memorandum, "Vices of the Political System of the U. States," in Rakove, *James Madison: Writings*, pp. 74–76.
10. John Adams, *Thoughts on Government* (Philadelphia, 1776), in *The Founders'*

Constitution, vol. 1, edited by Philip Kurland and Ralph Lerner (University of Chicago Press, 1987), p. 108.

11. Max Farrand, *Records of the Federal Convention of 1787,* vol. 1 (Yale University Press, 1966), p. 151.
12. Ibid., p. 154.
13. Ibid., p. 168.
14. Ibid., p. 218.
15. Ibid., p. 214.
16. Ibid., p. 361.
17. Ibid., pp. 468–69.
18. Ibid., p. 484.
19. Ibid., p. 486.
20. Ibid., pp. 527–28. Madison originally wrote "delusion" in his notes, then replaced it at some later point with "alternative."
21. Ibid., p. 554. Madison's notes of his own remarks for this date do not make this point, but William Paterson's notes confirm King's summary. Ibid., pp. 555–56.
22. Farrand, *Records of the Federal Convention of 1787,* vol. 2, pp. 9–10.
23. Ibid., pp. 630–31. After his original motion failed, Sherman proposed eliminating Article V entirely, which would make the equal state vote and every other clause unamendable.
24. "I have known one man where his State was represented by only two & were divided oppose Six States in Cong. on an import[ant] occasion for 3 days, and finally compelled [them] to gratify his Caprice in order to obtain his suffrage." I have not worked out when this might have been. On David Howell's disruptive role, see Jack Rakove, *The Beginnings of National Politics: An Interpretive History of the Continental Congress* (New York, 1979), pp. 313–17.
25. *Federalist* No. 62, in Rakove, *James Madison: Writings,* pp. 338–40.
26. Ibid., pp. 340–44.
27. *Federalist* No. 63, in Rakove, *James Madison: Writings,* p. 347.
28. Madison, "Observations on the 'Draught of a Constitution for Virginia,'" circa October 15, 1788, in Rakove, *James Madison: Writings,* p. 409.
29. *Federalist* No. 63, in Rakove, *James Madison: Writings,* p. 352.

Eight

ON THE MUTABILITY OF AMERICAN LAWS

MARTHA A. DERTHICK

$\mathcal{T}$he federalism that the United States has today is not the federalism that James Madison foresaw. In *Federalist* No. 10, Madison said that "great and aggregate interests" would be referred to the national legislature and the "local and particular" to the state legislatures.[1] In *Federalist* No. 45, he observes that the federal government would be concerned mainly with "external objects"—war, peace, negotiation, and foreign commerce, with which the power of taxation would be connected. The several states would address the "ordinary course of affairs," which would concern the "lives, liberties, and properties of the people, and the internal order, improvement, and prosperity of the State."[2] By contrast, the antifederalist Brutus proved to be on the mark when he predicted a national government with authority extending "to every case that is of the least importance."[3]

Whether Madison would object strongly to today's thorough intermingling of federal and state government functions is not clear. In *Federalist* No. 46, he waxed philosophical on the question of whether the federal government or the states would gain at the expense of the other over time:

> The federal and State governments are in fact but different agents and trustees of the people, constituted with different powers and designed for different purposes. . . . The ultimate authority . . . resides

129

in the people alone, and . . . it will not depend merely on the comparative ambition or address of the different governments whether
either, or which of them, will be able to enlarge its sphere of jurisdiction at the expense of the other. Truth . . . requires that the event
in every case should be supposed to depend on the sentiments and
sanction of their common constituents.

I suspect, however, that Madison would nonetheless find much to disapprove of in the grant-in-aid regimes that since the late nineteenth century
have been the principal instrument of intergovernmental relations in the
United States.[4] In *Federalist* No. 62, constructed to make the case for the
Senate, he argues with passion the importance of stability in law:

The facility and excess of lawmaking seem to be the diseases to
which our governments are most liable. . . . To trace the mischievous
effects of a mutable government would fill a volume. . . . It will be
of little avail to the people that the laws are made by men of their
own choice if the laws be so voluminous that they cannot be read, or
so incoherent that they cannot be understood . . . or undergo such
incessant changes that no man, who knows what the law is today, can
guess what it will be tomorrow. . . . No government . . . will long be
respected without being truly respectable; nor be truly respectable
without possessing a certain portion of order and stability.

The major grant-in-aid programs have become monuments to the mutability of the federal government's laws.

In fiscal year 2011, the federal government had more than 200 intergovernmental grant programs, providing $607 billion to state and local gov-
ernments. Those funds accounted for 17 percent of federal outlays and a
fourth of spending by state and local governments. Not all of the 200 are
important, but a few are hugely so, with profound consequences for state and
local governments and the citizenry. By far the most consequential is Medicaid, which offers health insurance coverage to low-income individuals and
families, including children and their parents, pregnant women, the disabled, and the elderly. In fiscal year 2011, an estimated 53 million people on
average were enrolled in Medicaid each month, accounting for $275 billion

in federal expenditures and $157 billion in spending by the states, which administer the program.[5] While far less expensive than Medicaid, a second very important grant-in-aid program is Title I of the Elementary and Secondary Education Act (ESEA), with federal expenditures exceeding $23 billion in fiscal year 2011. This program provides aid to schools based on a formula that emphasizes assistance to children who live in poverty. As amended in 2001 under the name No Child Left Behind (NCLB) Act, this act has proved deeply disruptive and controversial in local school districts throughout the nation. These two programs illustrate key features of policymaking in the U.S. system of extremely interdependent governments.

RAPID GROWTH WITH REPEATED AMENDMENTS

Rather than gridlock, the putative ill of modern American government, both Medicaid and ESEA, after their enactment in 1965, promptly became examples of hyperlexis, or overactive lawmaking, to borrow a phrase from the late Bayless Manning.[6] For the next thirty-five years Congress revised them incessantly. Starting with Social Security amendments in 1967, Congress had enacted sixty significant changes in Medicaid payment policies in twenty-three different laws by 2010.[7] The typical vehicle for change was an omnibus budget reconciliation act, as occurred eight times, but sometimes the law was freestanding, as with the Medicare Catastrophic Coverage Act of 1988, which, among other provisions, required states to cover pregnant women and infants meeting a federally defined level of poverty. The prime driver of expansion after 1979, when he became chairman of the Subcommittee on Health and the Environment of the House Committee on Energy and Commerce, was a gifted and persistent policy entrepreneur named Henry Waxman, a Democrat from Westside, an urban region of Los Angeles County that includes West Hollywood. With his leadership, Congress repeatedly expanded the program between 1984 and 1990. More than a half-million pregnant women, between 4 and 5 million children, and millions of low-income elderly and disabled Medicare beneficiaries were made eligible for Medicaid. Maternity and pediatric benefits were expanded, and the enrollment process was changed to make access to coverage easier.[8] The states reinforced these expansive congressional initiatives by exploiting loopholes in Medicaid laws and regulations that shifted costs to the federal government.[9]

Amendments to Title I of ESEA also began immediately after enactment, with a revision of the allocation formula in 1966 that enhanced benefits for the poorest states. A more ambitious change occurred in 1970, when eligibility criteria were liberalized and new programs of grants were added that aimed to strengthen local education agencies, enhance education planning and evaluation capabilities, fund advisory councils, and promote projects to improve nutrition in public and nonpublic schools. That law extended the act for three years, thus beginning a pattern of periodic reauthorizations accompanied by the fine-tuning of allocation formulas, revised eligibility standards, and ever more categories of aid. The new programs funded innovative teaching techniques, energy conservation curriculum development, and a biomedical enrichment program to provide science instruction to minority students at the secondary school level. The multiplying categories were occasionally consolidated on a limited scale, but Republican presidents never succeeded in getting the wholesale consolidation that would have culminated in a block grant. Major reauthorizations with revisions took place in 1974, 1978, 1981, 1988, and 1994. Federal education spending rose beyond what presidents had wanted, although not to the same extent as the overwhelming enlargement that took place in Medicaid. In fiscal year 1980, Title I grants ("compensatory education for the disadvantaged") totaled $3.3 billion, while Medicaid grants totaled close to $14 billion. By 1990 the compensatory education grants amounted to $4.4 billion and Medicaid grants to $41 billion; by 2000, the amounts were $8.5 billion and $117.9 billion respectively.[10]

Grant statutes and their expansion are an inviting vehicle for members of Congress who want to achieve grand policy objectives incrementally, with little scrutiny or debate, as Waxman did, and for those who merely take credit for minor additions to the vast catalog of federal grants for state and local governments.

MUTABILITY BY DESIGN: MEDICAID WAIVERS

Provisions of law that authorize deviations from other laws are called waivers. They are not unknown in other federal laws, but they have acquired particular importance in grant statutes because they make possible adaptations to the varied circumstances of the states and they invite entrepreneurship by the state governments. During the administrations of Bill Clinton and George W. Bush, waivers were used extensively by the states to enlarge and otherwise modify the Medicaid program.[11]

Congress began to provide waiver authorities in 1962, when Congress added section 1115 to the Social Security Act to authorize experimental demonstrations by state governments in shared health and welfare programs, including Medicaid. In 1981, with support from the Reagan administration, Congress enacted a second important waiver provision, called section 1915c for its place in Medicaid law, to encourage states to provide home and community-based services (HCBS)—as distinct from institutional care—primarily in nursing homes. For a quarter-century, presidential administrations approved few demonstrations, but beginning with President Clinton's administration, federal practice changed, and states were quick to respond. By the end of the Bush administration, nearly every state had submitted a waiver proposal and more than 150 of them had been approved.

Contrary to the usual requirements of Medicaid law, HCBS waivers enabled states to concentrate services in defined geographic areas, target services to particular categories of beneficiaries (for example, specific categories of the developmentally disabled), cap the number of recipients, and establish waiting lists. Nearly all of the states used those waivers, and most used them for the benefit of the most expensive enrollees. The annual average expense per waiver beneficiary in 2006 was more than $24,000.

Section 1115 waivers were used more broadly. Many states used them to move recipients from fee-for-service to managed care, to expand coverage of adult populations, and to incorporate market-based features. States that wanted to charge premiums or impose other costs on Medicaid beneficiaries also gained some freedom to do so. In fact, out of thirty-three demonstration waivers approved or renewed during the Bush administration, 70 percent featured some mix of premiums, deductibles, or copayments. A Florida demonstration approved in 2005 when Jeb Bush, the president's brother, was governor sought to have Medicaid enrollees choose among alternative plans offered by private insurance companies. It was launched in two counties, Broward and Duval, which combined contained nearly 10 percent of the state's population.

Waivers were ambitious also in making possible innovative statewide programs. The Oregon Health Plan expanded coverage to all uninsured residents with incomes of up to 100 percent of the federally defined poverty level (FPL), moved almost all nondisabled enrollees into managed care, and set up a prioritized list of services to define the program's benefit package. Tennessee's waiver, called TennCare, made all uninsured residents eligible but required premium payments that were correlated to enrollees' income. Residents with incomes below the FPL paid no premiums. Both of the plans proved too ambitious and had to be modified. The most durable of the statewide waiver applications ultimately came from Massachusetts, where Governor Mitt Romney was seeking to achieve near-universal health care coverage.

Presidential Breakthroughs: No Child Left Behind and the Patient Protection and Affordable Care Act

Both K-12 education and Medicaid have been targeted by newly elected presidents for major policy reform, education in the case of George W. Bush and Medicaid by Barack Obama. Their efforts contain different lessons about the mutability of grant-in-aid laws. Seeking to revise the position of his party, which had resisted federal intervention in local schools, Bush campaigned on a promise of education reform and repeated it in a position paper sent to Congress immediately after his inauguration: "Bipartisan education reform will be the cornerstone of my Administration."[12] Despite having spent billions of dollars on K-12 education since 1965, the federal government had not achieved excellence in the nation's schools. Bush sought to enhance "accountability," which had become the watchword of education reform. States, districts, and schools that improved student performance would be rewarded. Failure would be sanctioned.

In response to his proposal, Congress enacted No Child Left Behind, though with many changes sought by Democrats because Bush both needed their support and wanted the reform to be bipartisan. It remains the latest of the periodic reauthorizations of Title I of ESEA. It passed in December 2001 with large bipartisan majorities, 381 to 41 in the House and 87 to 10 in the Senate. With its demands for annual testing for grades 3–8 in reading and math and proof of "adequate yearly progress" for student subgroups defined by race, ethnicity, socioeconomic status, disability, and English language proficiency, it carried federal prescription much farther than any previous law. And it threatened sanctions against schools that failed to make the required progress. All students had to attain proficiency in reading and math by 2013–14, and all teachers had to be "highly qualified" by the end of the 2005–06 school year. At the beginning of 2002, Bush's secretary of education warned a meeting of chief state school officers at Mount Vernon, President Washington's estate in Virginia, that enforcement would be strict: there would be no waivers, "not in this century, not in this country."[13]

After forty years of amendment, chapter 70 ("Strengthening and Improvement of Elementary and Secondary Schools") now occupies more than 300 pages in the *U.S. Code*, more than 30 times the size of Title I in 1965 when it appeared in the *U.S. Statutes-at-Large*. Toward the end of chapter 70, section 7861 grants authority to the secretary of education to waive statutory and regulatory requirements under the act, subject to certain restrictions. The secretary cannot, for example, waive the formula for the allocation of funds, or maintenance-of-effort requirements imposed on states, or civil rights requirements, or provisions relating to parental participation and involvement. But the authority is quite broad, and in the fall of 2011 the Obama administration announced that it was inviting state education agencies to apply for waivers of many of the most onerous and unrealistic provisions of No Child Left Behind. As a condition for receiving waivers, states would have to develop plans and make promises stipulated by the administration. In effect, the executive would now define grant-in-aid conditions under Title I.[14] For example, the administration pushed the states to adopt a common set of academic standards and include measures of student performance in their evaluation of teachers.[15]

By the late summer of 2013, the administration had granted waivers to forty-one states and the District of Columbia. Waiver requests were outstanding from four other states, and five states had not yet filed requests or had filed but withdrawn them. One of the five was California, but there, in a groundbreaking innovation, the administration had granted waivers to eight local school districts, including Los Angeles and San Francisco.[16] The administration could not have done that had Congress renewed authorization of the ESEA in a timely way. Reauthorization was due in 2007, and Congress recognized that revision was desirable, but the rival political parties were unable to reach agreement. That they had agreed on NCLB in the first place was attributable partly to aggressive promotion by a newly elected president, whose leadership many Republicans in Congress felt obliged to follow whatever their private reservations, and partly to the extraordinary effects of the terrorist attacks of September 11, 2001. Work on the legislation was suspended after the attack, and when it resumed the legislature felt pressure to act simply in order to prove to the public that it was capable of acting. Party leaders now believed that passing a law would reassure the public that its government was unified and functioning.[17] According to a high-ranking member of the Bush administration's Department of Education, "Suddenly stumbling blocks that had impeded progress for months were cavalierly resolved, and consensus emerged over what had been the most contentious issues only weeks earlier . . . concern for unintended consequences was discarded."[18]

Law in this case was unstable because it was defective in its conception. Many schools throughout the country, even schools with excellent reputations, were perversely condemned as failures because they did not make "adequate yearly progress," and it became necessary, as 2013–14 approached, to acknowledge that universal proficiency was a utopian fantasy. Conditions in the federal government's early grant-in-aid programs—in, say, the first half of the twentieth century—typically applied to administrative features of state governments. States were required to provide matching funds, to formulate statewide plans, and to adopt merit systems of personnel administration. They were subject to financial audits to assure the federal government that funds were not being used fraudulently.[19] But as federal government ambitions grew, particularly in the 1960s, conditions were directed toward more overtly political objectives—such as, for example, the addition of citizen participation requirements in order to affect the distribution of political power.[20] They promoted policy change and, through grant-in-aid conditions that were written into income support programs, even went so far as to prescribe behavioral outcomes such as the reduction of out-of-wedlock births or, as in No Child Left Behind, the improvement of student achievement. That is a far reach for intergovernmental grant-in-aid programs, which are by no means magic wands. The offer of money is usually an effective tool. It induces state governments to respond, but the conditions attached to the money are blunt. As they become more exacting and prescriptive, they risk goal-displacing responses that falsify results. There were well publicized cases, notably in Atlanta, of school administrators and teachers cheating on tests in order to meet the demands of NCLB, for example.[21]

President Obama's plans for using Medicaid law to expand health insurance coverage encountered a very different obstacle, in the form of the federal judiciary. Expansive and expensive as Medicaid had become, it still did not reach many low-income adults, and it varied among the states. In most states, adults without dependent children historically had not received Medicaid. The Patient Protection and Affordable Care Act of 2010 (Affordable Care Act/ACA) called for expanding eligibility and making the income standard uniform across the country, with benefits for individuals with incomes of up to 138 percent of the federal poverty level. That was expected to allow Medicaid to reach millions of adults not previously covered by the program. As an incentive to state governments to participate, the law offered to cover 100 percent of the cost of newly eligible recipients between 2014 and 2016 and a declining share thereafter, but not less than 90 percent. That was a higher matching rate than prevailed in the existing program, in which the federal share ranged from 50 to 83 percent. A further incentive— indeed, a threat—lay in a provision that would withdraw all federal Medicaid grants from states that declined to participate in the expanded program.

Many state governments brought suit, and while the Supreme Court did not strike down the Medicaid portion of the act, it ruled that states must be given the choice of whether to participate without the threat of losing all their Medicaid grants if they did not. Grants that states are free to accept voluntarily are constitutionally permissible; coercion is not. Chief Justice John Roberts wrote in *National Federation of Independent Business* v. *Sebelius* that Congress had put a "gun to the head" of the states in the ACA, and by a vote of 7 to 2, the Court said to drop it. Given the option of taking on the added caseload, as of the fall of 2013 half of the states had agreed to do it and half had not. Most of the participants were on the West Coast and in the upper Midwest and parts of New England. Southern states and the

Plains states resisted. Perhaps they would join eventually; it was hard to predict.

The Growing Chaos of Agency Guidance

Following the enactment of a law, the federal government agency charged with administering it releases its interpretation of the law. No doubt, Madison would have wished this process also to exhibit economy of expression, stability, and clarity. In the Administrative Procedure Act (APA) of 1946, which was a response to the expansion of federal government agencies during the New Deal, Congress attempted to introduce order, discipline, and accountability in the conduct of federal government administration. It distinguished between adjudication and rulemaking and defined procedures for rulemaking. Before issuing regulations, agencies must publish notice and permit interested parties to submit their views in writing for agency consideration. The process thus prescribed, called "notice and comment rulemaking," became deeply entrenched, and resulted in a very thick *Federal Register* and *Code of Federal Regulations,* in which the rules were published. However, as federal government regulation expanded in the 1970s and 1980s, this process came under stress and began to be observed in the breach. In 2000 in *Appalachian Power* v. *EPA* , a case well known to students of administrative law, the U.S. Court of Appeals for the District of Columbia Circuit described the evolving situation as follows:

> Congress passes a broadly worded statute. The agency follows with regulations containing broad language, open-ended phrases, ambiguous standards and the like. Then as years pass, the agency issues circulars or guidance or memoranda, explaining, interpreting, defining and often expanding the commands in regulations. One guidance document may yield another and then another and so on. Several words in a regulation may spawn hundreds of pages of text as the agency offers more and more detail regarding what its regulations demand of regulated entities. Law is made, without notice and comment, without public participation, and without publication.[22]

In an attempt to acknowledge this situation and cabin the proliferation of guidance that does not undergo the process prescribed in the APA, the Office of Management and Budget (OMB) in 2007 issued the *Final Bulletin for Agency Good Guidance Practices,* which defines a guidance document as "an agency statement of general applicability and future effect . . . that sets forth a policy on a statutory, regulatory, or technical issue or an interpretation of a statutory or regulatory issue." OMB did not intend "to indicate that a guidance document can impose a legally binding requirement."[23]

Websites of the Centers for Medicare and Medicaid Services (CMS), which administers Medicaid grants, and the Department of Education, which administers grants under Title I of ESEA, indicate how they have responded to OMB in the matter of agency guidance to state and local governments, citizens, and other interested parties. The two agencies have taken contrasting approaches. Without referring to OMB, the CMS identifies on its website four categories of policy guidance applicable to Medicaid.[24] The most formal and prescriptive are *regulations,* which "codify policies based on statutory provisions of the Social Security Act." They proceed through the formal steps—notice of proposed rulemaking, issuance of an interim final rule open for public comment, and a final rule—contemplated in federal law. Less formal are *official letters* sent to state Medicaid directors and state health officials, which are used "to provide states with guidance and clarification" on statutory changes pertaining to policy and financing for Medicaid and CHIP (Children's Health Insurance Program). Apparently less formal still are *informational bulletins,* which are designed to "highlight recently released policy guidance and regulations and also to share important operational and technical information." The fourth, seemingly casual category, is *frequently asked questions,* which is used to provide information or guidance not otherwise to be found. Frequently asked questions, known as FAQs, are informal but not unimportant. On the contrary, they often address matters of utmost importance, and they appear to be used when regulation, though arguably more appropriate, would take too much time to produce. CMS issued streams of FAQs as it prepared to carry out the Affordable Care Act.

Logging onto CMS's website early in 2014, a user could search by selecting among the several types of policy guidance and twenty topics arrayed alphabetically from "Affordable Care Act" to "Tribal Issues." Alternatively, one could scroll through a chart with 640 entries arrayed by date, each providing information on guidance type, title, and topic(s). Heading the chronological table on the day I logged on were two items for January 24, 2014. One was a two-page informational bulletin with the title "Implementation of Hospital Presumptive Eligibility," and the other was a related nine-page set of twenty-nine frequently asked questions beginning with "What is hospital presumptive eligibility, and how is it different from presumptive eligibility (PE) for pregnant women and children?" and ending with "Must the hospital complete the PE application and determination before services can be covered by Medicaid?" Those questions arose out of the extension of Medicaid to a much larger adult population under the Affordable Care Act. The answer to the first question began as follows:

> For years, states have had the option to use presumptive eligibility (PE) to connect pregnant women and children to Medicaid. Hospitals were often key to implementing PE for those populations. Starting in January 2014, the Affordable Care Act gives qualified hospitals a unique new opportunity to connect other populations to Medicaid coverage. Under this new PE authority, hospitals will be able to immediately enroll patients who are likely eligible under a state's Medicaid eligibility guidelines for a temporary period of time. . . . Like other forms of PE, hospital PE aims to: Assure timely access to care while a final eligibility determination is made.

The answer to the twenty-ninth question was "Yes, an individual has to be found presumptively eligible (the PE application is submitted and a determination made) for services to be covered during the hospital PE period."[25]

By contrast to CMS, the Department of Education's page on policy guidance makes explicit reference to the OMB bulletin. As of September 2013, the department had posted a 19-page list of 155 significant guidance documents, issued between 1970 and 2013, that had been judged to meet OMB's definition. Of the 155, only 119 were current; 36 had been withdrawn in the preceding year. They were divided among 8 subject areas, of which elementary and secondary education was by far the longest. Many of the documents appear to be quite informal, taking the form of answers to frequently asked questions or a "Dear Colleague" letter. Some say "non-regulatory guidance."

All invite comment from users of the site as well as complaints about whether the department is complying with OMB's bulletin.[26]

Alexis de Tocqueville, one of the wisest students of American government, wrote of its federalism:

> Among the vices inherent in every federal system the most visible of all is the complication of the means it employs. . . . The federal system . . . rests, whatever one does, on a complicated theory whose application requires of the governed a daily use of the enlightenment of their reason. . . . When one examines the Constitution of the United States, the most perfect of all known federal constitutions, one is frightened . . . by the quantity of diverse knowledge and by the discernment that it supposes in those whom it must rule. The government of the Union rests almost wholly on legal fictions. The Union is an ideal nation that exists so to speak only in minds, and whose extent and bounds intelligence alone discovers.[27]

Toqueville was writing before the Civil War, which ended by substituting a new reality for the legal fictions on which the union had rested. American political development since then has steadily, if sometimes slowly, reinforced the legal and financial supremacy of the federal government. Madison may have supposed that federal revenue would come from tariffs, but the Sixteenth Amendment, added in 1913, enabled the federal government to collect income taxes, which ultimately became a rich and expansive source of revenue that nourished today's grant-in-aid programs. Madison may have thought that the encroaching branch would be the legislature, but twentieth-century presidents, with rare exceptions, have emerged as tribunes of the people and aggressive setters of a national policy agenda. Medicaid and ESEA were both products of Lyndon Johnson's Great Society, after all. Madison may have supposed, innocently, that wars would be rare, but they have become perpetual, so that the pursuit of national security can be used to justify virtually any encroachment of the national on the local. Even education reform borrowed from the language of national security when it was given impetus in the 1980s by the federal government report entitled *A Nation at Risk*.

Leaving aside the observation that the union was a legal fiction, Tocqueville's characterization of American federalism is startling for its freshness—except that it would be more apt if it were inverted to say that it is the officeholders in government, more than the governed, who must daily use their reason and possess a great quantity of diverse knowledge, along with discernment, if the federal constitution is to function well. The pervasive overlapping of functions, the vast amount of law and lawmaking—which is augmented by a comparably vast volume of regulation and informal guidance from the federal government—cannot possibly be intelligently comprehended by the citizenry. They perceive the law only as it is applied to their lives by the holders of public office. Most of that application is done by administrators in state and local governments.

Citizens' experience of the law depends very much on the wisdom and discernment of lawmakers and the quality of cooperation between administrators at the different levels of government. Both lawmaking and interactions among governments have become a difficult struggle in K-12 education, as the recent experience of No Child Left Behind shows. One reason that the law proved unworkable except through waivers was that its congressional authors overlooked state legislators and administrators, at least in the form of their professional organizations, which were sidelined as the legislation was prepared.[28] In 2013, both houses worked on bills on reauthorizing Title I of ESEA, and by a narrow margin the House actually passed a bill, but Democrats and Republicans were far apart. Senate action did not get beyond the committee stage.

With Medicaid, lawmaking has become so complicated and challenging that Congress in 2009 tried contracting it out to a nonpartisan seventeen-member commission charged with making semiannual reports with recommendations to Congress, the secretary of health and human services, and the state governments for the entire array of Medicaid policies—eligibility, enrollment, benefits, payments, access to care, and quality of care. The new commission, whose members are appointed by the Comptroller General, is known as MACPAC, the acronym for the Medicaid and CHIP Payment and Access Commission. (In fiscal year 2011, CHIP, closely related to

Medicaid, provided $9 billion in federal grants.) Of course, it was no part of MACPAC's charge to give advice to the Supreme Court, which turned out to be a major player in the making of Medicaid policy with its decision in 2012 that gave states the option of declining the newly expansive Medicaid grants contained in the Patient Protection and Affordable Care Act of 2010 ("Obamacare").

MACPAC has approached its task carefully, with more attention to research and analysis than policy recommendations. Its first report, released in March 2011, was "foundational," giving priority to development of "key baseline data."[29] A more recent report, released in June 2013, selected six subjects for analysis:

—eligibility and coverage of maternity services in Medicaid and CHIP (almost half of all births in the United States were paid for by the two programs in 2010)

—a provision in the Affordable Care Act that requires state Medicaid agencies to increase payment rates for primary care physicians in 2013 and 2014

—a review of research on access to care for disabled adults under age 65 who are enrolled in Medicaid and living in the community

—an update on Medicaid and CHIP data for policy analysis and program accountability

—an update on efforts to improve program integrity—that is, to prevent improper payments, waste, and abuse—in Medicaid

—an update of MACStats (Medicaid and CHIP Program Statistics) that are not otherwise readily available.

Medicaid is so large and grew so fast that the government has found it difficult to stay informed about it. An early attempt was publication of a "yellow book," comparable to the Green Book that the House Ways and Means Committee has published periodically since 1981 to provide "Background Material and Data on the Programs within the [Committee's] Jurisdiction."[30] In November 1988 and January 1993, the Subcommittee on Health and the Environment of the House Committee on Energy and Commerce released a similar document that had been prepared by the Congressional Research Service at the request of Representative Waxman.[31]

However, it did not develop into a regular series, and MACStats holds the promise of at least becoming a reliable source of information, which is presumably an indispensable first step in the making of public policy.

WHAT WOULD MADISON THINK?

Were Madison to read this chapter, I expect that he would grant my argument about the facility and excess of lawmaking. But I am not sure that to him it would be the most troubling part of my story, even if I have chosen to make it the central part. I expect that he might be more deeply troubled by the incidental evidence of faulty deliberation in the legislature—shown, for example, in the way that Medicaid was hugely expanded by the ingenious agency of one influential member of the House and by the indifference to contentious and unresolved issues as No Child Left Behind was passed. He would have questions about the degree of discretion exercised by administrative agencies. How much law is being made outside of legislatures, not just in waivers that have some warrant in law but also in answer to questions that are (or might be) "frequently asked"? How can a citizen, or even a judge, tell what is supposed to be legally binding? And he would certainly be puzzled and curious about the features of American federalism today. Just how is one to characterize a federalism in which the national government prescribes a schedule of tests for students in local elementary schools but allows state governments discretion in regard to a broad expansion of a program as important as Medicaid? Putting together the growth of federal government power with the growth of executive power, he would quite likely recall his warning that this would happen—that consolidating the states into one government would result in enlarging executive power because the national legislature would lack the competence to regulate the many objects belonging to local governments under the original design.[32]

Notes

1. Edward Mead Earle, *The Federalist: A Commentary on the Constitution of the United States* (New York: Modern Library, 1937), p. 60.
2. Ibid., p. 303.
3. Herbert J. Storing, *What the Anti-Federalists Were For* (University of Chicago

Press, 1981), pp. 10–11. More fully, Brutus said: "The powers of the general
legislature extend to every case that is of the least importance—there is nothing
valuable to human nature, nothing dear to freemen, but what is within its
power. It has authority to make laws which will affect the lives, the liberty, and
property of every man in the United States; nor can the constitution or laws of
any state, in any way prevent or impede the full and complete execution of every
power given." "Essays of Brutus," in *The Anti-Federalists: Selected Writings and
Speeches*, edited by Bruce Frohnen (Washington: Regnery Publishing, 1999),
Essay 1, pp. 375–76.

4. For the early-twentieth-century history of grants-in-aid, see Jane Perry Clark,
   The Rise of a New Federalism: Federal-State Cooperation in the United States
   (Columbia University Press, 1938), chapter 6.
5. Congressional Budget Office, "Federal Grants to State and Local
   Governments," March 2013 (www.cbo.gov/publication/43967). For a succinct
   scholarly summary by a political scientist, see Michael J. Rich, "Grants-in-
   Aid," in *Federalism in America*, vol. 1, edited by Joseph R. Marbach, Ellis Katz,
   and Troy E. Smith (Westport, Conn.: Greenwood Press, 2006), pp. 294–96.
6. Bayless Manning, "Hyperlexis and the Law of Conservation of Ambiguity:
   Thoughts on Section 385," *Tax Lawyer*, vol. 36, no. 1 (http://heinonline.org.
   proxy.its.virginia.edu/HOL/Page?handle=hein.journals.txlr36). Manning, an
   expert in corporate law, taught at both Yale and Stanford and was dean of the
   law school at Stanford.
7. Medicaid and CHIP Payment and Access Commission (MACPAC),
   "Report to the Congress on Medicaid and CHIP," March 2011, pp. 177–
   81. This source is a table entitled "Timeline of Major Medicaid Payment
   Policy Developments." It can be compared with "Medicaid: A Timeline of
   Key Developments, 1965–2009," prepared by the Kaiser Family Foundation
   (https://kaiserfamilyfoundation.files.wordpress.com/2008/04/5-02-13-
   medicaid-timeline.pdf). Charles Brecher and Shanna Rose liken the growth
   of Medicaid to the "miraculous transformations" achieved by Mother
   Nature though metamorphosis. "Medicaid's Next Metamorphosis," *Public
   Administration Review*, vol. 73 (September-October 2013), pp. S60–S68.
8. Jean Donovan Gilman, *Medicaid and the Costs of Federalism, 1984–1992* (New
   York: Garland Publishing, 1998).
9. Shanna Rose, *Financing Medicaid: Federalism and the Growth of America's Health
   Care Safety Net* (University of Michigan Press, 2013), especially chapter 5.
10. Data are from *Congress and the Nation*, vols. 2–9 (Washington: Congressional
    Quarterly), and the *Statistical Abstract of the United States*.
11. The information on waivers is taken from Frank J. Thompson, *Medicaid Politics:
    Federalism, Policy Durability, and Health Reform* (Georgetown University Press,
    2012), chapters 4 and 5.
12. White House, "Foreword by President George W. Bush," *No Child Left Behind*.

13. Paul Manna, *Collision Course: Federal Education Policy Meets State and Local Realities* (Washington: CQ Press, 2011), p. 43.

14. "Letters from the Education Secretary or Deputy Secretary," September 23, 2011 (www2.ed.gov/policy/gen/guid/secletter/110923.html). Detailed guidance was provided in "ESEA Flexibility," September 23, 2011, updated June 7, 2012 (www.ed.gov/esea/flexibility).

15. Lauren Smith, "Congress Left Behind," *CQ Weekly*, March 12, 2012, pp. 490–94.

16. "Obama Administration Approves NCLB Flexibility Request for Pennsylvania," August 20, 2013 (www.ed.gov/news/press-releases/obama-administration-approves-nclb-flexibility-request-pennsylvania); Lyndsey Layton, "Calif. School districts Are Granted No Child Left Behind Waivers," *Washington Post*, August 7, 2013, A11.

17. Patrick J. McGuinn, *No Child Left Behind and the Transformation of Federal Education Policy: 1965–2005* (University Press of Kansas, 2006), p. 176.

18. Eugene Hickok, *Schoolhouse of Cards* (Lanham, Md.: Rowman & Littlefield, 2010), p. 73.

19. See, for example, Martha Derthick, *The Influence of Federal Grants: Public Assistance in Massachusetts* (Harvard University Press, 1970).

20. On the growth of grant-in-aid conditions and other forms of federal regulation of state and local governments, see Advisory Commission on Intergovernmental Relations, *Regulatory Federalism: Policy, Process, Impact and Reform*, Report A-95 (Washington: February 1984).

21. Kim Severson and Alan Blinder, "Test Scandal in Atlanta Brings More Guilty Pleas," *New York Times*, January 7, 2014, p. A9; Motoko Rich and Jon Hurdle, "Erased Answers on Tests in Philadelphia Lead to a Three-Year Cheating Scandal," *New York Times*, January 24, 2014, p. A16.

22. *Appalachian Power* v. *Environmental Protection Agency*, 208 F.3d 1015, 1029 (D.C. Cir. 2000), p. 8.

23. *Federal Register*, vol. 72, no. 16 (January 25, 2007), pp. 3432–440. My quotation from the Third Circuit is taken from this document, which gives the source as *Appalachian Power*, 208 F. 3d, 1019. For an account of one agency's evasion of APA requirements, see R. Shep Melnick, "The Odd Evolution of the Civil Rights State," *Harvard Journal of Law and Public Policy*, vol. 37, no. 1 (2014), pp. 113–34. The agency is the Office of Civil Rights in the Department of Health, Education, and Welfare, after 1979 in the Department of Education. Melnick describes a regulatory regime that "governs the conduct of nearly every employer, school, and unit of state and local government in the country" but "is notable for its lack of transparency and accountability."

24. "Federal Policy Guidance" (www.medicaid.gov/Federal-Policy-Guidance/Federal-Policy-Guidance.html).

25. Ibid.

26. "Significant Guidance Documents" (www2.ed.gov/policy/gen/guid/significant-guidance.html).
27. Alexis de Tocqueville, *Democracy in America*, translated, edited, and with an introduction by Harvey C. Mansfield and Delba Winthrop (University of Chicago Press, 2000), p. 155.
28. Elizabeth H. DeBray, *Politics, Ideology, and Education: Federal Policy during the Clinton and Bush Administrations* (Teachers College Press, 2006), pp. 148–51; Jesse H. Rhodes, *An Education in Politics: The Origins and Evolution of No Child Left Behind* (Cornell University Press, 2012), p. 153.
29. MACPAC, *Report to the Congress on Medicaid and CHIP*, p. iv.
30. Since 2011 the Green Book has appeared only on the Internet. The most recent edition may be found at http://greenbook.waysandmeans.house.gov/2012-green-book.
31. *Medicaid Source Book: Background Data and Analysis*, Committee Print 100-AA, U. S. House of Representatives, Committee on Energy and Commerce, 100 Cong., 2 sess. (November 1988), and *Medicaid Source Book: Background Data and Analysis (A 1993 Update)*, Committee Print 103-A, U. S. House of Representatives, Committee on Energy and Commerce, 103 Cong., 1 sess. (January 1993). The Kaiser Commission on Medicaid and the Uninsured published one successor: *The Medicaid Resource Book* (July 2002).
32. "Consolidation," in the *National Gazette*, December 5, 1791, in *James Madison: Writings* (New York: Library Classics of the United States, 1999), p. 498. The thought is echoed in "Report on the Alien and Sedition Acts," January 7, 1800, wherein Madison observes that were federal power to extend to every subject falling within the idea of the "general welfare," one consequence would be to enlarge the discretion of the executive. "In proportion as the objects of legislative care might be multiplied, would the time allowed for each be diminished, and the difficulty of providing uniform and particular regulations for all, be increased. From these sources would necessarily ensue, a greater latitude to the agency of that department which is always in existence." Ibid., p. 619. I am indebted to Sidney Milkis for calling my attention to the relevance of these passages.

Nine

JAMES MADISON AND
THE CHARACTER OF AMERICAN EDUCATION

Eugene Hickok

*T*rying to determine what James Madison might think of contemporary education policy in the United States is something of a fool's errand. It is tantamount to asking what the Framers would think about the modern U.S. political and governmental state of affairs. Madison and his political associates inhabited a world so completely different from ours that it may be folly to relate their thinking to it. However, they did produce a constitution that continues, perhaps only peripherally, to shape modern American government and politics; therefore, seeking to determine how their views on public, political, or social issues might be reflected in current events and how they might look upon contemporary public policy should be an exercise worth undertaking.

Among the Framers, James Madison stands out. Although the Constitution, created in Philadelphia in 1787, was the product of many minds, long hours of debate and deliberation, and many compromises, it is not without good reason that Madison is regarded as the Father of the Constitution. He was the moving force behind the Constitutional Convention, prevailing upon George Washington to attend and working diligently with his Virginia colleagues in the days leading up to it. More important, Madison devoted hours of preparation and study in his library at Montpelier attempting to determine the nature of the problems that had plagued not only the Articles of Confederation but republics throughout history. It was in that library that he drafted the proposals that Edmund Randolph introduced early in the proceedings of the convention—proposals that became the document that helped to set the terms of the debate for the entire summer. Madison's Virginia Plan, although not adopted by the delegates, made the Constitution that was adopted possible.

Madison also merits our gratitude for having kept a daily journal of the proceedings of the Convention. His notes, published years later, provide a window through which one can get a sense of what the issues were, how they were resolved, and who said what, when, and to whom. Scholars and others can debate whether Madison's notes have any real authority regarding the "intent of the Framers," but as a source of information and insight into the Constitutional Convention, they are invaluable. Madison also was a member of the First Congress and introduced what became the Bill of Rights. He served as secretary of state for President Thomas Jefferson. And, of course, he was the nation's fourth president. It seems more than appropriate to consider him among the dominant political figures of his time. Madison, the diminutive, soft-spoken Virginian, was a giant among the founding generation.

That being said, one must exercise caution when attempting to apply Madison's thinking to contemporary public policy issues. He was, as we all are, a product of his time and circumstances. The task is made even more treacherous with regard to education policy because Madison's thoughts on the topic are not among those that dominate his papers. What Madison does provide is a sense of what he thought an educated person should know and which values education in the young republic should reflect and promote. His own education, his work with Jefferson in creating and overseeing the University of Virginia, and his writings thus provide a glimpse into his thinking regarding education in the early republic.

The challenge in relating Madison's views on education to contemporary education policy and politics in America is made more difficult by the fact that the United States does not really have a national education policy. Sure, Congress enacted the Elementary and Secondary Education Act in the 1960s and reauthorized it several times over the intervening years. Congress has also passed legislation dealing with higher education, special edu-

cation, and vocational and technical education. President Jimmy Carter elevated what was at the time a relatively small component of the Department
of Health, Education, and Welfare to cabinet status, but the Department
of Education still remains one of the smaller cabinet agencies. Although
it issues rules and regulations and oversees billions in spending on education policies, it has only limited influence on American education—perhaps
more than in the past but still limited.

Education in America remains primarily a state and local concern. Federal dollars might account for around 10 percent of what states spend on
K-12 education. National dollars going to higher education—to institutions
and to student grants and loans to attend those institutions—are only a
fraction of the revenues underwriting American colleges and universities.
Moreover, the character of education differs from state to state. How states
govern their education systems, raise their education revenues, spend their
education dollars, and determine student and institutional achievement are
all shaped in state capitals and statehouses. Moreover, the politics of education varies among the states. In some, teachers' unions and professional
associations dominate the political landscape. In others, school boards and
boards of trustees set the terms of the discussion. In short, it is fair to say the
United States has a highly decentralized education system, even as Washington has sought to assert greater influence over it in recent years. Therefore, any attempt to holistically describe contemporary education policy in
America runs into the disparities and complexities that accompany such a
decentralized and diverse "system."

Finally, American education operates on a number of levels and, depending on how one looks at it, a number of economic models. Fundamentally,
there exist elementary and secondary education (K-12) and postsecondary
and higher education. In most states the two sectors exist separately for all
political, governmental, and economic purposes; they hardly interact in
any serious and systematic way, except perhaps when institutions of higher
learning prepare students to teach in K-12 classrooms. Then there are the
public schools and postsecondary institutions and the nonpublic, or private,
schools and postsecondary institutions. More recently, for-profit postsecondary institutions have grown in number and influence. Home schooling
also has increased in recent years. It is hard to imagine how James Madison or any of his contemporaries would view the dizzying array of institu-

tions, programs, policies, and politics that constitute education in modern America. Perhaps it is best to start by considering Madison's thinking about education in general.

Madison's Education

Not much is known about James Madison's early education. His family owned numerous books dealing primarily with agriculture, farming, and the management of large plantations—books that Madison was likely exposed to at an early age. According to Ralph Ketcham, the author of an important biography of Madison, by the time of Madison's eleventh birthday, "he had acquired the rudiments of learning, and had probably read as well much of the miscellaneous printed matter available in this father's house."[1]

In June of 1762, Madison began more formal schooling under Donald Robertson, a graduate of the University of Edinburgh who had established a secondary school in King and Queen County, Virginia. Under Robertson's tutelage, according to Ketcham, Madison received instruction in English his first year and then Latin, reading the works of Cicero and Virgil after mastering the grammar and language. He probably also studied Horace, Justinian, Ovid, and others. At some point, Madison studied Greek, which at the time was considered something of a prerequisite for admission to college. His education also included studies in mathematics, algebra, geometry, geography, French literature, Italian, Spanish, and logic. Madison spent five years with Robertson.[2]

In 1767, Madison returned to Montpelier to receive advanced tutoring from the Reverend Thomas Martin, a graduate of the College of New Jersey. Martin lived in the Madison home during this time and was a constant source of instruction and mentoring for Madison. Surely, he had some influence on the decision to send Madison to the College of New Jersey rather than the College of William and Mary. In any event, at the age of eighteen, James Madison left the piedmont of Virginia for Princeton, New Jersey. According to Ketcham, he was "serious, bookish, and confident in his family standing and in his good education."[3]

The College of New Jersey (now Princeton University) must have been a tonic for the young intellectual. Madison attended John Witherspoon's classes and lectures and studied moral philosophy, which included such topics as economics, political science, history, and current events. He read the works of Grotius, Puffendorf, Cumberland, Selden, Hobbes, Machiavelli, Locke, and Sidney. He also became familiar with the writings of Adam Ferguson, Lord Kames, and Hume. But the College of New Jersey offered something more than instruction in the classics. It offered Madison a vision of enlightenment and liberty that would influence him—and through him, the nation—for the rest of his life. In Ketcham's words, "the College of New Jersey in Madison's day *was* the seedbed of sedition and nursery of rebels Tory critics charged it with being, but that is not all: it was as well a school for statesmen trained to seek freedom and ordered government through the pursuit of virtue."[4] Madison graduated in 1771 but remained at the college for an additional year to complete what we might refer to as "graduate education." Leaving New Jersey, he was "a paragon of the well-educated scholar" possessing an education founded in "history, wisdom, lore of Greece and Rome" and the Christian tradition.[5]

Upon returning to Virginia and Montpelier, Madison began his lifelong journey in public affairs. He concerned himself with the pursuit of religious freedom through service in local and state offices and combined his intellectual pursuits with a keen sense of the possibilities of practical politics. He emerged as a moving force among that group of influential men who shaped the early republic—Madison, Jefferson, James Wilson, Benjamin Franklin, Alexander Hamilton, and George Mason among them—individuals who were unique to America and to that time. They were, Gordon Wood wrote, "intellectuals without being alienated and political leaders without being obsessed with votes."[6]

MADISON AND JEFFERSON ON EDUCATION
IN THE YOUNG REPUBLIC

Madison and Thomas Jefferson formed a lifelong association that continues to influence American government and politics. But their friendship extended even beyond that. Jefferson lived at Monticello, in Albemarle County, Virginia, which is adjacent to Orange County, where Madison lived at Montpelier, and as "neighbors" they shared their ideas and thinking on a vast array of topics and concerns, including education.

Jefferson is rightly considered the founder and creative force behind the University of Virginia. But he did not center his efforts only on the university; he was also very instrumental in the creation of the system of public education that developed, over time, in Virginia and was influential elsewhere, and James Madison was his collaborator in those endeavors. In 1818, both Jefferson and Madison watched with interest as the Virginia General Assembly debated a general education bill. It called for primary education throughout the state, the creation of colleges or academies to be located in nine "districts" within the Commonwealth, and a single university to cap the system.[7] It was not a debate focusing on the intellectual energy that such an education system might provide for the residents of Virginia. Rather, the concerns were quite practical. Jefferson, with Madison's support, proposed "primary schools established with public support throughout the state that teach the rudiments of learning, so that all citizens would be able to transact their own affairs, understand the elements of morality, and be trained in the responsibilities of community life and of citizenship."[8] Both men saw a public education system as essential to the cultivation of responsible and moral individuals capable of self-government. To them, education was a public necessity.

Around the same time that the General Assembly was debating education, Jefferson was pursuing his dream of establishing a university for Virginia. At a time when almost all of the existing colleges and academies had religious roots and affiliations, Jefferson wanted to create a nonsectarian institution for higher learning. He felt that the teaching of religious doctrine, whatever form it took, too often instilled a sense of obligation, even fear, in the student and too often led to punishment of those who might stray from its dictates. Jefferson felt that education should contribute to the creation of men of good character not through punishment but through the instruction that they received, the books that they read, and the values and principles that they were taught. He "hoped that 'pride of character, laudable ambition, and moral dispositions,' could replace the degrading motive of fear."[9] Neither Jefferson nor Madison was hostile to religion. But they were both wedded to the separation of church and state and the free exercise of individual conscience. As Ketcham puts it, "They were determined to keep inviolate the separation of church and state in Virginia and to nourish at the university an atmosphere of impartial, undogmatic inquiry rather than the shrill defense of sectarianism that engulfed so many of the religiously founded colleges of their day."[10]

In a letter to Edward Everett written in 1823, Madison explained his views on the subject. Commenting on the nonsectarian character of the University of Virginia, he argued that a sectarian institution might become a "sectarian monopoly," while an institution composed of "professorships of rival sects" could become "an Arena of Theological Gladiators." To Madison, a nonsectarian approach might exhibit some irreligious tendencies, but that outcome would be more manageable than the two aforementioned options. "On this view of the subject," he wrote Everett, "there seems to be no alternative but between a public University without a theological professorship, and sectarian Seminaries without a University."[11]

Jefferson envisioned a university that would provide instruction in ten "divisions": ancient languages, modern languages, pure mathematics, physics, chemistry, biology, anatomy and medicine, government, law, and humanities. Within the humanities would be philosophy, ethics, rhetoric, literature, and fine arts. The great challenge would be finding able scholars to teach at such a university.[12] Jefferson was most concerned with the need to avoid "politicization" in the teaching of law and government. He did not want faculty to be partisans of stronger, consolidated government, something that he had fought against during his time in government, or of extreme "states' rights." Fearing that, he proposed a required reading list that he felt might mitigate the tendency of faculty to espouse their personal political beliefs. The list was to include the *Declaration of Independence*, *The Federalist*, and the 1798 and 1800 Virginia Declarations and "Report," along with the works of Locke and Sidney.[13]

Madison agreed with Jefferson regarding his concerns but was less sanguine about the possibility that required readings would mitigate faculty "politics." In a letter to his friend, Madison agreed with Jefferson, saying that "it is certainly very material that the true doctrines of liberty as exemplified in our Political System, should be inculcated on those who are to sustain and may administer it" but confided that texts probably would do little to combat "constructive violations" of constitutions. He admitted that even *The Federalist* did not enjoy a reputation as an authoritative text among all scholars. The problem, as Madison saw it, was that texts still left room for interpretation and construction by professors. Where they are too general, he wrote, they do not provide enough information; where they are too specific, they "divide and exclude where meant to unite and fortify." It would be difficult to find texts, Madison felt, that would be "both guides and guards for this purpose."[14]

Still, Madison understood and agreed with Jefferson's concerns and suggested adding *Washington's Farewell Address*. But he still was of the opinion that "the most effectual safeguard against heretical intrusions into the School of Politics, will be an Able and Orthodox Professor, whose course of instruction will be an example to his successors, and may carry with it a sanction from the Visitors [the university's board of trustees]."[15] Jefferson and Madison both shared the view that the best form of government was free, republican government and that students should be instructed to support and administer that form of government. They did not believe in what has come to be called "the marketplace of ideas." Rather, they felt that such an approach was less than practical and potentially dangerous in so young and fragile a republic.

Jefferson became the first rector of the University of Virginia and considered the university one of his greatest achievements and lasting legacies. Upon Jefferson's death, Madison became rector, serving for eight years. The university prospered during Madison's tenure; its enrollment was stable, its library holdings increased, and in 1832 it awarded its first master's degree.[16] During his career, Madison was supportive of other institutions too, among them Princeton, Allegheny College, and Hampden-Sydney College, where he had served on the founding board of trustees (along with Patrick Henry) in 1775, although he never attended a meeting of the board. His devotion to the education and intellectual nourishment of Virginians and his fellow countrymen was a concern throughout his public life. But it was a concern driven, in large part, by his recognition of the need for a practical education that would help individuals meet their day-to-day needs and responsibilities as well as foster in them the sense of civic duty essential to the maintenance of republican government. He did not see colleges as "ivory towers" where academics might pursue their scholarly interests as they taught and mentored students. Rather, they were to be places of enlightenment where young men might develop the intellectual and practical talents necessary for pursuing a livelihood and practicing self-government.

DEAR SIR

Madison provides a more complete picture of his ideas for education in a letter that he sent to William T. Barry of Kentucky in August of 1822. Barry was lieutenant governor of Kentucky at the time and also was taking up new duties as a professor of law and politics at Transylvania College in Lexington. He had written Madison seeking his thoughts regarding establishing a system of public education for the people of Kentucky. Madison's response provides a rather comprehensive vision for such a system, touching on some of the same themes that he and Jefferson talked and wrote about so often. Madison begins his letter by applauding the Kentucky legislature for its liberal appropriation to create a public education system. He then gets right to the point:

> A popular Government without popular information, or the means of acquiring it, is but a Prologue to a Farce or a Tragedy, or, perhaps both. Knowledge will forever govern ignorance; and a people who mean to be their own Governors, must arm themselves with the power which knowledge gives.[17]

Madison encourages Barry to be deliberate when approaching the issue and not to assume that the people have no interest in such a system. That opinion might be justified should the plan call for the "establishment of Academies, Colleges, and Universities, where a few only and those not of the poorer classes can obtain for their sons the advantages of superior education." Surely it is unjust that all should be taxed to pay for a plan for "the benefit of a part, and that too the part least needing." It is critical, Madison counsels, to take everyone into consideration.

> It is better for the poorer classes to have the aid of the richer by a general tax on property, than that every parent should provide at his own expense for the education of his children, it is certain that every

Class is interested in establishments which give to the human mind its highest improvements, and to every Country its truest and most durable celebrity.[18]

For Madison it seemed beyond doubt that everyone should want to support the creation of educational institutions. "Learned Institutions," he writes, "ought to be the favorite objects with every free people. They throw light over the public mind which is the best security against crafty & dangerous encroachments on the public liberty." He then provides examples of the benefit such institutions provide. They are "nurseries of skilled teachers" and "schools for the particular talents required for some of the Public Trusts, on which the able execution of which the welfare of the people depends." They increase the number of educated people from among whom the people elect their agents, "especially those who are to frame the laws."

Those with meager means, Madison writes, should be interested in a "system which unites with the more Learned Institutions, a provision for diffusing through the entire Society the education needed for the common purposes of life." He then cites the 1779 Virginia "Bill for the more general diffusion of Knowledge" which states, according to Madison, that talented youths whose parents cannot afford it should "be carried forward at public expense from seminary to seminary, to the completion of his studies at the highest." Both the wealthy and the poor should support such an approach—the wealthy because it will provide for their descendants, the poor because such a system will make it more possible that their descendants will not be poor.

To Madison, education was the responsibility of government. "The American people owe it to themselves, and to the cause of free Government" to prove to the rest of the world, "that their political institutions," which are being observed from "every quarter,"

are as favorable to the intellectual and moral improvement of Man as they are conformable to his individual & social Rights. What spectacle can be more edifying or more seasonable, than that of Liberty & Learning, each leaning on the other for their mutual & surest support?[19]

Being a bit hesitant to second-guess what officials in Kentucky might be thinking regarding topics and subjects to be taught and mindful of the relatively sparse population there and the uniqueness of every state, Madison nonetheless offers his suggestions. In addition to "Reading, Writing, and Arithmetic" the poor should get some "Knowledge of Geography; such as can easily be conveyed by a Globe & Maps" in order to "expand the mind and gratify curiosity." They should be taught something about "the Globe we inhabit" and "the Nations among which it is divided, and the character and customs which distinguish them." This, along with travel, will tend to "weaken local prejudices and enlarge the sphere of benevolent feelings." He closes his letter with the observation that "a general taste for History" is "an inexhaustible fund of entertainment & instruction" and encourages "any reading not of a vicious species must be a good substitute of the amusements too apt to fill up the leisure of the labouring classes."[20]

Madison's letter to Barry reflects his overall concern that education be encouraged and expanded so that not only the wealthy but also the poor might benefit. It is a view of public education—education funded through tax dollars and provided by the government—as a means of offering opportunities that might lead to upward mobility while also serving the general interest of the state by creating citizens with the learning and tools necessary for making informed judgments and governing themselves. There are limits to Madison's framework, surely—for example, he mentions education for men but not women, and he seems almost patronizing when he writes of the poor. But the former is merely a reflection of the times and the latter should be seen more as a genuine concern for the interest of the poor rather than any condescension toward them. In short, Madison viewed education—at any and all levels—as essential to a rich and full life. Furthermore, he viewed it as no less essential to the future success of the young republic in the world—a world that was watching the nation with growing interest.

THE EVOLUTION OF AMERICAN EDUCATION

In 1790, the population of the young United States of America was nearly 4 million people. Nineteen percent were blacks, almost 90 percent of them living in the South. Native Americans were not counted.[21] In 1835, the population exceeded 14.5 million. In 2013, upward of 315 million people called America home.[22] When young Madison was attending the College of New Jersey at Princeton, there were fewer than ten or so other institutions that he might have chosen. Harvard had been around since 1636, the College of William and Mary, in Madison's Virginia, since 1693. Having been established in 1746, Madison's institution of choice was relatively young when he arrived there.

Today there are more than 4,000 postsecondary institutions in the United States with more than 17.5 million students enrolled. They form a richly diverse sector of the American economy. Public four-year institutions (numbering 629) exist alongside private four-year institutions (numbering 1,845). Public two-year institutions (1,070) compete for students with private two-year institutions (596). Interestingly, more than 57 percent of students enrolled in postsecondary and higher education institutions are female, and almost 62 percent consider themselves full-time. More than 30 percent come from minorities; more than 3 percent are foreign.[23]

In 2011, the graduation rate for full-time, first-time undergraduate students at four-year, degree-granting institutions was 59 percent within six years. Graduation rates were better at private institutions (65 percent) than public (57 percent). The graduation rate for the growing, private, for-profit postsecondary sector hovered around 42 percent.[24] In 2013, the average cost to attend a four-year public institution was over $10,500 a year for in-state students and almost $17,900 for out-of-state students. The average cost of attending a private four-year institution approached $40,000 a year.[25]

Madison would undoubtedly find all of this stunning. However, he would be even more amazed at the size and costs of elementary and secondary education in America. In 2013, more than $591 billion was spent on K-12 education, around $11,800 per student. Teachers employed in the nation's 15,746 school districts made an average of around $56,000 a year. Almost 100,000 public schools educate almost 35 million elementary students and 14.5 million high school students. Enrollment in private schools totals nearly 5.4 million.[26]

By almost any measure, then, Americans take education seriously. They are willing to allocate taxpayer dollars, pay tuition, and take out loans in order to get an education. In 2013 the nation's student loan debt eclipsed credit card debt. The idea of public schools being supported by the taxpayers and available to all, an idea Madison embraced, has become part and parcel of the American experience. The idea of establishing institutions of advanced learning so that those with the ability and the desire (and the resources) might extend their education to its fullest extent, an idea that Madison embraced, has likewise become, if not completely a part of the America experience, certainly part of the American dream.

Education policy in the United States has evolved over time, of course. During Madison's time, education was reserved for those who could afford it. Young men, generally from wealthy families, would get schooling or tutoring in order to continue and enlarge the family holdings. Some would go on to higher education. The early colleges, as Madison and Jefferson noted, were largely private sectarian or church-related institutions. Over time, states adopted systems of public education funded by taxpayers, and public institutions of higher education were established; all were state and local efforts funded by state and local revenues. As recently as 1902, state and local government spending on education accounted for about 1 percent of the gross domestic product (GDP) of the country, most of which was devoted to K-12 schooling. It continued to grow, with some decreases, during the Great Depression and World War II. By 1950, K-12 spending was around 2.1 percent of GDP and higher education spending was .38 percent. Both sectors experienced increases over time. By the 1970s, K-12 spending was around 4 percent of GDP and higher education spending reached 1.5 percent. In other words, in twenty-five years, K-12 spending almost doubled and higher education spending almost quadrupled in relation to GDP. Into the 2000s, K-12 spending has fluctuated around 3.5 to 3.8 percent of GDP and higher education has increased to around 1.6 to 1.8 percent of GDP.[27]

Spending on education, at all levels, remains primarily a state and local responsibility, but Washington's role has increased over time. The national government's first major attempt at framing a "national" education policy is the Morrill Land-Grant Colleges Act of 1862. Originally proposed by Justin Smith Morrill of Vermont in 1857, it passed in 1859 but was vetoed by President James Buchanan, who argued that education was a state responsibility. Morrill tried again in 1861, this time including the teaching of military tactics as well as agriculture and engineering at the proposed institutions. President Lincoln signed the legislation on July 2, 1862. The Morrill Act allocated land to states based on the size of their state congressional delegations: 30,000 acres per member, based on the 1860 census. States that had seceded from the union were excluded. The mission of the institutions to be created by the states under the act was, "without excluding other scientific and classical studies," to teach "in such manner as the legislatures of the States may respectively prescribe, in order to promote the liberal and practical education of the industrial classes in the several pursuits and professions in life."[28] At the start of the twentieth century, many states had a land-grant institution. There were two in the South of the old Confederacy.

The Morrill Act provided the foundation for a more active role for the federal government in education. For example, during the Great Depression, New Deal programs helped to construct hundreds of buildings on college and university campuses and helped keep students in college through financial aid and work-study programs. During World War II, the nation's war effort led to billions in spending on military and defense research, which continues to be an important part of federal grants and aid to America's institutions of higher education. The end of the war led to a second landmark piece of legislation that further increased Washington's role in education: the G.I. Bill. Officially the Servicemen's Readjustment Act of 1944, the G.I. Bill provided a variety of benefits for veterans returning from World War II. Every active-duty veteran who served at least ninety days, whether in combat or not, and who was honorably discharged was eligible to receive low-interest loans for home mortgages, low-interest loans to start a business, and cash payments for tuition and living expenses in order to attend colleges, high schools, and vocational schools. By 1956, millions of veterans had taken advantage of the educational opportunities that the G.I. Bill made available. The law helped to transform higher education in the country and was a key part of the economic transformation that took place immediately after the war. Several successive versions of the G.I. Bill have extended benefits to veterans of the Korean War, the Vietnam War, and the wars in Iraq and Afghanistan.[29]

Washington also became more involved in American K-12 education as a result of the Supreme Court's ruling in the landmark case *Brown* v. *Board of Education*, which called for an end to school segregation by race "with all deliberate speed." Over many years of ongoing legal and political battles, the federal government forced state and local officials to integrate their schools. *Brown* was followed by cases dealing with forced busing to end de facto segregation and a host of related issues, virtually transforming the face of public education in much of the country, particularly in the South. The ramifications of the *Brown* decision can be seen even today in the various equal protection and affirmative action cases related to race, gender, and ethnicity with regard to education.[30]

These three defining events helped to usher in a larger role for the federal government in American education. In addition, legislation passed by Congress in the 1950s and 1960s solidified the national government's role. In 1958, the National Defense Education Act put Washington in the student loan business. In 1965, the Elementary and Secondary Education Act (ESEA), part of Lyndon Johnson's War on Poverty, extended the government's reach into America's classrooms. That same year, the Higher Education Act (HEA) increased government loan programs and added a mix of loans and grants. Both the ESEA and the HEA have been reauthorized by Congress several times, extending and revising various provisions and spending authorizations. Perhaps the most controversial version of ESEA was passed during President George W. Bush's first term. Entitled No Child Left Behind, the law put in place accountability policies that required testing of all children in certain grades and embraced the ambitious goal of making sure that all students were proficient in reading and math by 2014. That goal was not achieved—many argue that it is impossible to achieve—and the law has been altered by the Obama administration without congressional action.

In 1975, Congress passed the Education for All Handicapped Children Act. At the time relatively few students with physical and mental disabilities were being educated in America's public schools; indeed, many states excluded such children from schools. The law, later revised as the Individuals with Disabilities Education Act (IDEA), changed that, requiring states accepting federal dollars to provide early intervention and special education and other services for children from birth to adulthood. It has done for these students and their families what *Brown* began to do for African American children and families.

Even given all of the policies, regulations, and dollars flowing from Washington in more recent years, education remains primarily the responsibility of state and local governments. Washington's influence is reflected in the decisions that state and local officials make, and the issue of "overreach" is often brought up by state officials eager to protect what they consider to be a state prerogative. But there is little chance that the federal government will retreat from its claim to authority and its interests with respect to education. Moreover, it can be argued that even though education is a state and local responsibility, it is a national priority and Washington therefore has an important role to play in making sure that it is available and affordable for every American. That is the philosophy on which much of the education policy emanating from the nation's capital is based. ESEA is aimed primarily at improving educational opportunities and achievement for low-income and at-risk children. HEA is concerned primarily with providing student financial assistance for postsecondary education. IDEA ensures that children with physical and mental disabilities get a "free and appropriate education."

Education policy at the national level has been, almost from the beginning, about democracy: It has been about making sure that people can get the education that they need to be good citizens; it has been about targeting at-risk and low- and middle-income students and families and communities for special assistance; and it has been about tying education to economic development and national competitiveness. Those represent core values in America, and it makes sense that they are reflected in national education policy. But just as Madison concerned himself not only with creating a constitution but also with governing, what matters with regard to national education policy is not only the structure and purpose of that policy but also its implementation and results.

THE NATION'S PERFORMANCE

Education, particularly elementary and secondary education, has been the focus of considerable political scrutiny at the national level for more than a generation. During the Reagan administration, the publication of *A Nation at Risk* initiated a national debate over the quality of public education in America. Under Reagan and continuing with every administration since, education reform proposals have been an integral component of a president's domestic policy agenda. George H. W. Bush had "Goals 2000," Clinton had "Improving America's Schools," George W. Bush had "No Child Left Behind," and Obama has touted the "Race to the Top." Central to each of these initiatives has been the belief that America's schools and students are underperforming, that many are failing, and that the nation therefore needs to mount a concerted effort at education reform. Most indicators of educational achievement do indeed suggest that student achievement in reading, math, and science has been flat for more than twenty years. Moreover, the performance of U.S. students is lower than that of students in many other countries.

All the while, however, spending on education has continued to increase, with federal spending increasing rather dramatically in the 2000s. In 1970, the total cost for a single student from kindergarten through twelfth grade was around $57,000; in 2010, it was around $164,400 per student. The United States spends $11,800 a year per student, more than any other nation, yet student and school achievement remains flat. There are many high-achieving schools and students, and the nation's best students can compete with students worldwide. But far too many schools and students, particularly in urban areas and very rural locations, are underperforming, and they have been for generations.[31]

Despite national initiatives to reform and improve schools, together with state-based efforts, achievement remains disappointing. Education remains a central concern in public opinion polls. Americans care about their schools and want them funded adequately; they also respect the teaching profession and want teachers paid well. Interestingly, they tend to think their own schools are doing all right, despite evidence to the contrary. A 2013 survey found that an overwhelming majority of the general public grades the nation's schools C or better; only 6 percent say that they are failing. Among teachers, 90 percent give America's schools a C or better; among parents, 80 percent do so. When asked about the schools in their own community, the responses are even more positive: 84 percent of respondents give their community schools a grade of C or better.[32]

What accounts for the disconnect between the public's perception of the quality of American education and the realities regarding student achievement? Probably many things. The accountability movement, with its emphasis on testing, is seen by its many critics as too narrow in its focus and testing as not a satisfactory indicator of student or school performance. In addition, testing is seen as crowding out other, very important curriculum and education concerns. Critics say that it tends to "dumb down" the curriculum and undermine the importance and value of courses and disciplines that are not tested. The emphasis on accountability leads to "teaching to the tests" and drilling students as test time approaches as opposed to working on critical thinking skills and creativity.

But there is something else at work here. Education is something that everyone can relate to and has an opinion about because everyone has gone to school. Everyone knows someone who has something to do with education: teachers, students, administrators, and school board members. Moreover, people develop relationships with their children's schools and teachers and do not like to think that their schools don't measure up. Just as polls report that people think poorly of Congress but think highly of their own senators and representatives, so too, it seems, people might be concerned about the overall quality of American education but feel pretty good about the schools that their own children attend. When parents were given the choice to send their children to better-performing schools under the provisions of No Child Left Behind, relatively few took advantage of the opportunity. Many said that they preferred to stay—they felt a sense of loyalty to their children's schools despite the schools' poor performance.

In contrast to elementary and secondary education, for years American postsecondary and higher education has enjoyed a solid reputation worldwide. More recently, however, it has become subject to widespread concern and criticism, for a number of reasons. The cost of attending colleges and universities has continued to climb rapidly, outpacing inflation—at some institutions by large margins. That has led to more families and students having to borrow to pay for their education, and for some, it has led to crushing student debt. On top of that, there is growing concern that students graduate lacking some of the knowledge and skills that they need in order to succeed in life. College graduates still make more money in their lifetime than non–college graduates. Still, there is growing concern that higher education is about to undergo major changes, driven in part by technology and in part by student and family discontent.

The evidence regarding popular attitudes toward higher education is mixed. A study reported in 2010 in the *Chronicle of Higher Education* suggested that public opinion on higher education was becoming more negative. The study reported that 60 percent of the public thought that colleges "mostly care about the bottom line" and 54 percent thought that they "could spend less and still maintain a high level of quality." On the other hand, a majority (55 percent) still thought that "a college education is necessary for a person to be successful in today's work world."[33] However, a 2012 study found that "more than 1.5 million new bachelor's degree holders reported being either unemployed or underemployed."[34] That same year, a Pew Survey saw wide-scale dissatisfaction with American higher education. According to Pew, 57 percent agreed that higher education "fails to provide students with good value for the money." An even greater majority (75 percent) felt that higher education is "too expensive for most Americans to afford." Yet 86 percent of the college students surveyed said that "college has been a good investment for them personally." But the costs and debt burden associated with obtaining a college education do not go unnoticed by students or their families, even though they might think that it is worth the financial strain. Twenty-five percent of those surveyed said that debt made it harder for them to buy a home, and even more said that it made it harder to pay other bills. According to the Pew survey, a college education was considered less important for success in the world than "a good work ethic" and "knowing how to get along with people."[35]

One multiyear study concerning the "civic literacy" of college graduates produced some disturbing results. According to the American Civic Literacy Program of the Intercollegiate Studies Institute, "College-educated adults were particularly ignorant of the Founding and Civil War eras, constitutional themes, and the essential features of a market economy." The study went on to conclude that a college education had almost no influence on students' understanding and awareness of civics and government. Rather, being active in such things as campaigns and contacting elected officials were more influential than a college education. That is of particular note given James Madison's concern that Americans get a good education in order to fulfill the responsibilities of self-government.[36]

WHAT WOULD MADISON THINK?

It would be easy to assume that James Madison would have a difficult time understanding education in America today. He was, after all, a member of the Virginia "aristocracy," born to privilege. He benefited from an early education that relatively few young men of his time could acquire and even fewer young women. He attended the College of New Jersey at Princeton, where he studied under some of the most eminent teachers and scholars of the era. He spent his life immersed in great books and applied his knowledge to the tasks of writing a constitution, forming a government, and governing. He interacted with a handful of men who quite rightly can be considered among the better educated and most influential and affluent of the time. When away from government, he and his wife, Dolley, lived at Montpelier, where they relied on slaves to manage the large plantation and family business. Surely such a man would have trouble comprehending the democratization of education in America.

Indeed, Madison had real apprehensions about democratic government in general. His analysis of the troubles that plagued the Articles of Confederation led him to believe that democracy entails certain problems, which he laid out and addressed in perhaps his most read and celebrated essay, *Federalist* No. 10. They are the problems associated with public opinion, majority rule, and factions—problems related to what many of the Framers referred to as the "excesses of democracy."

In Madison's mind, democracies had always been undermined by factions that seek to advance their own interests against the long-term interest of the country or the rights of others. Indeed, in perhaps the single best sentence in *The Federalist*, Madison asserts in another essay that even "had every Athenian citizen been a Socrates; every Athenian assembly would still have been a mob."[37] Madison's response to all this was to turn political theory on its head and call for a "large, extended republic" in the United States that might be governed by public opinion while at the same time not be subject to the problems so often associated with it. In such a republic, public views could be "refined and enlarged" through the deliberations of representatives so that the true public interest might be served. It is the difference between merely responding to public opinion and seeking to improve on it. *Federalist* No. 10 presents Madison's proposed solution to the problems associated with democracy, and, he argues, that solution is the premise on which the new Constitution is based.

One can argue, by the way, that Madison was not only right but also prescient in his analysis of democratic government. In contemporary American politics and government, the influence of public opinion—delivered by polls, 24/7 news coverage, and social media—has made the country more democratic than ever while at the same time making it more difficult for elected officials to get beyond responding to public opinion in order to make decisions that may not be popular but are nevertheless necessary. There are a lot of reasons behind the dysfunction in Washington—strident partisanship, warring ideologies, institutional rivalries, and so forth—but one is surely the very democratic nature of the country. Madison was correct: democracies have a difficult time governing.

It might easily be assumed that Madison would also have a difficult time with the nation's emphasis on equality in education. He was, after all, a slave owner. His plantation depended on slave labor and he lived around slaves his entire life. How could anyone associated with such a horrible institution begin to understand, let alone appreciate, the principle of equality? However, it is necessary to understand Madison's thinking regarding slavery. While he indeed depended on slaves for Montpelier to continue to exist as a successful business enterprise, Madison understood the evils of slavery. According to Ketcham, he treated his slaves humanely and instructed his overseer to treat them with "humanity and kindness." By the 1790s, although "Madison had been forced to abandon his hope to be free of the slave system, and even had to take part in maintaining it, he still did what he could to lessen its harshness and degradation."[38]

Madison's worries about the moral evil of slavery intensified over the years. He saw slavery as incompatible with the Declaration of Independence, even as it gained greater prominence as cotton became the cash crop of the South. But he knew that it was politically impossible to end the institution. Moreover, Madison felt that slaves, even if freed, would confront prejudice and suffering for generations because of their status as "freed slaves" and what he saw as the inherent distinctions among the races. He felt the more humane and practical thing would be to support relocating freed slaves to Africa. He was among a handful of men to form the American Colonization Society to promote the idea. Still, as Ketcham points out, "that a man of Madison's realism and integrity should in this instance adhere to such an insufficient and compromised program is painful evidence of the virtually insoluble dilemma posed for him." Madison never freed his slaves, either during his lifetime or upon his death. He "failed utterly to do anything about what he regarded as a moral evil and an economic catastrophe."[39]

By contemporary standards, Madison falls far short when it comes to equality in America. But he reflected the times in which he lived. This is not to excuse Madison; it is to understand him. Slavery, whenever and wherever it exists, is morally outrageous. Madison knew that, but he failed to act on it. In his later years he came to understand fully not only the implications of that failure but of the institution of slavery in the United States generally and sought a way to resolve the growing political and economic problems associated with it.

In his writings, Madison argued that education should be made available to the poor as well as the rich and that it should be provided by the government. He saw education as critical to personal growth and success and to the exercise of self-government. He would be surprised, surely, by the degree to which equality has been such a central principle in the evolution of American education. He might wonder at the sight of men, women, African Americans, members of other minorities, and special-needs students sitting next to one another in American classrooms. He might wonder at the number, size, and character of the nation's institutions of higher education and the students and faculty who study and teach there. That equality in American education—the character of equality, what it means, what has been done to promote it—has evolved in the way that it has might surprise Madison. But he would not be surprised that the principle of equality has been such a compelling force in education and in the United States generally.

Given Madison's own hunger for knowledge and his lifelong study of history, politics, and government, the fact that education is such a central concern in this country would please him. It is beyond speculation to consider what he would make of the costs associated with education and the massive systems and organizations and institutional infrastructure that go into education in America. Madison's understanding of the relationship between education and self-government might lead him to be concerned about the relatively mediocre performance of so many of America's schools and students. He might be even more concerned about the relative ignorance of so many of the nation's students when it comes to civics, history, government, and politics. But the overall character of education in the country, indeed, the character of the country itself, is something that Madison might find heartening yet troubling, satisfying yet perhaps discomforting. That the republic that he helped to create has accomplished so much would please him, surely. That its health and security remain threatened would trouble him but not surprise him. That the hope for its future remains tied to education would merely reflect his own understanding of the needs of a democratic people. That the future of the republic will be challenged by forces seen and unseen would cause him to urge vigilance.

Madison believed that education made the republic possible and could help to ensure its health and future. It has made possible all that this country has achieved and provides the key to its future. The fact that education in America has become what it is says volumes about what the country values and what sets it apart. James Madison's contributions to the foundation and early years of the republic helped to establish those values. The Constitution that he helped to create did not make contemporary education in the United States inevitable. It does make it possible.

Notes

1. Ralph Ketcham, *James Madison* (University of Virginia Press, 1990), p. 19.
2. Ibid., p. 20.
3. Ibid., p. 24.
4. Ibid., p. 44.
5. Ibid., pp. 44-45.
6. Gordon Wood, "The Democratization of Mind in the American Revolution," in *The Moral Foundations of the American Republic,* edited by Robert Horwitz (University Press of Virginia, 1977), p. 103.
7. Ketcham, *James Madison,* p. 647.
8. Ibid., p. 648.
9. Ibid., p. 649.
10. Ibid., p. 652.
11. Letter to Edward Everett, March 19, 1823, in *Letters and Other Writings of James Madison,* vol. 3, *1816–1828* (Philadelphia: J.P. Lippincott, 1867), p. 307.
12. Ketcham, *James Madison,* p. 648.
13. Ibid., p. 654.
14. See Ketcham, *James Madison,* pp. 654–55.
15. Ibid., p. 655.
16. Ibid., p. 658.
17. Letter from Madison to W. T. Barry, August 4, 1822, in *Letters and Other Writings of James Madison,* p. 276.
18. Ibid., p. 277.
19. Ibid., p. 279.
20. Ibid., p. 280.

21. See U.S. Census Bureau (www.census.gov/prod/www/decennial.html).
22. See U.S. Census Bureau, U.S. and World Population Clock, April 2, 2015.
23. National Center for Education Statistics, *Digest of Education* (Department of Education, 2006).
24. National Center for Education Statistics, "The Condition of Education 2013," NCES 2012-037 (Department of Education, May 2013) (http://nces.ed.gov/pubs2013/2013037.pdf).
25. Carole Feldman, "Education in America: Facts and Figures as Students Head Back to School," *Huffington Post*, August 31, 2013.
26. See National Center for Education Statistics, "Fast Facts" (U.S. Department of Education, 2013) (http://nces.ed.gov/fastfacts/).
27. See "U.S. Education Spending History from 1990" (www.usgovernmentspending.com/education_spending).
28. 7 U.S.C. § 304.
29. P.L. 78-346, 58 Stat. 284 m.
30. 345 U.S. 483 (1954).
31. U.S. Department of Education, *Digest of Education Statistics*, and National Assessment of Educational Progress, "Long-Term Trends, 17-Year-Olds, 2013."
32. See Michael Henderson and Paul Peterson, "The 2013 Education Next Survey" (http://educationnext.org/category/government-and-politics/public-opinion/).
33. See Eric Kilderman, "Public Opinion of Higher Education Continues Downward Slide," in *Chronicle of Higher Education*, December 12, 2010.
34. Bill Path, "Has the Tipping Point for Higher Education Occurred?," *Huffington Post*, July 1, 2013.
35. "Is College Worth It?" (Pew Research Center, May 15, 2012) (http://www.pewsocialtrends.org/2011/05/15/is-college-worth-it/).
36. Intercollegiate Studies Institute, American Civic Literacy Program, "Enlightened Citizenship 2011" (www.americancivicliteracy.org).
37. *Federalist* No. 55, in *The Federalist* (Wesleyan University Press, 1961), p. 374.
38. Ketcham, *James Madison*, p. 375.
39. Ibid., p. 629.

Ten

COURTING PUBLIC OPINION

James Madison's Strategy for Resisting Federal Usurpations

LYNN E. UZZELL

On March 23, 2010, President Barack Obama signed into law the Patient Protection and Affordable Care Act (which would soon be dubbed "Obamacare" by friends and foes alike). The battle over the bill in Congress had been bitterly contested; the vote had split sharply down party lines; and the final passage of the law brought cheers of jubilation from some quarters and howls of protest from others. Opponents of the new law claimed among other things that it was an unconstitutional exercise of federal power. In particular, the "individual mandate"—which requires people to have health insurance or pay a penalty—was deemed to lie outside even the most expansive reading of the Commerce Clause found in Article I, section 8, of the Constitution. After opponents lost the fight in Congress, they did what aggrieved parties are wont to do. They called their lawyers.

Within moments of President Obama's signing ceremony, attorneys general in numerous states began filing lawsuits.[1] Proponents of the new law were at first confident and dismissive of any legal challenge. The question of constitutionality had first been broached while the bill was still under consideration. When a reporter asked Speaker of the House Nancy Pelosi what part of the Constitution authorized Congress to impose the individual mandate, she famously quipped, "Are you serious? Are you serious?"[2] As it turns out, they were serious, and the legal challenge that they mounted was formidable. By the time that the case was argued before the Supreme Court, twenty-six states had joined the lawsuit and the legal winds were at their back. One appeals court decision had been in their favor; the administration's counsel (according to some) had done a poor job of defending the law; and many of the questions coming from the bench had seemed sympathetic to the plaintiffs.

As the Supreme Court was poised to deliver its opinion, the pundits, prognosticators, and bookies began laying odds that substantial portions of the health care law would be overturned; the only question remaining seemed to be whether it would be overturned in its entirety or merely gutted beyond salvaging. Then, in a surprise twist, Chief Justice John Roberts led a 5-4 decision siding with the administration (though not with their arguments), ruling that the individual mandate was within the taxing powers of Congress. Once again, the cheers and howls were heard from their respective quarters, and President Obama went on national television to declare that "the highest court in the land has now spoken" and that "with today's announcement, it's time to move forward."[3] Opponents were left to lick their wounds and rejoin the battle on different fronts.

I do not propose to revisit the question of whether the Affordable Care Act was or was not constitutional, and I am even less interested in examining whether or not it is good policy. Rather, I wish to use this one example of a contretemps between state and federal authorities as a springboard to examine and evaluate the various possible *strategies* for resolving disagreements over the authoritative interpretation of American federalism. And in the interest of probing the depths of that perennially fascinating inquiry, "WWJD?"—"What Would 'Jemmy' Do?"—I explore how James Madison responded to similar perceived abuses of federal power and why he chose the avenues that he did. In this way, we may catch a glimpse of how the Father of the Constitution believed that a constitutional fracas should be resolved. And to the degree that his reasons are persuasive and his actions worthy of emulation, we may be armed with a guiding principle for how future battles over federalism should be waged.

There can be no question that Madison believed that the federal courts were a legitimate and even (in one sense) a final arbiter for determining the boundaries of federal authority. On that question he never wavered. When attempting to untie "the Gordian knot of the . . . collision between the federal and State powers," the federal courts must have the last word, because all other roads would lead to anarchy and disunion.[4] Toward the end of his life, he recalled that he had defended the supremacy of the federal courts when he wrote the *Federalist* essays "and I have never ceased to think that this supremacy was a vital principle of the Constitution, as it is a prominent feature of its text."[5] But even if the Supreme Court would sometimes be called on as final arbiter of certain questions of federalism, it was clearly not the only arbiter, nor (and here is the nub) was it necessarily the best one. Both in theory and in practice, Madison preferred appealing to the people, either directly or through their representatives, rather than resorting to litigation. And that preference was not rooted in shortsighted considerations of achieving immediate political success for the question at hand; rather, it proceeded from his considered opinion of what was needed to make America's experiment in republican government work.

Constitutionalism and Federalism in the Service of Popular Rule

Madison's commitment to and understanding of both federalism and constitutionalism were grounded in his more fundamental dedication to popular rule. That is not to say that he believed that every passing whim of a majority of the citizenry should be indulged. Such an indiscriminate attachment to majority rule would inevitably subvert the rights of some minority party and would ultimately cause popular government to self-destruct. Rather, he sought ways to refine and arrange popular institutions so that they might yield that rarity in political history: a stable, just, and durable republic. A few years after his retirement from public service, Madison shared with his brother-in-law the political philosophy that informed his earliest reflections on national supremacy as well as some alterations in his thinking that had taken place since then:

> For myself, having, from the first moment of maturing a political opinion down to the present one, never ceased to be a votary of the

principle of self-government, I was among those most anxious to rescue it from the danger which seemed to threaten it; and with that view, was willing to give to a Government resting on that foundation as much energy as would insure the requisite stability and efficacy.[6]

Throughout Madison's political career, the various political principles that he advocated—whether for an extended sphere of republican government, for checks and balances on the branches of government, or for a faithful interpretation of the Constitution—always served the primary goal of ensuring that a popular form of government could succeed.[7] And many Madisonian scholars have subsequently gone off the rails because they have viewed his principles as a succession of discrete parts rather than seeing them within the interconnected and organic hierarchy in which he placed them.

Madison's initial preference for a sovereign national government and his eventual embrace of the national halfway house that the Constitution created were both grounded in his commitment to making republican government work. Heading into the Constitutional Convention, Madison had become convinced that a dramatic shift in powers from the state governments to the central government was necessary, not only to preserve the union but also to rescue republican government itself from the many ills that threatened its survival in the states.[8] He explained to Virginia's governor, Edmund Randolph, that he believed that it was "a fundamental point that an individual independence of the States, is utterly irreconcileable with the idea of an aggregate sovereignty." His idea for a new constitution, therefore, would have established "a due supremacy of the national authority" while leaving in place the authority of the state governments only insofar "as they can be subordinately useful."[9]

The individual proposals that Madison offered in his Virginia Plan and defended throughout the Constitutional Convention would have admirably accomplished the goal of subordinating the states to a national government with unambiguous sovereignty. But many of the other Framers balked at the most nationalistic tendencies of his plan, and that unequivocal supremacy that he wished to see in the federal government was precisely what he failed to get. Privately, he confided to Jefferson that his failure to achieve his objects would probably doom the success of the Constitution.[10] Publicly, however, he defended the "partly federal and partly national" character of the Constitution like a true believer. His *Federalist* No. 39 is a model of chastened nationalism. The federal government was supreme over "certain enumerated objects only," he explained, and the state governments retained "a residuary and inviolable sovereignty over all other objects."[11]

There was nothing peculiar or esoteric about Madison's interpretation of American federalism during the ratifying period. Even Alexander Hamilton—who never saw a restraint on national powers that he liked— had defended the Constitution in the same way.[12] At the time, the defenders of the new Constitution had spoken with one voice on the subject of federalism. And in case anyone possessed lingering uneasiness that the "inviolable sovereignty" of the states was not clear enough in the original Constitution, the 1st Congress added the Tenth Amendment for good measure. Nevertheless, howsoever clearly the *principle* of federalism may have been stated in the Constitution, the devil is in the details. Boundary disputes over the legitimate spheres of state and federal authority arose almost immediately and continued to bedevil the new government for years to come. America's first parties formed in large measure over differing views on the proper extent of federal authority. In particular, the Federalist Party began interpreting the Necessary and Proper Clause in ways that endowed the federal government with far-reaching power, and the Democratic Republicans frequently kicked at those incursions into the states' sovereignty. Given Madison's earlier predilections for a strong national government, some were surprised (and some continue to express surprise) that he sided with the Republicans.[13] But the stance that he took was of a piece with his fundamental commitment to republican government.

Madison may have originally submitted to the Constitution's compromise of divided sovereignty with some misgivings, but he would thereafter and throughout his life defend it with resolute determination.[14] That apparent U-turn is the first clue to understanding Madison's approach to constitutional questions. So long as the formation of the Constitution was an open question—so long as the Framers had a free hand in constructing its outlines—Madison would fight stoutly to codify his own opinions about federal power in the proposed plan of government. But once the Constitution had been ratified—once it was no longer a lump of clay to be molded but an authoritative expression of the people's deliberate will—then Madison defended the arrangement that had received the people's consent. The constitutional interpretation that Madison sought and defended was "the sense in which the Constitution was accepted and ratified by the nation" because "in that sense alone it is the legitimate Constitution."[15]

Therefore, when Madison came to believe that the people's own "sense of the Constitution" was under assault by Congress, he viewed it as more than simply a threat to the rule of law (although he certainly saw it as that); in his view, it was also an assault on popular government itself. Both Madison and Hamilton had wanted a much stronger central government than the Constitution gave them. Both had thought that the inherent weaknesses in the Constitution might doom its success, but both nonetheless defended it during the ratification debates because they thought that it was better than nothing. Where they parted ways was how they responded to their disappointed hopes for the Constitution after it was ratified. According to Madison's account of the rupture, Hamilton continued to fight for a version of the Constitution that he had always wanted, and he did so by interpreting certain clauses more expansively than they had been understood at the time the Constitution was adopted. By contrast, Madison had submitted to the Constitution that had received the people's consent.[16] If Madison had continued to cling to his own opinions of national supremacy after the people had definitively rejected them, then he would have been sacrificing the *end* of republican government to his preferred *means* of salvaging it. So long as the people had not yet definitively spoken, he sought to influence their choice. After they had made their solemn and deliberate choice, he was always prepared to sacrifice his private judgment to their will. That pattern would repeat itself throughout his career.

And just as preserving the people's sense of the Constitution was for Madison a question of upholding republican principles, so should the strategies adopted for its preservation be republican. Madison's strategic thinking on this question was already fully formed before it was ever tried in the crucible of public policy debates. When he tackled the abstract question of the inevitable clashes between the state and federal governments in *The Federalist*, he accused the antifederalists of having "lost sight of the people altogether in their reasonings on this subject." The rival ambitions of state and federal officials might goad them to attempt mutual encroachments— that was only natural—but "the ultimate authority, wherever the derivative may be found, resides in the people alone." Therefore, the success or failure of any attempt at encroachment will "depend on the sentiments and sanction of their common constituents."[17] The surest defense of the federal structure of the Constitution would be the "ultimate authority" of all political power: the people themselves. And the country had not been under the new government for long before Madison had the opportunity to put his abstract theories to the test.

Within ten years of the adoption of the Constitution, Madison witnessed two measures pass Congress—the bill instituting a national bank and the Alien and Sedition Acts—that he believed were nothing less than bald-faced usurpations of powers that had never been granted to the federal government under the Constitution. With each perceived invasion he attempted different strategies for defending what he believed was the states' legitimate authority. But each of his strategies had this in common: they bypassed the courts and aimed ultimately at influencing that original font of power, the people.

It may be argued that Madison's decision to take his case before the court of popular opinion rather than federal judges was merely pragmatic. Since no federal court had yet exercised the power of judicial review at the time that these issues were being settled, some contemporaries may have doubted that they possessed the authority to strike down federal laws at all. Furthermore, at least insofar as the Alien and Sedition Acts were concerned, Madison may have had reason to believe that the federal courts would be unfriendly to his position. Be that as it may, Madison (along with many others at the time) never doubted that the courts did possess that power. Yet Madison's preference for the people as the ultimate arbiters and guardians of federal limits displays a consistency that can be seen from the ratifying period until his dying day: his position was not dictated by circumstances. Pragmatic considerations may have influenced his choices, but his republican principles were ever his lodestar.

The National Bank

When Treasury Secretary Alexander Hamilton introduced his sweeping proposals for economic reform in 1790, he met with unexpectedly fierce opposition from his erstwhile ally, James Madison, who was then the leading voice within Congress. By the time that Hamilton recommended the creation of a national bank in 1791, Madison's opposition to Hamilton's policies was already firmly established. Many historians who write about Madison's constitutional objections to the Bank Bill therefore insist that his stance was little more than a smokescreen to cover his real antagonism to the oligarchical and urbanizing trend of Hamiltonian economic policy and its potential for introducing corruption into the national councils.[18] There may be much to be said for their reflections on Madison's opposition to those economic measures in general. But these peripheral reasons should not be allowed to overshadow the stubborn fact that Madison's fiercest arguments against a national bank were grounded in a principled objection to its constitutionality, not policy considerations.

The principal point of departure on this question for Madison and Hamilton lay in their respective interpretations of the Necessary and Proper Clause. Hamilton gave it an expansive reading that would have justified almost any power that was useful or even merely convenient in exercising Congress's enumerated powers. Madison read the clause much more narrowly, and he claimed that his narrower reading was warranted not only from the plain meaning of the text but from the manner in which the words were understood by the people who adopted the Constitution:

> The explanations in the state conventions all turned on the same fundamental principle, and on the principle that the terms necessary and proper gave no additional powers to those enumerated. (Here he read sundry passages from the debates of the Pennsylvania, Virginia and North-Carolina conventions, shewing the grounds on which the constitution had been vindicated by its principal advocates, against a dangerous latitude of its powers, charged on it by its opponents.)[19]

It was during those debates that Madison first gave a clear articulation of the link that he saw between a faithful interpretation of the Constitution and the cause of republican government itself. As Colleen Sheehan has written, to Madison,

> No opinion in the regime, however widespread and popular, is superior to the voice of the people expressed in its most sovereign capacity in this document. . . . He viewed Hamilton's broad construction of

the Constitution as more than a point of legal debate—it struck at the very philosophical basis of republican government.[20]

The written record of Madison's speech in Congress merely states vaguely that "he read sundry passages from the debates" at the state conventions in order to prove that the people who ratified the Constitution construed this clause in the narrower fashion that he advocated. But it is possible that among the passages that he read were arguments that he himself had delivered at Virginia's Ratifying Convention to refute Patrick Henry's dire warnings that the Necessary and Proper Clause would one day be rendered into a "sweeping clause" that would be used to justify every conceivable federal power. Madison's narrower interpretation of the Necessary and Proper Clause was not newly manufactured in 1791 to meet the immediate crisis of defeating Hamiltonian economic policies; it was consistent with the interpretation that he had given to the clause when he was actively mollifying the Constitution's opponents in Virginia.[21] If Congressman Madison were to countenance a broader interpretation of this clause just three years after he had given assurances that it could never be interpreted in that way, then he would indeed have betrayed what his own experience told him was "the sense in which the Constitution was accepted and ratified by the nation." And the zeal with which Madison threw himself into foiling that impending betrayal is evident in the closing salvo of his speech before Congress. The proposed national bank, Madison was quoted in notes of the debates as saying, "was condemned by the rule of interpretation arising out of the constitution; . . . was condemned by the expositions of the friends of the constitution, whilst depending before the public; was condemned by the apparent intention of the parties which ratified the constitution; . . . and he hoped it would receive its final condemnation, by the vote of this house."[22]

It didn't. And no Tea Party Republican could have suffered greater agonies over the final passage of the Affordable Care Act than Madison felt as he witnessed the Bank Bill sail through Congress by a comfortable majority, supplied overwhelmingly by Northern representatives. But Madison had one ace up his sleeve that Republicans in 2010 did not have: the sympathetic ear of the president. As he had already described in *Federalist* No. 44, in the event that Congress "should misconstrue or enlarge" the power vested in them by distorting the "true meaning" of the Necessary and Proper Clause, then the line of defense "in the first instance . . . will depend on the executive and judiciary departments."[23] And he had reason to hope that President Washington, who had a high regard for Madison's political opinions, would refuse his assent to the bill. Madison's arguments against the bank's constitutionality were therefore duly recycled in the report issued to Washington by Secretary of State Jefferson. And at first Washington was genuinely ambivalent about the question. Giving fresh encouragement for hope, the president asked Madison to draft a veto message for him, just in case he might need it. He didn't. In the end, Washington sided with Hamilton's arguments, signed the bill, and the Bank Bill became the law of the land.

Having lost the fight in the legislative and executive departments, Madison's next move is instructive. He did not choose to continue the fight in the federal judiciary, though he might have. Instead, he went over their heads and took his case directly to the people. As *Federalist* No. 44 had already made clear, whereas the executive and judiciary departments are remedies to congressional overreach "in the first instance, . . . in the last resort a remedy must be obtained from the people who can, by the election of more faithful representatives, annul the acts of the usurpers."[24] Bypassing the third branch, he turned instead to the fourth estate.

The same year that the Bank Bill passed Congress, Madison urged a former college friend of his, Philip Freneau, to start a newspaper in Philadelphia called the *National Gazette*. It would not be long before the paper was seen as an engine for propagating the Republican Party's party line, but in its earliest days it maintained a pretense of impartiality. Madison contributed several articles for his friend's paper, all published anonymously. But those opinion pieces were far from being the eighteenth-century version of talk-radio tirades. Like the *Federalist* essays a few years earlier, they were often short, reflective treatises that examined abstract principles of government, and the early ones in particular were divorced from the immediate context of contemporary policy debates. Unquestionably, they ultimately aimed to achieve a political end, but their modus operandi had the unmistakable stamp of education rather than sophistry: they sought to engage the minds of the citizenry rather than inflame their passions.

Within those essays, Madison attempted to interest the American public in the cause of maintaining the distinct spheres of power lodged in the state and federal governments. In the essay "Consolidation," Madison warned of the dangers inherent in concentrating powers within the central government at the expense of the state governments. If those "local organs" were destroyed, then "neither the voice nor the sense" of the people could be heard or heeded by the distant Congress, "leaving the whole government to that *self-directed course*, which, it must be owned, is the natural propensity of every government." To avoid this fate, "let it be the patriotic study of all, to maintain the various authorities established by our complicated system, each in its respective constitutional sphere." Guarding the proper boundaries of federalism was difficult, but it was also imperative, because no less than the cause of popular rule was at stake. The reader of "Government of the United States" was presented with a similar message and the same stirring call to arms: "Those who love their country, its repose, and its republicanism, will therefore study to avoid [consolidation of the states into one government], by elucidating and guarding the limits which define the two governments."[25]

The two essays had looked outward, examining the citizen's duty to preserve the federal structure of the Constitution. But in "Public Opinion," Madison turned introspective. He seemed to be tipping his hand to reveal how he perceived his own duty, the motivation that prompted him to write these essays:

> Public opinion sets bounds to every government, and is the real sovereign in every free one.
> As there are cases where the public opinion must be obeyed by the government; so there are cases, where not being fixed, it may be influenced by the government.

In a free government (in other words, a republican government), public opinion is the ultimate ruler. But once again, to Madison, not every transitory shift in the public opinion polls deserves a reflexive obedience. Instead, only when public opinion was clearly the fixed and deliberate disposition of the people should it command the rulers' submission. Ephemeral inclinations might still be subject to education or persuasion. And whatever facilitates the free exchange of ideas—"and particularly a *circulation of newspapers through the entire body of the people*"—promotes free government.[26] Madison—acting as full-time legislator and part-time journalist—was doing his bit to promote republicanism. In these articles he was trying to influence public opinion—and to fix it—on the version of federalism that he believed to be essential to free government.

If Madison had hoped that his newspaper articles would inspire a groundswell of popular resistance to the Bank Bill and lead the electorate to clamor for its repeal, then again, his project was a failure. But Madison's dedication to government by consent is always even more apparent in defeat. When President Madison later found it necessary to sign a national bank into law, he was, of course, charged with hypocrisy by his critics. But according to Madison, the principle undergirding both decisions was his commitment to popular rule. He later insisted that "the inconsistency is apparent, not real" because in the intervening years numerous subsequent elections had convincingly demonstrated that the people had disagreed with Madison's interpretation of the Constitution.[27] More than twenty years of public support for a national bank had provided "the requisite evidence of the national judgment and intention" on the question of the bank's constitutionality.[28] He nonetheless stipulated that even the weight of popular opinion is not sufficient to repeal or alter a provision in the Constitution (that is what the amendment process is for). However, if a long train of elections and legislative precedents is not sufficient to "fix the interpretation of a law," then nothing else can be. Once "evidence of the public judgment" can be ascertained, then "individual opinions" on the subject must be sacrificed.[29] On the question of the national bank, it was the public's interpretation of the Constitution, not his own private judgment, to which Madison finally yielded.

THE ALIEN AND SEDITION ACTS

In his next great battle against federal encroachments, Madison tried different tactics and met with greater success. During the first half of the 1790s, conflicting interpretations of American federalism had been truly in play, but toward the end of the decade the tide had turned decidedly in the direction of the Federalists. With the adoption of the controversial Alien and Sedition Acts, however, the Federalists had clearly overplayed their hand. Authoritarian both in form and execution, the acts became increasingly unpopular among the people. It was in response to that crisis and while the Republican Party was languishing in the political wilderness that Madison harnessed the authority of the state legislatures as a vehicle for driving public opinion.

Once again, Madison did not adopt his tactics as a response to immediate circumstances; he was simply following the playbook that he had detailed earlier when he penned his essays under the name Publius. In *Federalist* No. 44 he insisted that if the federal government tried any unconstitutional funny business at the expense of the state legislatures, they "will be ever ready to mark the innovation, to sound the alarm to the people, and to exert their local influence in effecting a change of federal representatives." In *Federalist* No. 45 he predicted that the state governments would always be a powerful defense against federal overreach because the people will be more attached to them than to any distant government. And, in a foreshadowing of the Virginia Resolutions, Madison predicted in *Federalist* No. 46 that "the embarrassments created by [state] legislative devices" could threaten federal officials with "difficulties not to be despised."[30]

So when the Adams administration passed the despicable Alien and Sedition laws, Madison anonymously drafted resolutions of protest to be passed by the Virginia legislature. (Jefferson had already written corresponding resolutions for Kentucky.) Madison denounced the Sedition Act because it fell afoul of the First Amendment's guarantee of free speech and press, the objection that seems most obvious to us today. But the preponderance of the protest was aimed at the loose construction of the Constitution and the encroaching nature of the federal government, of which the Alien and Sedition Acts were only the latest examples. It concluded with an appeal to the other states to join Virginia, "in confidence that they will concur with this Commonwealth in declaring, as it does hereby declare, that the acts aforesaid are unconstitutional."[31]

The immediate response to the Virginia and Kentucky Resolutions was not propitious. No other state formed common cause with Virginia and Kentucky, and several officially rebuked what they viewed as an invitation to disunity. After all, if individual states could declare federal laws unconstitutional, then they would be thrown back to the days of lawlessness that they had escaped when they scrapped the Articles of Confederation. (Part of the virulence of the other states' reactions may have been in response to the more intemperately worded Kentucky Resolutions, with which—to

Madison's lasting chagrin—his Virginia Resolutions would always be inextricably linked.) In an attempt to salvage the situation, Madison, who stood for election to the Virginia legislature in 1799, drafted a "report" that endeavored to explain and vindicate the previous year's resolutions. Easily twenty times longer than the original resolutions, the report explained in painstaking detail the pernicious tendencies of the Alien and Sedition Acts and the reasons why they were unconstitutional.[32] Perhaps even more important, Madison felt that he had to explain and defend the act of passing the resolutions as a legitimate form of state protest.

Madison hoped to convince his readers that the Virginia Resolutions were not an attempt to undermine the constitutional order. He affirmed, once again, that the judicial department is empowered to decide "in the last resort" all constitutional questions placed before it. But the judiciary, like any other branch, may decide wrongly. (Was it not the case that the federal courts had been busily prosecuting journalists and even a congressman under the Sedition Act?) The finality of the Court, therefore, was relative:

> this resort must necessarily be deemed the last in relation to the authorities of the other departments of the government; not in relation to the rights of the parties to the constitutional compact [in other words, the people themselves], from which the judicial, as well as the other departments, hold their delegated trusts.

Consequently, the Virginia legislature had done no more than its duty when it had volunteered "expressions of opinion" that the Alien and Sedition Acts were unconstitutional. It had never claimed for itself the final authority to decide or enforce the question of constitutionality; it had merely sought to influence the public's "opinion, by exciting reflection." The final determination of whether the Virginia and Kentucky legislatures had judged correctly could safely be left in those hands that were most truly and absolutely the last resort: "the temperate consideration and candid judgment of the American public." To view the courts as final arbiters in all respects would be as subversive to republican government as instituting a monarchy. "The authority of constitutions over governments, and of the sovereignty of the people over constitutions, are truths which are at all times necessary to be kept in mind."[33]

If it was true that Madison's ultimate audience was not the other state legislatures but the American people, then his strategy on this occasion must be deemed a triumph of the first order. In the election of 1800 (which came to be known as the Revolution of 1800), the Federalists suffered a rout from which they never fully recovered. The administrations of Jefferson and Madison were able to curb most of the federal excesses that had previously encroached on state sovereignty; indeed, their interpretation of federalism retained its ascendency until Southern Democrats began to overreach and clamor for the rights of nullification and secession. (Unfortunately, they tried to claim the mantle of Madison in the process.) That ultimate vindication by the electorate was enough to convince Madison that—in spite of being initially rebuffed by the other state legislatures—the Virginia Resolutions had achieved their intended purpose.[34]

CONCLUSION

So, how would Madison judge the strategy adopted by Obamacare's opponents, those who immediately took their dispute to the courts in 2010? He certainly would not claim that they had done anything illegitimate or unconstitutional. But he might have considered that approach ill-advised. By attempting to make an end run around the American people they were, in the first place, acting contrary to the spirit of the Constitution, because they preferred an authoritative decision from an unelected branch of the government to securing the consent of the governed for their position. They gave the president every justification to declare, with the authoritative finality of a gavel hitting a sounding block, that "the highest court in the land has now spoken" and that "with today's announcement, it's time to move forward." In the second place, this shortcut is unlikely to be a winning strategy in the long run. By failing to convince the public that their version of federalism was the correct one, they missed an opportunity to form a lasting corrective to what they deemed to be federal incursions on state sovereignty.

Madison's newspaper submissions of 1791–92 offer us the first lesson in what it takes to make American federalism work. The system, he said, is complicated and it cannot be sustained in a situation in which the citizenry becomes ignorant of or indifferent to the legitimate spheres of power of the federal and state governments. In order to work, "let it be the patriotic study of all" of those who live within the system "to maintain the various authorities . . . each in its respective constitutional sphere."[35] It is therefore the duty of the American people to defend their complicated system of divided sovereignty, and it is the duty of public servants to educate the citizenry about its true meaning.

If the advocates of states' rights find Madison's first lesson in federalism to be a bitter pill to swallow, his second lesson is even more likely to stick in their craw. If the public's impulse to concentrate power in the federal government should become a part of their fixed opinion—rather than a transitory passion—then even a victorious case before the Supreme Court would be at best only a temporary interruption of the people's sovereign will. In the face of sustained public opposition (at least in matters of doubtful constitutional interpretation), the duty of public officials is to subjugate their private opinions to that of their constituents. It is the inexorable logic of republican government: if a given interpretation of federalism has the people's ready understanding and voluntary acquiescence, then the support of the judiciary is not necessary. If that interpretation fails to win their support, then no tribunal, no matter how august, will long be able to withstand their choice. In any contest between state and federal authorities, neither side is going to achieve a decisive victory without receiving the "sanction of their common constituents."[36]

But as of this writing, the ultimate arbiter of Obamacare—"the temperate consideration and candid judgment of the American public"—has not yet issued its final judgment. Some people are still predicting that the law will collapse under the weight of its own unpopularity and legislative pressure. If that is the case, popular opinion will have had the last say, although probably not because the people were weighing the conflicting claims of federalism in the balance. Beyond the particular question of health care, there may be increasing signs of pushback to other examples of expansive federal legislation. With recent referendums legalizing marijuana in some states, in defiance of federal prohibitions, we may be seeing a novel form of "grassroots nullification" of federal law.[37] Rather than waiting for the state legislatures "to sound the alarm to the people," the new vanguard for states' rights may be proceeding from the individual initiative of citizens.

Notes

1. Sheryl Gay Stolberg and Robert Pear, "Obama Signs Healthcare Overhaul Bill, with a Flourish," *New York Times*, March 23, 2010 (www.nytimes.com/2010/03/24/health/policy/24health.html?_r=0).

2. "Flashback: When Asked Where the Constitution Authorizes Congress to Order Americans to Buy Health Insurance, Pelosi Says: 'Are You Serious?,'" December 13, 2010 (http://cnsnews.com/news/article/flashback-when-asked-where-constitution-authorizes-congress-order-americans-buy-health).

3. Bill Mears and Tom Cohen, "Emotions High after Supreme Court Upholds Health Care Law," June 28, 2012 (www.cnn.com/2012/06/28/politics/supreme-court-health-ruling/index.html).

4. Letter from James Madison to Spencer Roane, June 29, 1821, in *The Mind of the Founder: Sources of the Political Thought of James Madison*, rev. ed., edited by Marvin Meyers (University Press of New England, 1973, 1981), p. 367.

5. Letter from James Madison to Nicholas P. Trist, December 1831, in *Letters and Other Writings of James Madison,* published by Order of Congress, 4 vols. (Philadelphia: J. B. Lippincott & Co, 1865), vol. 4, p. 211, cited in the American Reference Library (Orem, Utah: Western Standard Publishing Company, 1998).

6. Letter from James Madison to James G. Jackson, December 27, 1821, in *Letters and Other Writings of James Madison*, vol. 3, p. 245; see also the opening paragraphs of *Federalist* No. 39, in *The Federalist Papers*, edited by Clinton Rossiter, with new introduction and notes by Charles Kesler (New York: Penguin Group, 1961,1999).

7. Lance Banning is especially good about recognizing the underlying consistency that informs so many of Madison's individual political opinions. See Banning, *Sacred Fire of Liberty: James Madison and the Founding of the Federal Republic* (Cornell University Press, 1995).

8. Madison's prognosis of those ills, his alarm for their consequences, and his proposed remedy are found in his "Vices of the Political System of the U. States," written around April 1787.

9. Letter from James Madison to Edmund Randolph, April 8, 1787, in *The Papers of James Madison Digital Edition*, edited by J. C. A. Stagg (University of Virginia Press, 2010) (http://rotunda.upress.virginia.edu/founders/JSMN-01-09-02-0197); hereafter referred to as *JMDE.*

10. Letter from James Madison to Thomas Jefferson, September 6, 1787, in *JMDE* (http://rotunda.upress.virginia.edu/founders/JSMN-01-10-02-0115).

11. *Federalist* No. 39, in *The Federalist Papers*, edited by Rossiter, p. 242.

12. Compare Hamilton's speech at the Constitutional Convention on June 18, 1787, with the reply that he gave to Melancton Smith in the New York Ratifying Convention on June 27, 1788, in *The Debates in the Several State Conventions on the Adoption of the Federal Constitution, as Recommended by the*

General Convention at Philadelphia, in 1787, 5 vols., edited by Jonathan Elliot (Philadelphia: J. B. Lippincott Company, 1901), vol. 5, p. 202, and vol. 2, pp. 355–56, cited in the American Reference Library (Orem, Utah: Western Standard Publishing Company, 1998). Compare also his *Federalist* No. 33.

13. Gordon S. Wood has bestowed an honorific on the scholarly befuddlement: Wood, "Is There a 'James Madison Problem'?," in *Liberty and American Experience in the Eighteenth Century*, edited by David Womersley (Indianapolis: Liberty Fund, 2006) (http://oll.libertyfund.org/title/1727/81746).

14. Drew McCoy presents a great analysis of the elderly Madison's frustrating attempts to teach the upstart younger generation the true meaning of federalism in McCoy, *The Last of the Fathers: James Madison and the Republican Legacy* (Cambridge University Press, 1989), pp. 130–51.

15. Letter from James Madison to Henry Lee, June 25, 1824, in *Letters and Other Writings of Madison*, vol. 3, p. 443; see also Letter from James Madison to Thomas Ritchie, September 15, 1821, and Letter from James Madison to Nicholas P. Trist, December 1831.

16. Nicholas P. Trist, "Memoranda," September 27, 1834, in *The Records of the Federal Convention of 1787*, rev. ed., 4 vols., edited by Max Farrand (Yale University Press, 1966), vol. 3, p. 534.

17. *Federalist* No. 46, in *The Federalist Papers*, edited by Rossiter, p. 291.

18. See, for instance, Wood, "Is There a 'James Madison Problem'?"; Ralph Ketcham, *James Madison: A Biography* (Newtown, Conn.: American Political Biography Press, 1971), pp. 319–23; and Andrew Burstein and Nancy Eisenberg, *Madison and Jefferson* (New York: Random House, 2010), pp. 221–24 and 555–56. Once again, Banning's *Sacred Fire of Liberty* provides a useful corrective; see especially pp. 325–33.

19. James Madison's speech on the Bank Bill, February 2, 1791, in *JMDE* (http://rotunda.upress.virginia.edu/founders/JSMN-01-13-02-0282).

20. Colleen A. Sheehan, "Madison versus Hamilton: The Battle over Republicanism and the Role of Public Opinion," in *The Many Faces of Alexander Hamilton: The Life and Legacy of America's Most Elusive Founding Father*, edited by Douglas Ambrose and Robert W. T. Martin (New York University Press, 2006), p. 182.

21. See Madison's speeches on the subject of the Necessary and Proper Clause in Virginia's Ratifying Convention on June 16 and 17, 1788, in *The Debates in the Several State Conventions on the Adoption of the Federal Constitution*, edited by Elliot, vol. 3, pp. 438–39 and 455.

22. James Madison's speech on the Bank Bill, in *JMDE*.

23. *Federalist* No. 44, in *The Federalist Papers*, edited by Rossiter, p. 282.

24. Ibid.

25. Madison's articles for the *National Gazette*, "Consolidation," December 5, 1791, and "Government of the United States," February 6, 1792, in *JMDE*. See http://rotunda.upress.virginia.edu/founders/JSMN-01-14-02-0122 and http://

rotunda.upress.virginia.edu/founders/JSMN-01-14-02-0190, respectively. Colleen A. Sheehan has undertaken a thorough examination of Madison's rhetorical exploits during this period. See Sheehan, "The Politics of Public Opinion: James Madison's 'Notes on Government,'" *William and Mary Quarterly*, vol. 49, no. 4 (1992), and "Madison v. Hamilton: The Battle over Republicanism and the Role of Public Opinion," *American Political Science Review*, vol. 98, no. 3 (August 2004). Although her conclusions paint Madison as more of an Aristotelian and classical republican than the evidence seems to support, she nonetheless deserves kudos for showcasing an underappreciated facet of Madison's political thought.

26. James Madison, "Public Opinion," December 19, 1791, in *JMDE* (http://rotunda.upress.virginia.edu/founders/JSMN-01-14-02-0145). Emphasis is in the original.

27. Letter from James Madison to Nicholas P. Trist, December 1831, in *Letters and Other Writings of Madison*, p. 211.

28. Letter from James Madison to Charles Jared Ingersoll, June 25, 1831, in *Mind of the Founder*, edited by Meyers, p. 393.

29. Letter from James Madison to Nicholas P. Trist, December 1831, in *Letters and Other Writings of Madison*, p. 211. Colleen Sheehan, in "Madison v. Hamilton," p. 414, goes out of her way to emphasize that when Madison submitted to "the public judgment," it was more precisely the judgment of "*the generation who ratified the Constitution.*" But that distinction, while factually true, is not made in Madison's writings.

30. *Federalist* Nos. 44, 45, and 46, in *The Federalist Papers*, edited by Rossiter; quotations on pp. 282 and 294.

31. Virginia Resolutions, December 21, 1798, in *JMDE* (http://rotunda.upress. virginia.edu/founders/JSMN-01-17-02-0128). This source and the one in note 32 also provide a good editorial introduction to the historical situation surrounding these documents.

32. "The Report of 1800," January 7, 1800, in *JMDE* (http://rotunda.upress. virginia.edu/founders/JSMN-01-17-02-0202).

33. Ibid.

34. Letter from James Madison to Edward Everett, August 28, 1830, reprinted in *The Virginia Report of 1799–1800: Touching the Alien and Sedition Laws; Together with the Virginia Resolutions of December 21, 1798, Including the Debate and Proceedings thereon in the House of Delegates of Virginia and Other Documents Illustrative of the Report and Resolutions* (Richmond, Va.: J.W. Randolph, 1850), pp. 249–56, esp. pp. 252 and 255–56.

35. "Consolidation," in the *National Gazette*, December 5, 1791. Alexis de Tocqueville made the same point in even starker terms in *Democracy in America*, trans. and ed. by Harvey C. Mansfield and Delba Winthrop (University of Chicago Press, 2000), pp. 155–56.

36. *Federalist* No. 46, in *The Federalist Papers*, edited by Rossiter, p. 291.
37. See Glenn Harlan Reynolds, "How Americans Can Kill Obamacare, Legalize Pot," *USA Today*, January 26, 2014 (www.usatoday.com/story/opinion/2014/01/26/obamacare-numbers-health-exchanges-insurance-obama-column/4913341/).

Eleven

MADISON'S VACILLATIONS—
AND MODERN AMERICA'S

Seeing a Founder, an Opposition Leader, a Muddle-
Through Executive, and a Wartime President in
Contemporary American Security Anxieties

BENJAMIN WITTES AND RITIKA SINGH

*A*mericans vacillate over national security and government power. They
want an effective intelligence community, but they do not want too much
surveillance or data collection. They want to rein in the National Security
Agency, but they are outraged when the intelligence community does not
connect the dots. They want to capture and interrogate the enemy, but they
want to close Guantánamo Bay. They want to kill the enemy, but drone
strikes make them uncomfortable. They berate their political leadership for
its exertions of power and also for its forbearance in exerting power. The
further they get from the attacks of September 11, 2001, the less tolerance
they show of strong government action to prevent future attacks—the very
actions that they demanded in the wake of the attacks, the very actions
that followed bitter recriminations for the inaction that preceded that day.
Americans grow less tolerant, that is, until an event like the Boston Mara-
thon bombing or the rise of the Islamic State happens, when they immedi-

ately want to know why the government did not know more and do more and act earlier and more decisively.

It is easy to regard such vacillations either as failures of nerve or as inconstancy with respect to the values that America professes as a society. Yet the truth is that they are honorable struggles, ones that reflect genuinely competing and not-always-compatible concerns in a political culture that is genuinely committed to limited government and personal liberty even as it often perceives the need to take muscular action to protect itself—and those principles—from those who would do them harm.

These vacillations are also very old. The contemporary literature and case law on the relationship between government security powers and civil liberties routinely goes back to the Civil War and earlier. The Founders themselves struggled with the problems of creating a government—and an executive branch within that government—with power adequate to protect the nation's security but bounded so as not to menace the liberty of the people or the sovereignty of the states that made up the union. They profoundly disagreed with one another about how to optimize security while also constraining federal power and while not granting imperial powers to the presidency within the national government.

Sometimes, those struggles—so closely related to those of the country today—took place within the personalities of individual founders over time. And perhaps no leader of prominence in the founding period vacillated more than did the Father of the Constitution himself. James Madison went back and forth over the course of his long career—as the Constitution's principal theoretician, as an opposition leader, as secretary of state in an administration committed to shrinking federal power, and finally as a wartime and postwar president—about how security should inflect the powers invested in government. In Madison's vacillations, Americans today can see fascinating harbingers of their own.

In this chapter, we look at Madison's rather uneven trajectory on this subject and try to relate that trajectory to Americans' contemporary struggles. We trace the evolution of his attitudes through four discrete periods of his career, periods in which his role changed significantly and his attitudes changed along with them—sometimes sharply, sometimes to a lesser degree. A cynic might regard these shifts as reflecting hypocrisy or situational approaches to matters of principle. But we argue that they actually reflect more honorable shifts between values that blend in different concentrations in different circumstances. Finally, we look at the current era, attempting to map Madison's different sensibilities onto different strains of public attitudes toward the relative importance of empowering government to protect security and restraining excesses of government power. We suggest that the various strains of Madisonian thought on the subject still persist in contemporary dialogue, each playing a discernible role in the post-9/11 debate over the governance of security.

ONE MAN, FOUR PERIODS

We remember Madison as among the greatest theoreticians of government in all of history. But Madison was not principally a theorist, at least not in the abstract sense. He was a practitioner, a politician, a person who had to think through governance questions because the society in which he played a leadership role over a number of decades required formative governance decisions. His theoretical views stemmed from uncommonly deep study of the history of governance, constitutions, and political arrangements in other countries. But that study flowed less from academic interest than from the need to react to the circumstances of the young country that he was helping to build. Those circumstances changed substantially over the course of his public life, and Madison's views and approaches changed with them. Madison the president faced problems different from those faced by Madison the imaginer of the ideal constitutional arrangement for a far-flung, decentralized country. Madison the opposition leader imagined federal power differently from Madison the concerned citizen of a country with virtually no central leadership.

We have broken Madison's career into four distinct periods. We rely extensively in the pages that follow on Ralph Ketcham's indispensable biography of Madison. We also use Ketcham's book as a road map to Madison's thinking on issues of executive power and security during these four periods, though we have generally drawn on the sources that Ketcham cites to flesh out those issues.[1] First, before and during the Constitutional Convention, Madison advocated for a stronger federal government. Second, during the era of Federalist government, Madison expressed anxiety about what he saw as excesses of federal power under Treasury Secretary Alexander Hamilton and President John Adams—and grave concern about abuses of civil liberty in the name of security. Third, as secretary of state under President Thomas Jefferson and then as president, he attempted to govern under the republican vision of limited federal power and a highly restrained executive within the federal system—although when practical exigencies forced him to make peace with powers that he had once decried, he did so without particular apology. Finally, as president during and after the War of 1812 with Britain, Madison had to govern as wartime commander in chief. Although he tried mightily to do so with a narrow conception of his role and showed remarkable restraint with respect to civil liberties in wartime, he also ultimately expanded the reach of the federal government and helped institutionalize key military and security powers that had once given him great anxiety.

MADISON AS FOUNDER

When Madison envisioned the ideal government for the nascent United States, national power played a key role in what he saw. As part of the Virginia delegation to the Constitutional Convention, in 1787, he was one of the most vocal supporters of a strong union. Both behind the scenes in the years leading up to the convention and during the bitter debates during the convention itself, Madison maintained that a strong federal government and a successful union were inextricably linked and that the authority vested in the government by the Articles of Confederation was insufficient to carry out the business of the country.

One of Madison's key motivations in trying to strengthen the federal government—though by no means the only one—was his concern about security. He was wary of humiliation by foreign powers and observed that absent federal power, the states would continue warring with one another—as they frequently did over issues of commerce—leaving countries like Spain, France, and England free to exploit the divisions among them. In a letter to James Monroe in 1785, Madison wrote angrily about the trading policies of Great Britain, which rendered the United States a "passive victim to foreign politics." According to Madison, the only way to correct that wrong was to achieve "harmony in the measures of the States," with "acquiescence of all the States in the opinion of a reasonable majority." That might seem like concern merely about trade policy, but Madison clearly saw the problem as creating something of an existential threat to the union. As he wrote portentously in the letter: "I apprehend danger to [the] very existence [of the Union] from a continuance of defects which expose a part, if not the whole, of the empire to severe distress."[2]

Madison believed that egregious "trespasses of the states on the rights of each other" threatened to provoke international conflict.[3] Those trespasses may have arisen because of the lack of regulation of trade and the absence of a uniform currency. But as he wrote in one of his most famous preconvention essays, the tensions, particularly to the extent that they involved "subjects of foreign powers," could drag "the Union in foreign contests."[4] If the nation were to comport itself effectively abroad and prevent itself from being exploited at home by foreign actors, it would have to speak with one, unified voice.

The decentralized structure of the Articles of Confederation created other problems. The states routinely violated international law and treaties when it suited their purposes—to such an extent that Madison worried during the convention that "complaints [were coming] from *almost every nation* with which treaties have been formed." Leaving this self-serving state behavior unchecked would surely bring about "foreign wars," he argued, and "a rupture with other powers is among the greatest of national calamities." An effective central authority was needed to ensure that "no part of a nation shall have it in its power to bring [that] on the whole."[5] The United States also had to be able to defend itself if it were invaded or attacked by foreign powers, and a cautionary lesson from the Revolutionary War—during which George Washington had insufficient independence from the Continental Congress and the Congress had insufficient power to fund his army—showed that a more robust federal power would be necessary. During the Virginia Ratifying Convention on June 16, 1788, Madison elaborated on the problem:

> Where is the provision for general defence? If ever America should be attacked, the states would fall successively. It will prevent them from giving aid to their sister states; for, as each state will expect to be attacked, and wish to guard against it, each will retain its own mi-

litia for its defence. Where is this power to be deposited, then, unless in the general government, if it be dangerous to the public safety to give it exclusively to the states?

The "safety of the Union," Madison insisted at the Constitutional Convention, depended on the ability of the government to "repel foreign invasions."[6]

The young country also faced no shortage of internal security concerns. During the Constitutional Convention, Madison made the case that the country had to be able to suppress insurrections and preserve its internal security, pointing to violence in Massachusetts at the time and the existence of slavery—and the possibility of slave revolts—as evidence of potential instability that might require federal power:

> The insurrections in Massts. admonished all the States of the danger to which they were exposed. Yet [there are] no provisions for supplying the defect of the Confederation on this point. According to the Republican theory indeed, Right & power being both vested in the majority, are held to be synonimous. According to fact & experience, a minority may in an appeal to force be an overmatch for the majority. 1. If the minority happen to include all such as possess the skill & habits of military life, with such as possess the great pecuniary resources, one third may conquer the remaining two thirds. 2. one third of those who participate in the choice of rulers may be rendered a majority by the accession of those whose poverty disqualifies them from a suffrage, & who for obvious reasons may be more ready to join the standard of sedition than that of the established Government. 3. where slavery exists, the Republican Theory becomes still more fallacious.[7]

The great arguments for federal power in *The Federalist Papers*, some of which sound themes of security as well, were generally written by Alexander Hamilton, but there is no doubt that Madison shared his concerns. If the story had stopped here, we would remember Madison—at least on this point—as a theoretician of expanded federal power.

MADISON THE OPPOSITION LEADER

Madison's enthusiasm for a strong federal power, however, did not survive the decade that followed ratification of the Constitution, and his anxieties about executive authority in the security sphere played an important role in his change of view. Scholars have long debated how much his attitudes really shifted and whether his views in those two periods are reconcilable. But at a minimum, the change was considerable. Over a period of less than a decade, he went from urging federal supremacy—including the authority of the national government to veto state laws—to leading the opposition to exertions of federal power and interpreting federal authorities under the Constitution narrowly. One of the major reasons for the change was the vision of executive power promoted by the Federalist powerhouse, Alexander Hamilton.

Hamilton had become secretary of the treasury under President Washington. Madison's relationship with Hamilton—cordial and cooperative at the convention because of both men's aspirations for a strong union—began to fray as Hamilton's ambitious plans for the country's finances unsettled Madison's notions of federal restraint. In his famous "Report on Public Credit," Hamilton proposed establishing the public credit of the country by using measures that Madison—who believed the secretary's plan to be a vast overreach of federal authority—considered unconstitutional. His discomfort was further heightened by Hamilton's plan to create a national bank. He now saw the darker side of having a strong, centralized federal executive authority, and he worried that the most cherished republican values—of separation of powers and limited federal power—were quickly eroding.

That attitudinal shift away from federal authority combined with a growing suspicion of concentrated presidential power, a matter that Madison had not previously focused on, to affect Madison's view of security matters. The two issues were deeply connected because in serving as the primary actor in foreign affairs, a strong federal government has to act through some branch of government. Hamilton took the view not only that the federal government should be supreme in this area but also that the executive branch should wield the foreign affairs authority. Madison, meanwhile, had grown anxious over both the scope of federal power and executive primacy in foreign affairs.

In the period leading up to the Jay Treaty with Great Britain, the man who only a few years earlier had argued for a strong central government capable of speaking with a single voice on foreign affairs now objected to Hamilton's views on executive hegemony in foreign affairs. Hamilton, a staunch admirer of Great Britain despite his role in the Revolutionary War, wanted to preserve British maritime hegemony because the young American economy depended so heavily on it, and he wanted a strong U.S.-British relationship. Madison, by contrast, took the view that a strong France would serve as a counterweight to British arrogance and that the rivalry between them would allow the United States to prosper.

In a series of articles signed "Pacificus" and published in the summer of 1793, Hamilton defended robust executive prerogatives in foreign affairs, stating that the president had the power under the Constitution to make and interpret treaties, receive ambassadors, and otherwise act as the primary executor of the laws of the United States.[8] Madison, however, vigorously opposed that interpretation. Responding under the name "Helvidius," he wrote that Hamilton's view struck at the "vitals of [the country's] constitution, as well as at its honor and true interest." He argued that the treaty power "is not an execution of laws [and] does not presuppose the existence of laws" to execute. "It is, on the contrary, to have itself the force of a *law*, and to be carried into *execution*, like all *other laws*, by the *executive magistrate*." In other words, making a treaty is a legislative act. "To say then that the power of making treaties, which are confessedly laws, belongs naturally to the department which is to execute laws, is to say, that the executive department naturally includes a legislative power. In theory this is an absurdity—in practice a tyranny." Similarly, "a declaration that there shall be war, is not an execution of laws" but is an "*enacting, as a rule for the executive, a new code* adapted to the relation between the society and its foreign enemy."[9] In "Letters of Helvidius No. 4," Madison continued to warn of the dangers of executive prerogative in matters of security:

> In no part of the constitution is more wisdom to be found, than in the clause which confides the question of war or peace to the legislature, and not to the executive department. Beside the objection to such a mixture to heterogeneous powers, the trust and the temptation would be too great for any one man; not such as nature may offer

as the prodigy of many centuries, but such as may be expected in the ordinary successions of magistracy. War is in fact the true nurse of executive aggrandizement. In war, a physical force is to be created; and it is the executive will, which is to direct it. In war, the public treasures are to be unlocked; and it is the executive hand which is to dispense them. In war, the honours and emoluments of office are to be multiplied; and it is the executive patronage under which they are to be enjoyed. It is in war, finally, that laurels are to be gathered; and it is the executive brow they are to encircle. The strongest passions and most dangerous weaknesses of the human breast; ambition, avarice, vanity, the honourable or venial love of fame, are all in conspiracy against the desire and duty of peace.[10]

In February 1793, Britain declared war on France. According to Richard Brookhiser, another Madison biographer, Britain refused to return escaped American slaves, trading with the British West Indies was a nightmare for American merchants, and British troops still controlled twenty American forts, "intriguing with Indians and menacing settlers."[11] Even as tensions grew and the country's security interests began to suffer, Madison refused to acknowledge that more power should accrue to the executive to prepare for war. And when news arrived of British misbehavior—of impressing American ships and exploiting and fomenting unrest among Native Americans on the western frontier—Madison did not support the increases in the army and navy called for by Hamilton and the Federalists.[12] Almost two decades later, as president, Madison would take a very different view of how to respond to what turned out to be persistent irritants in the U.S.-British relationship.

Madison held the same line during the Whiskey Rebellion in the summer of 1794. Despite the quite real and quite troublesome domestic unrest that existed in western Pennsylvania, Madison did not want government force to be the answer and he specifically opposed it, believing that it would set an unhealthy precedent of central high-handedness in enforcing the law. The same Madison who only seven years earlier had cited domestic insurrection as one reason that the Constitution should create a strong central government now argued in a letter to James Monroe that insurrections usually caused an "increase [in] the momentum of power." Madison was certain that had the rebellion not ended on its own terms, "a formidable attempt would have been made to establish the principle that a standing army was necessary for enforcing the law."[13] The insurrection, once the justification for federal power, had now in Madison's view become a lesser threat than the power to put it down.

When John Jay returned from London, having negotiated a treaty governing the terms of American commerce with Great Britain, Madison and his allies were enraged. Just as they had feared, the Jay Treaty was—in their view—far too favorable to Britain and wholly insufficient in addressing American maritime grievances. Along with his fellow members of the House of Representatives, Madison called for President Washington to make public the papers of the negotiations related to the treaty. The Hamiltonians again contended that such a request threatened executive prerogatives in foreign policy. Some of Madison's opponents went even further, accusing Madison of being unprincipled; during the Constitutional Convention, they argued, he had urged adoption of the powers that President Washington was now claiming. Madison pushed back, saying that this interpretation of executive authority threatened simple republican government.

The apogee of Madison's period as an antifederalist leader arose not over the issues of state versus federal power or separation of federal powers but over a classic conflict between civil liberties and government security authority. The Alien and Sedition Acts, passed under President John Adams in 1798 as the United States was on the verge of war with France, were enacted during a period in which Madison had stepped back from political life. While he was disquieted by Adams's calls for domestic military preparedness as tensions with France grew, he reentered national politics only because he found the Sedition Act so appalling. The Sedition Act criminalized criticism of the federal government and its policies, making it a crime to "write, print, utter or publish . . . any false, scandalous, and malicious writing against the government of the United States, or either House of Congress, or the President, with intent to defame, or bring either into contempt or disrepute."[14] Madison quickly became one of the primary opponents of the law. He authored the famous Virginia Resolution of 1798 and, as a member of the Virginia Assembly, wrote the "Report on the Resolutions" in 1800—both of which assailed the Sedition Act on constitutional grounds.[15]

Interestingly, Jefferson—who concurred with Madison's disapproval of the Alien and Sedition Acts and who authored the Kentucky Resolution of 1799—was too extreme in his opposition for Madison's liking. Jefferson touted state supremacy over the powers of the federal government and argued that each state legislature had the right to oppose those federal laws that it deemed unconstitutional—an argument that presaged later Southern pro-slavery arguments that states had "nullification" powers with respect to federal laws to which they did not consent.[16] Although Madison also strongly advocated for limited government power and fully agreed that the Alien and Sedition Acts were unconstitutional, he framed his arguments largely in terms of free speech and balked at veering so far from his original position on a unified country.

In short, by the time that the Jeffersonians assumed power in 1801, Madison had developed significant anxieties along three separate axes that have echoed down through the ages in discussions of security policy. He worried that the federal government had too much power vis-à-vis the states and the people. He worried that the executive branch had too much power vis-à-vis the legislative branch given whatever quantum of power the federal government as a whole might have. And he worried that Congress was transgressing the Bill of Rights in its legislative enactments. While Madison the Founder had dreamed of a powerful central government capable of securing the country, Madison the opposition leader had grown fearful of the Leviathan that he saw emerging.

MADISON IN POWER

When Jefferson ascended to the presidency in 1801, Madison was at his side as his most trusted adviser and counselor—and as his secretary of state. In the eight years that followed and well into Madison's own presidency, the pair governed the country while attempting to adhere to cherished republican ideals of a restrained executive and limited federal government. But they also struggled to reconcile what was a frankly unrealistic vision of federal power with the realities that they faced, which shaped a great deal of their behavior in practice. The commitment to scaling back what the

Jeffersonians saw as excessive Federalist commitment to central power was sincere. One of Madison's first acts as secretary of state was to downsize the department—from eight employees to seven—a step that Ketcham explains as an "economy move."[17] The size of the armed forces was reduced too, and the judiciary was scaled back under the Judiciary Act of 1801.

But like any opponents of government power who suddenly find themselves in power, they also had to govern. To do so without engaging in gross hypocrisy, they had to make do with the rudimentary tools that their ideology left them. The trouble was that the country faced genuine problems that required national attention—and sometimes national action. British impressment of American ships was still an issue, as was the need to navigate between the ambitions of two great powers—Britain and France—as well as lesser powers like Spain. Attempts at navigation did not always prove consistent with the Jeffersonian vision of highly circumscribed federal and presidential power. Madison's arguments at the Constitutional Convention about why the country needed central power turned out to have merit, after all.

The first real test of the administration's interpretation of federal power arose when James Monroe negotiated the purchase of Louisiana in a deal that, from the point of view of the national interest, could hardly have been better. It more than doubled the landmass of the country, it diminished American involvement in foreign power struggles by removing France from the North American continent, and it diminished U.S. dependence on foreign powers for trade. It also was a bargain: all of that cost a mere $15 million. What the Louisiana Purchase was not, however, was a creature of an executive who saw himself as Congress's magistrate in international affairs and who adhered strictly to those powers enumerated in the Constitution. It was instead the work of an energetic administration that took a leadership role in foreign policy and saw itself as the chief actor in building the new nation.

That disparity caused President Jefferson a great deal of concern. He had wanted to amend the Constitution before moving forward with the Louisiana Purchase, but he was talked out of it. Madison, too, struggled with reconciling the twin desires of having a restrained executive and of sustaining and expanding the union—but he did not doubt that opportunities such as the Louisiana Purchase were consistent with legitimately republican goals. He wrote to John Quincy Adams, Ketcham recounts, that "the Constitution didn't cover the case of the Louisiana Purchase, but that it was necessary to remember 'the magnitude of the object,' and to trust 'the candor of the country' to approve the deed."[18]

Later, during his own presidency, Madison also engineered the takeover of what is now Florida, which was then two separate territories. Although Spain technically controlled the territory of West Florida, it was almost entirely inhabited by American settlers, who had risen up against the Spaniards. In ordering the governor of the Orleans Territory, William Claiborne, to take over West Florida using as many militiamen as necessary, Madison made one of the most muscular executive decisions that he would make during his time in office. He then made plans to take over East Florida so that a similar crisis would not arise there.[19] In a letter to William Pinkney, Madison wrote that "the occupancy of [West Florida] was called for by the crisis there, and is understood to be within the authority of the Executive. East Florida, also, is of great importance to the United States, and it is not probable that Congress will let it pass into any new hands."[20]

Madison knew that his actions were antithetical to Republican conceptions of presidential power. His justification, Ketcham explains, was the necessity of thwarting the "extralegal domination of West Florida [by a third party] and excluding foreign powers [from gaining influence] there."[21] To put the matter simply, Jefferson and Madison had their scruples, but they did not shrink from strong action when the national interest, as they saw it, called for action. Nor did Jefferson and Madison declare war on all of the Hamiltonian institutions that they had previously decried. Hamilton's once-detested national bank was kept in place, and the two did not go out of their way to limit federal borrowing and spending power by constitutional amendment. As Lynn Uzzell explains in her chapter in this volume, that was not hypocrisy. Madison regarded the issue of the bank has having been settled—and his side having lost. Ketcham summarizes more generally:

> The Republicans were not blind doctrinaires. They remained cautious about broad construction and desisted on principle from countless acts of aggrandizement about which the Federalists would have had no qualms, while at the same time they recognized that the

Constitution was not a strait jacket, but rather was an instrument for governing a nation.[22]

One problem for the Republicans was that while they were downsizing the government and its security functions, British policy had not changed. The British had formally authorized—even expanded—impressment of American sailors and generally did not respect the young country's independence or interests. Ultimately, Jefferson and Madison had to begin making plans to improve the national defense. And the more they sought to confront the British, the more they had to use federal power to do so. On July 2, 1807, the administration issued a proclamation ordering all British ships to leave American harbors and refusing British ships aid and supplies. Jefferson ordered Virginia governor William Cabell to ready the militia should the British decide to shell American ports. And Madison called for a complete embargo on all American shipping in the Embargo Act of 1807 in the hope that completely freezing trade between the two countries would encourage the British to come to the negotiating table.

Enforcing the act proved a frustrating and fruitless endeavor. Secretary of War Albert Gallatin simply did not have the federal power needed to stop smugglers from violating the terms of the embargo. He recognized, says Ketcham, that "Congress must either invest the Executive with the most arbitrary powers and sufficient force to carry the Embargo into effect, or give it up altogether."[23] Whether or not it was possible to make the embargo effective, the Jefferson administration never mustered the political will to try. And the policy failed to change British behavior. Nor did Madison and Jefferson put special energy into getting Congress to appropriate money for war preparations, and Congress left the country altogether ill-prepared when, a few years later, Madison as president sought a declaration of war. The problem continued into Madison's presidency, and he never dealt with it effectively. When in 1810 he requested an increase in defense appropriations, Congress—in a Tea Partyesque move to achieve a balanced budget—*reduced* appropriations instead.

Things ultimately changed as continuing tensions with Great Britain rendered war inevitable and the new session of Congress contained many more so-called War Hawks, who were less reticent about taking decisive action. Madison also changed. The man who had opposed military readiness during the 1790s for fear of federal power, Ketcham recounts, now "recommended enlarging the army, preparing the militia, finishing the military academy, stock-piling munitions, expanding the navy, and increasing [tariffs] to encourage trade and manufactures vital to the national interest." In an even further departure from his old philosophical commitments, the president understood that "war would require both new taxes and large loans."[24]

But Madison was late to the game, and Congress went with him only so far. It passed six resolutions ordering "an increase of ten thousand in the regular army, a levy of fifty thousand volunteers, altering the militia, full outfitting of the navy, and . . . the arming of merchant ships."[25] The president still faced vehement resistance, both from "Old Republicans," who opposed measures to increase the army and navy, and from Federalists, who opposed war with Britain. The result, as Stephen Budiansky, author of a naval history of the war, vividly illustrates, was dire under-preparation when war was finally declared in June 1812:

> At the start of the conflict, the U.S. Navy had twenty warships, by extremely generous counting; the Royal Navy had nearly 1,000, including some ninety already on station in and around North American waters. The Royal Navy was in fact as large as all of the rest of the world's navies combined. In 1812 it had 145,000 sailors and marines; it had nearly as many lieutenants (3,100) as the U.S. Navy had seamen altogether (3,600). The imbalance in land forces was, if anything, even more one-sided. At the start of the war, the U.S. Army had fewer than 7,000 soldiers to Britain's quarter-million regulars under arms.[26]

Madison in this period is a complicated figure, as only someone who has both thought deeply about governance and tried to govern can be complicated. It is easy to find actions in the Jefferson administration that Madison the opposition leader would have denounced. It is also easy to find broad areas of consistency with the philosophy that he expressed in the 1790s. At the end of the day, however, it is hard to escape the conclusion that his principled commitment to republican philosophy made him late and weak in displaying the sort of national leadership that the country needed in the run-up to a conflict and without which it faced war altogether unprepared. This principled commitment was at some level admirable. But it was not good leadership.

MADISON AS WARTIME PRESIDENT

Madison's story at the helm of government during the War of 1812 is one of remarkable restraint. As we describe in detail elsewhere, generally speaking his conduct defied the notion that presidents violate civil liberties in wartime and use wars to aggrandize executive powers.[27] The story is especially striking because the War of 1812 saw the most concerted domestic opposition to any war that the country has ever fought. Historian Donald R. Hickey describes it as "America's most unpopular war," noting that "it generated more intense opposition than any other war in the nation's history, including the war in Vietnam."[28] The Federalists of the New England states were especially strident in their opposition. The federal government faced concerted resistance to efforts to collect taxes, recruit military officers, mobilize militias, enforce court orders, regulate trade, and even deploy the army and navy. Some of the activity was frankly treasonous: Federalist leaders marshaled state resources to oppose federal policy, openly sided with the enemy against Washington, and at one point gathered a convention that contemplated the dissolution of the union. What's more, the country's situation was fairly dire. The War of 1812 did not go well for the United States, which was lucky at the end to scrape by with a stalemate; at one point, the British marched to Washington and burned down the White House, leaving the president a homeless refugee.

Yet despite the unquestionable domestic impediments that he faced, Madison rejected on principle proposals to repress internal dissent, staying true to the position that he had taken toward dissent and criticism of public officials while the Federalists were in power. The Sedition Act had been used barely a decade earlier against members of his own political party by the very Federalists who were now opposing the president's policies, and other leaders of the time saw the act as a useful precedent. But Madison rebuffed all suggestions to repress dissent. He also showed a remarkable unwillingness to detain U.S. nationals in military custody or to subject them to military trials. In fact, during the War of 1812, Madison deferred to habeas judgments not only by federal courts but by state courts ordering the release of U.S. citizens suspected of spying for the enemy. What's more, he seems to have willingly accepted that the military lacked the authority to detain such suspects and try them before military tribunals, except with congressional authorization.

Madison's conduct during the War of 1812, in short, was that of a president who did the minimum—who did not take strong executive action to ensure an American victory and who was willing to incur and tolerate risks to maintain his principles. The federal government's weakness was, in part, a reflection of Madison's own philosophical commitments, and the inertia of the executive was a reflection of his core beliefs about executive power in a republic. Madison's adherence to the proper role of the republican executive, as he conceived it, arguably held the country back from decisively winning the War of 1812. Yet the only president who sought to fight a war without augmenting federal power ultimately took critically important steps to do just that—although notably, not at the expense of civil liberties. As Budiansky writes,

> The war's outcome almost instantaneously forged a new consensus at home that embraced a standing army and navy as an essential expression of American national strength, prestige, and diplomatic influence in both the Western Hemisphere and Europe. Two decades earlier, Alexander Hamilton had promoted that characteristically Federalist view of military power. . . . That kind of thinking had been anathema to Republicans. But now all of the speeches about militarist "adventurism" and "tyranny" evaporated almost overnight and Republican opposition to the navy was hardly to be heard. In a passage that Alexander Hamilton himself might have written, Madison acknowledged in his message to Congress announcing the end of the war that a chief lesson of the conflict was that "a certain degree of preparation for war is not only indispensable to avert disasters in the onset but affords also the best security for the continuance of peace."

In the wake of the war, Congress authorized an increase in the navy, allocating "$1 million a year over eight years for construction of a substantial fleet." It bolstered the army and authorized reforms to its structure. Under James Monroe, Madison's successor, West Point was revived. Republicans had moved away from the "short-lived era of military power as conceived by the framers of the Constitution—who thought armies and navies would be raised only when needed and promptly disbanded at the end of a war—to a more modern conception of military power as an inextricable component of national foreign policy even in peacetime."[29]

Modern America's Several Inner Madisons

Madison's attitudes in each of the four periods of his career can be seen today in various strains of thought in the post–September 11 period. Unlike Madison, Americans now experience these strains of thought concurrently, not sequentially, and it's hard to identify any single modern individual who embodies as many of them as Madison did in his time. Yet they are all there, woven into the current discourse on law and security. All of Madison's periods represent themes that sometimes recede and sometimes come to the foreground today.

Much security-oriented legislation, for example, reflects Madison the Founder, keenly aware of how the absence of certain government powers threatens security and of the need for new structures to empower government to protect the population. Of course, Americans also think about how to restrain government in the exercise of those powers, but like Madison at the Constitutional Convention, they approach the Patriot Act or the FISA Amendments Act or the Military Commissions Act or any number of other pieces of legislation with the fundamental idea of empowering government to secure the country.

At the same time, Madison the opposition leader also is very much alive. He lives in the constant resistance to government security measures from civil libertarians and dissenting members of both political parties in Congress—all of whom invoke the fear of overweening government power that strong counterterrorism measures might lead to. He lives in the insistence on the part of the courts on reviewing the constitutionality of certain powers and ensuring that their exercise complies with legal norms. He also lives in the skeptical press, which takes as a baseline premise that federal security powers—and executive powers within the federal system—are ripe for abuse and threaten other values. He lives in Americans' fear of the structures of power that the country has built, the limitations built into those structures, and the occasional dismantling of them. He inhabits the side that retreated from the excesses of the early years of the war on terror—the side of the George W. Bush administration, even when in power, that rebelled against the neo-Hamiltonianism of its most extreme flank.

Madison in power—the man who muddled through highly conscious of his values but who also was unapologetic about the Floridas and Louisiana and willing to seek from Congress money for war preparations that he once opposed—lives as well. His sensibility is very much the sensibility of, for example, the Obama administration. Obama, after all, came into office— much as the Jeffersonians did—promising to restore American values in the wake of what he saw as the dangerously Hamiltonian vision of executive authority promulgated by his predecessor. Like Madison's, Obama's commitment to retrenchment of executive authority—to greater submission to Congress's will—was sincere. And like Madison, Obama took some significant steps that genuinely reflect a more modest conception of his role. Yet just as Madison did not abandon Hamilton's national bank, Obama did not fundamentally alter the course of the war against al Qaeda begun by Bush.

Indeed, while the Federalists lost every battle with the Republicans— to the point that they actually went extinct as a political party—they ultimately won the war. The Republicans became them. To the extent that Hamilton and Madison disagreed, America today reflects, in most respects, Hamilton's vision, not Madison's. And the early Republican administrations, Madison's included, were pivotal in developing consensus on the essential features of national power. Similarly, it was Obama's embrace of key aspects of Bush's war on terror that have institutionalized them. Madison made his peace with the national bank; Obama has made his peace with the Authorization for the Use of Military Force (AUMF).

Madison the wartime president—the man who refrained from exercising the substantial power available to him yet ultimately expanded federal power—still inhabits the country too. For just as Madison did not take certain huge steps that he might have taken, there are steps that Americans might take today on which they have turned their backs. They have turned their backs on coercive interrogation. They, like Madison, have never subjected U.S. citizens to trial before military commissions.[30] They have adopted restrictive rules on drone strikes that permit targeting the enemy with lethal force in only a tiny subset of the cases in which the law would countenance lethal force.[31] The Obama administration has generally eschewed claims of inherent presidential power, preferring to frame its actions in terms of congressional authorization. The list of things that Americans do not do in modern counterterrorism operations is very long. It exists not only because of constitutional constraints but because, like Madison, Americans today put limits on themselves in the conduct of war because of a limited vision of executive authority. And while the country certainly does not go as far as Madison did in that regard, it does not always live at the margins of its power either.

At the same time, there is no doubt that—also like Madison—the United States is building in the long term an edifice of federal war-making power unlike anything that it has ever had before and unlike anything that it would profess in Platonic prospective terms to want. Obama back in May 2013 gave a moving speech about the end of the conflict, in which he insisted that "this war, like all wars, must end." He even quoted Madison on the subject, warning the public that "we must define the nature and scope of this struggle, or else it will define us. We have to be mindful of James Madison's warning that 'No nation could preserve its freedom in the midst of continual warfare.'" Obama in that speech assailed the idea of perpetual detention of suspects at Guantánamo Bay, saying that

> history will cast a harsh judgment on this aspect of our fight against terrorism and those of us who fail to end it. Imagine a future—10 years from now or 20 years from now—when the United States of America is still holding people who have been charged with no crime on a piece of land that is not part of our country. Look at the current situation, where we are force-feeding detainees who are being held on a hunger strike. . . . Is this who we are? Is that something our Founders foresaw? Is that the America we want to leave our children? Our sense of justice is stronger than that.[32]

This is the same Obama who has ramped up drone strikes, effectively creating a new form of remote warfare. It is the same Obama who has interpreted the AUMF broadly enough to encompass military operations in Somalia and Yemen and strikes against the Islamic State and whose Defense Department informs Congress that it sees no end to the conflict with al Qaeda in the foreseeable future. And it is the same Obama who has defended in court the power under the AUMF to detain on a long-term basis those very Guantánamo suspects whose detentions the president bewails. Like Madison, in short, Americans refrain from a great many exertions of power but also are building an edifice of power that must concern the part of them that remembers that they once raised principled objections to the acquisition of such power.

CONCLUSION

In many ways, the Founder whose vision most closely anticipated modern America is Hamilton: unrepentantly nationalist in the state-federal divide, commercial and urban in the urban-agrarian divide, and deeply antislavery in the country's regional divide. But with respect to national security, it is Madison's struggles, not Hamilton's, that presage America's struggles today. Madison was by no means the first figure to object to power and then to have to wield it. He is, however, the only member of the founding generation who both participated in the Constitutional Convention and had to run a war under the Constitution written at that convention. He is the only member who both theorized about a federal government empowered to protect the nation's security and then had to use those powers while he was in many ways still reticent about their exercise. He is the only member who both wielded an army and insisted on the right to dissent from the war that he led—a mainstay of modern attitudes toward dissent in security matters.

In our essay on Madison and civil liberties during the War of 1812, we reflected on the fact that no president since Madison has really replicated his solicitude for civil liberties in wartime. Subsequent presidents, in very different ways, have pushed the envelope of their power. Madison, by contrast, left his envelope unstuffed. Subsequent presidential behavior, we wrote, reflects the "total victory of the Hamiltonian vision of the executive over the one that Madison championed." The United States may speak Madison's language about executive power, we argued, but today it is Hamiltonian in practice.

That is true, but it does not mean that the anti-Hamiltonian strains of Madisonian thought and practice on security have died. They may not dominate the way that presidents behave or public expectations of the presidency, but they show up constantly in other aspects of political culture. Madison's concern about dissent, for example, lies at the heart of modern First Amendment law. And the country has developed complex mechanisms for protecting many of the values that he embedded in his republican conception of the executive.[33] Madison's answer to fundamental security concerns differed profoundly from those offered today. But his struggles across time are a window into the present. In critical respects, he spoke for today's America—in all of its many diverse and warring voices.

Notes

1. Ralph Ketcham, *James Madison: A Biography* (New York: Macmillan, 1971).
2. Letter from James Madison to James Monroe, August 7, 1785, in *Letters and Other Writings of James Madison*, vol. 1 (New York: R. Worthington, 1884), pp. 169–73.
3. James Madison, *Vices of the Political System of the U. States*, vol. 2, in *The Writings of James Madison: 1783–1787*, edited by Gaillard Hunt (New York: G.P. Putnam's Sons, 1901), pp. 361–69.
4. Ibid.
5. Madison's speech to the Federal Convention, June 19, 1787, in *Debates in the Federal Convention of 1787*, edited by Gaillard Hunt and James Brown Scott (Buffalo, N.Y.: Prometheus Books, 1987), p. 122.
6. "Virginia Ratifying Convention, June 16, 1788," Constitution Society (www.constitution.org/rc/rat_va_13.htm).
7. *The Debates in the Federal Convention*, June 19, 1787.
8. Alexander Hamilton, "Pacificus No. 1," June 29, 1793, in *The Founders' Constitution* (http://press-pubs.uchicago.edu/founders/documents/a2_2_2-3s14.html).
9. James Madison, "Letters of Helvidius No. 1," August 24, 1793, in *The Founders' Constitution* (http://press-pubs.uchicago.edu/founders/documents/a2_2_2-3s15.html).
10. James Madison, "Letters of Helvidius No. 4," September 14, 1793, in *The Founders' Constitution* (http://press-pubs.uchicago.edu/founders/documents/a2_2_2-3s15.html).
11. Richard Brookhiser, *James Madison* (New York: Basic Books, 2011), p. 123.

12. Ketcham, *James Madison*, p. 351.
13. Letter from James Madison to James Monroe, December 4, 1794, in *Letters and Other Writings of James Madison*, vol. 2 (New York: R. Worthington, 1884), pp. 23–27.
14. "Sedition Act," Constitution Society (http://constitution.org/rf/sedition_1798.htm).
15. James Madison, "Virginia Resolution of 1798," December 24, 1798, Constitution Society (www.constitution.org/cons/virg1798.htm), and "Report on the Viriginia Resolutions," January 1800, *The Founders' Constitution* (http://press-pubs.uchicago.edu/founders/documents/v1ch8s42.html).
16. Thomas Jefferson, "Kentucky Resolution of 1799," December 3, 1799, *Constitution Society* (http://constitution.org/cons/kent1799.htm).
17. Ketcham, *James Madison*, p. 410.
18. Ketcham, *James Madison*, p. 422, citing the memoirs of John Quincy Adams.
19. Stephen F. Knott, *Secret and Sanctioned: Covert Operations and the American Presidency* (Oxford University Press, 1996), pp. 87–104.
20. James Madison, Letter to William Pinkney, October 30, 1810, in *Letters and Other Writings of James Madison*, vol. 2 (New York: R. Worthington, 1884), pp. 485–89.
21. Ketcham, *James Madison*, p. 501.
22. Ibid., p. 422.
23. Ibid., p. 461.
24. Ibid., p. 510.
25. Ibid., p. 513.
26. Stephen Budiansky, "The War of 1812 and the Rise of American Military Power," in *What So Proudly We Hailed: Essays on the Contemporary Meaning of the War of 1812*, edited by Pietro S. Nivola and Peter J. Kastor (Brookings, 2012), p. 38.
27. Benjamin Wittes and Ritika Singh, "James Madison, Presidential Power, and Civil Liberties in the War of 1812," in *What So Proudly We Hailed*, edited by Nivola and Kastor.
28. Donald R. Hickey, *The War of 1812: A Forgotten Conflict* (University of Illinois Press, 1989), p. 255.
29. Budiansky, "The War of 1812 and the Rise of American Military Power," p. 39.
30. Wittes and Singh, *James Madison, Presidential Power, and Civil Liberties in the War of 1812*; and Ingrid Brunk Wuerth, "The President's Power to Detain 'Enemy Combatants': Modern Lessons from Mr. Madison's Forgotten War," *Northwestern University Law Review* vol. 98, no. 4 (2003–04), pp. 1567–616, 1568.
31. For an elaboration of the circumstances in which the United States permits drone strikes, see Kenneth Anderson and Benjamin Wittes, *Speaking the Law:*

The Obama Administration's Addresses on National Security Law (Stanford, Calif.: Hoover Institution Press, 2013), pp. 137–83.

32. Barack Obama, "Remarks by the President at the National Defense University," May 23, 2013 (www.whitehouse.gov/the-press-office/2013/05/23/remarks-president-national-defense-university); and James Madison, "Political Observations," April 20, 1795, in *The Papers of James Madison*, vol. 15, edited by Thomas A. Mason, Robert A. Rutland, and Jeanne K. Sisson (University Press of Virginia, 1985), pp. 511–34.

33. Jack Goldsmith, *Power and Constraint: The Accountable Presidency after 9/11* (New York: W.W. Norton, 2012).

CONTRIBUTORS

MARTHA A. DERTHICK
Professor Emeritus, Department of Politics, University of Virginia

JOHN J. DIIULIO JR.
Frederic Fox Leadership Professor and Professor of
Political Science, University of Pennsylvania, and
Nonresident Senior Fellow, Brookings Institution

WILLIAM A. GALSTON
Ezra K. Zilkha Chair in Governance Studies and
Senior Fellow, Brookings Institution

EUGENE HICKOK
Member of the Board of Directors, Montpelier Foundation,
and former U.S. Deputy Secretary of Education

R. SHEP MELNICK
Thomas P. O'Neill Jr. Professor of American Politics, Boston College

PIETRO S. NIVOLA
Senior Fellow Emeritus, Brookings Institution

JACK N. RAKOVE

William Robertson Coe Professor of History and American Studies and
Professor of Political Science and (by courtesy) Law, Stanford University

JONATHAN RAUCH

Senior Fellow, Brookings Institution

RITIKA SINGH

Graduate student, Edmund A. Walsh School of
Foreign Service, Georgetown University

LYNN E. UZZELL

Scholar in Residence, Robert H. Smith Center for the Constitution
at James Madison's Montpelier and Senior Fellow, Robert A.
Fox Leadership Program, University of Pennsylvania

BENJAMIN WITTES

Senior Fellow, Governance Studies, Brookings
Institution, and Editor in Chief, *Lawfare*

INDEX

Note: page numbers followed by n refer to notes, with note number.